INDIANS OF THE PLAINS

American Museum Science Books are published for The American Museum of Natural History by The Natural History Press. Directed by a joint editorial board made up of members of the staff of the Museum and Doubleday, this series is an extension of the Museum's scientific and educational activities, making available to the student and general reader inexpensive, up-to-date, and reliable books in the life and earth sciences, including anthropology and astronomy. The Natural History Press is a division of Doubleday and Company, Inc., and has its editorial offices at The American Museum of Natural History, Central Park West at 79th Street, New York 24, New York, and its business offices at 501 Franklin Avenue, Garden City, New York.

About the Author

DR. ROBERT H. LOWIE, one of the most distinguished anthropologists in America, spent the greater part of his teaching career at the University of California, Berkeley, where he was visiting associate professor of anthropology from 1917 to 1918, associate professor from 1921 to 1925, professor from 1925 to 1950, and, subsequently, professor emeritus.

Dr. Lowie came to America at the age of ten, received his A.B. degree from the College of the City of New York in 1901 and his Ph.D. from Columbia University in 1908, where he studied anthropology under Franz Boas. From 1907 to 1921 he was a member of the staff of The American Museum of Natural History, where he worked closely with Dr. Clark Wissler.

A summary of part of Dr. Lowie's work among the Indians was first published in 1935 under the title, *The Crow Indians*. He also did a considerable amount of work among the Indians of the Great Basin and the Southwest.

In 1948 Dr. Lowie delivered the Thomas H. Huxley Memorial Lecture before the Royal Anthropological Institute in England and was awarded the Huxley Memorial Medal. He was a member of the National Academy of Sciences and the American Philosophical Society. He received the degree of Sc.D. (*hon. causa*) at the University of Chicago in 1941 and the Wenner-Gren Medal and $1000 award in 1947.

INDIANS OF THE PLAINS

Robert H. Lowie

ORIGINALLY PUBLISHED AS AN
ANTHROPOLOGICAL HANDBOOK BY
THE AMERICAN MUSEUM OF NATURAL HISTORY

AMERICAN MUSEUM SCIENCE BOOKS
Published for The American Museum of Natural
History

The Natural History Press
GARDEN CITY, NEW YORK

The line illustrations for this book were prepared by the Graphic Arts Division of The American Museum of Natural History. The photographs were supplied by The American Museum of Natural History unless otherwise acknowledged.

INDIANS OF THE PLAINS was originally published by the McGraw-Hill Book Company, Inc., in 1954. The American Museum Science Books edition is published by arrangement with The American Museum of Natural History.

American Museum Science Books edition: 1963

Copyright, 1954,
by The American Museum of Natural History

All rights reserved
Printed in the United States of America

FOREWORD

When little boys play Indian, they often don feather headdresses and, if Santa Claus has been bountiful, costumes suggesting deerskin jackets and leggings decorated with fringe. When our European friends come to our shores, they sometimes expect to see, shouting war whoops, I suppose, along Broadway, Indians not unlike the ones that used to roam our Plains. Most of us, when we think of Indians, envision such items as tipis, war bonnets with trailing feathers, Sitting Bull, ponies, and buffaloes. In other words, we have all come to think of the Plains Indians as the genuine Indian, the ideal Indian—the very quintessence of Indian-ness. In many ways, however, the Plains Indians were a highly distinctive group and lived in a rather specialized way or at least in a manner quite different from other kinds of Indians. They were no more typical of the American Indian than the Navajo, the Hopi, or the Iroquois. Yet through the accidents of history, perhaps also by their own role, often heroic, in the epic of the West or indeed as the result of the insistent stereotype of the movies, they have come to usurp in the public mind all other Indians and to represent *the* Indian way of life.

But if in our symbolic use of the Indian we have rubbed out the fascinating local differences, the product of ages of development, and created an image not quite reflecting the Indian of the Plains, we have shown equally little understanding of these very Plainsmen, the variety in their tribal lives and the significance of their customs.

Since the Sioux, the Crow, the Blackfoot, and other tribes of the Plains have achieved a predominant position in the national symbolism—the justice of which I shall not deal with here—let us, at least, see the Plains Indians as they were and understand what it was that made them the product of their environment and their history. For it is these Indians that many of us want to know more about.

There was, in my opinion, no one as qualified to help us do this as Robert H. Lowie, the author of this book. During his curatorial association with The American Museum of Natural History, he carried on a series of brilliant and painstaking studies of the Plains Indians; subsequently as Professor of Anthropology at the University of California he lectured about them; and throughout his long and outstanding career he constantly thought about them. I feel very fortunate that he consented to do this book for the Museum. He was *the* authority.

Harry L. Shapiro
Chairman and Curator
of Physical Anthropology

The American Museum of Natural History
New York, New York

CONTENTS

Foreword ix

1 INTRODUCTION 1
   The Plains Tribes 4
   Plains Culture 6
   Political, Linguistic, Cultural Units 10
   Population 11

2 MATERIAL CULTURE 15
   Food and Stimulants 15
      Hunting 15
      Fishing 19
      Wild Plants 20
      Agriculture 21
      Preparation of Food 25
      Tobacco 27
   Settlement and Dwellings 31
      The Tipi 32
      The Earthlodge 34
      Grass Lodges 38
      Osage House 39
   Domestic Animals and Transportation 39
   Dress and Personal Decoration 49
      Clothing 49
      Headgear 52
      Hairdressing 52
      Adornment and Mutilation 55

INDIANS OF THE PLAINS

Tools and Artifacts — 56
    Tools — 56
    Crafts — 59
    Weapons — 72

3 SOCIAL ORGANIZATION — 79
Marriage and the Family — 79
The Life Cycle — 86
Bands, Clans, Phratries, Moieties — 91
    Local Units — 92
    Kinship Units — 95
Kinship Terms — 103
Clubs and Societies — 105
Warfare — 114
Rank, Law, and Government — 123
Trade; Economic Values — 127

4 RECREATION — 131
Games — 131
Storytelling — 137
Clowns — 142

5 ART — 143
Painting on Skins — 143
Rawhide Decoration — 148
Embroidery — 151
Designs and Symbolism — 156
Music — 162

6 SUPERNATURALISM — 167
Beliefs — 167
    The Supernatural — 167
    Visions — 170
    Shamans — 175
    Priests — 179

CONTENTS

Hereafter	180
World View	182
Ceremonialism	183
Elements of Ceremonialism	185
Major Ceremonials	189
Crow Tobacco Society	191
The Sun Dance	197
Modern Movements	199
7 PREHISTORY AND HISTORY	205
8 ACCULTURATION	219
9 CONCLUSION	225
Hints for Further Reading	235
Index	239

LIST OF ILLUSTRATIONS
Figures

1.	Map of North American Indian culture areas	xx
2.	Map of Indian tribes in the Plains and surrounding areas	3
3.	Assiniboin buffalo pound	17
4.	Blackfoot willow fish trap	19
5.	Diagram of a Hidatsa cache pit	24
6.	Crow firedrill	26
7.	Blackfoot stone mauls	27
8.	Man's pipe from the Comanche	29
9.	Blackfoot medicine pipe	30
10.	Diagram of Hairy-coat's father's Hidatsa earthlodge	35
11.	Diagram of a twelve-post earthlodge, Hidatsa	37
12.	Blackfoot travois	41
13.	Three types of cradles used in the Plains	47
14.	Blackfoot woman's dress	50
15.	Patterns for Plains Indian moccasins	51
16.	Blackfoot hairbrushes	53
17.	Plains Cree tattoo designs	55
18.	Crow stone-headed war club	57
19.	Chipped stone knives and bone knife, Blackfoot; Pawnee arrow-smoothers	57
20.	Some tools used by Plains Indians	59
21.	An Arapaho wood carving	63
22.	A pattern for a parfleche	64
23.	Painted rawhide parfleche, bag, and container for ritual objects, Blackfoot	65
24.	A painted rawhide trunk from the Hidatsa	66
25.	Bead-decorated soft skin pouch, Arapaho	68
26.	An Arapaho bone tool	71
27.	Bows and quiver from the Blackfoot and Nez Percé	73
28.	Crow shields	77
29.	The Cheyenne camp circle	93
30.	War episodes as depicted on a Blackfoot tipi cover	120
31.	The capture of horses, recorded on a Blackfoot tipi cover	121
32.	Crow stick dice and plum-stone dice	133
33.	Ring, hoop, and dart for the Crow hoop-and-pole game	135

34.	Assiniboin cup-and-ball game	137
35.	Ceremonial carving, Crow Lumpwood Society	143
36.	Ceremonial carving, Crow Hot Dance	144
37.	Three patterns often used on buffalo robes	145
38.	Designs painted on parfleches	149
39.	Painted rawhide cases from the Arapaho	150
40.	Moccasin designs, Arapaho and Crow	154
41.	Dakota design elements	156
42.	Blackfoot skin rattle	163
43.	Shoshone drum and Hidatsa wooden rasp	165
44.	Tobacco bags used in the Crow Tobacco Ceremony	192

Photographs

1. Plains Cree fish weir
2. Detail showing entrance to weir
3. Hidatsa agricultural implements
4. Hidatsa burden baskets
5. Hidatsa corn-drying scaffold
6. Hidatsa woman pounding corn
7. Hidatsa horn rake and bone hoe
8. Grass-covered lodge and shade, Wichita
9. Painted tipi, Arapaho
10. Hidatsa woman paddling a bullboat
11. Crow couple in costume, about 1915
12. Sun Dance headdress, Blackfoot
13. Costume and hairdress from the Crow
14. Hair roach, shown on Missouri and Oto Indians, and a Ponca chief
15. Mandan pottery vessels
16. Assiniboin warrior with shield and bow spear
17. Hidatsa Dog dancer
18. Mandan Half-shaved Head Dance
19. Mandan Bull Society Dance
20. Two young warriors returning with their first scalps
21. Assiniboin Scalp Dance
22. Cree double-ball shinny game
23. Hidatsa hoop-and-pole game
24. Painted buffalo-skin robe depicting battle that took place in 1797
25. Quill-decorated saddlebag from the Dakota
26. Dakota moccasins
27. Beaded and quilled pipe and tobacco bags from the Dakota

LIST OF ILLUSTRATIONS

28. Dakota woman's bead-ornamented leggings
29. Crow sacred rock and offerings
30. Blackfoot medicine man
31. Altar in Adoption Lodge, Crow Tobacco Ceremony
32. Entrance to Adoption Lodge, Crow Tobacco Ceremony
33. Leader of the procession, Crow Tobacco Ceremony
34. Procession to the Adoption Lodge, Crow Tobacco Ceremony
35. Arapaho Sun Dance
36. Sacred doll of the Crow Sun Dance

INDIANS OF THE PLAINS

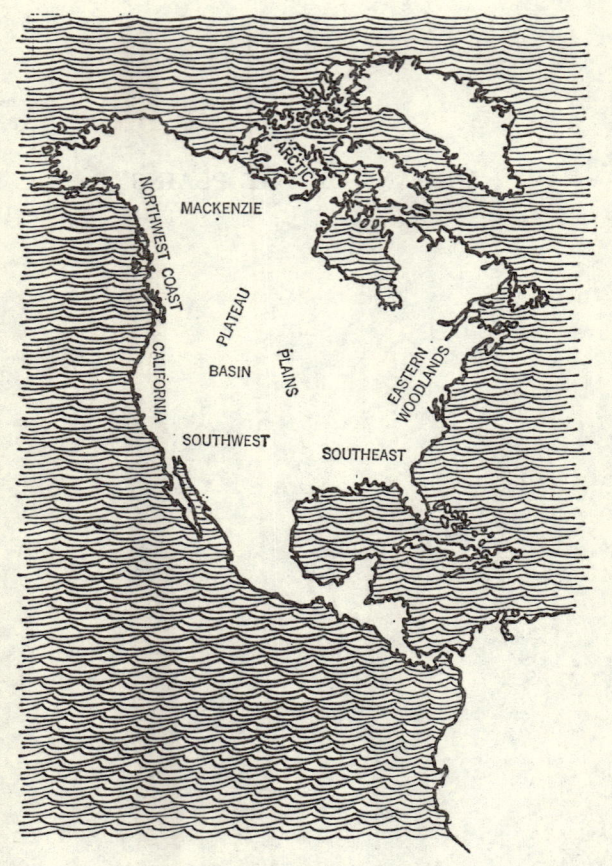

Fig. 1. North American Indian culture areas.

1 INTRODUCTION

The theme of this book is the culture of the Plains Indians from the time of their discovery until their virtually complete assimilation of the White man's ways. "Plains" is a geographical term that may be construed loosely to include the area between the Mississippi and the Rocky Mountains, along with adjacent parts of Canada. Or it may be limited so as to exclude the "Prairie" belt. However, it is not possible to apply the narrower definition at all strictly. The Plains proper are supposed to be marked off by their short-grass vegetation, a result of aridity; and the Prairie soil is allegedly distinguishable by its dark color. However, neither of these criteria is absolute. The shift in the character of the soil is gradual as one travels eastward, so that any line of demarcation drawn on this basis would be arbitrary. The true Plains are arid, with an average rainfall of less than 20 inches a year against 30 inches or more in other farming regions of our country. Hence the lack of trees and the dominant part of drought-resisting grama and buffalo grass in the vegetation. However, in this respect also no rigid definition will hold. In 1894 the town of Hays, Kansas, had a precipitation of only 11.80 inches, whereas in another year it rose to 35.40 inches. In some years the whole area will suffer from exceptional drought or share unusual humidity, but more frequently there will be no such uniformity in the several sections of the Plains. In consequence of such fluctuation the difference in vegetation from the Prairies may disappear, wet years bringing taller species of grass. Great variation also occurs with reference to temperature; in the same year subareas differ noticeably, so that in Texas the mercury may rise to 100° Fahrenheit for 30 consecutive days, whereas in North Dakota there may be only two such days during the same month; in the following year the figures may be reversed.

Even within a restricted section of the territory, appreciable differences are found. In South Dakota the southeastern valleys have an elevation of 1,100 feet against that of 5,000 feet in the Black Hills; and while the annual precipitation in the former district averages 30 inches, it drops to only 14 in the northwestern part of the state.

It is thus impossible to give a strict definition of the Plains Area in geographical terms. Culturally it would be even more arbitrary to set up absolute boundaries, for it is a matter of historical record or trustworthy tradition that many tribes of the Plains emigrated into them from the Prairies and Woodlands of the east. Hence we cannot confine ourselves to the short-grass regions, but shall include in our survey the natives of southern Alberta, Saskatchewan, and Manitoba; of Montana, Wyoming, Colorado, the Dakotas, Nebraska, Kansas, Oklahoma, and northern Texas; and of Minnesota, Iowa, Missouri, and Arkansas. As a matter of fact, it will not be possible to avoid mention of adjoining dis-

Fig. 2. Indian tribes in the Plains and surrounding areas. The dotted line outlines the Plains culture area.

tricts in any direction, their natives being conveniently referred to as "marginal."

The Plains Tribes

Primitive peoples are most conveniently classified according to their linguistic affiliations. Groups whose speech is so similar that they are able to communicate with each other, notwithstanding minor differences, are said to be speaking *dialects* of the same language; if the differences are too great for mutual intelligibility, we speak of distinct *languages*. However, in many instances of the latter kind, the languages show many resemblances that can be explained only on the assumption that they have diverged from a common parental tongue, perhaps centuries or even millenniums ago. This holds true for English, Dutch, and Swedish, but even Russian proves to be connected with these languages when their vocabularies and grammars are closely examined. Such ultimately related languages jointly form a *family (stock)*. In a large family it may happen that two or more of the languages are closer to each other than to the rest, in which case the family is for convenience divided into *branches*. Thus, most European languages plus certain Asiatic ones form the Indo-European family, which comprises the Germanic, Romance, Slavic, and other branches, most of them composed of several distinct languages, which in turn may split up into various dialects.

This mode of grouping, when applied to the Plains Indians leads to the recognition of six families. If we hyphenate the names of political groups speaking identical or virtually identical languages, we arrive at the following tabulation:

ALGONKIAN FAMILY	Blackfoot (Piegan–Blood–Northern Blackfoot) Cheyenne Arapaho–Gros Ventre	Plains Cree Plains Ojibwa (Plains Chippewa)
ATHABASKAN FAMILY	Sarsi	Kiowa Apache
CADDOAN FAMILY	Pawnee–Arikara	Wichita
KIOWAN FAMILY	Kiowa	
SIOUAN FAMILY	Mandan Hidatsa Crow	Dakota–Assiniboin Iowa–Oto–Missouri Omaha–Ponca–Osage–Kansa
UTO-AZTECAN FAMILY*	Wind River Shoshone–Comanche	Ute

* Although modern linguists recognize the relationship of these languages with Aztec and other Mexican languages, those spoken north of the Rio Grande are still sometimes conveniently referred to as "Shoshonean."

Though the several Plains tribes spoke so many different languages, they were not without a common medium of communication, *viz.*, a sign language not identical with that of deaf-mutes, but comparable to it. The gestures employed to designate various ideas were generally understood throughout the Plains. To illustrate the system, "cold" was indicated by clenching both hands and crossing the forearms in front of the chest with a trembling motion. "Chief" was represented by raising the forefinger, pointing it vertically upward, then reversing the finger and bringing it down. For "rain" or "snow" the gesture was to hold the hands at the level of the shoulders, the fingers hanging down, the palm down, and then to push downward. Though it might seem that this was an inferior system of communication, its possibilities were far greater than might be supposed. A Cheyenne could thereby recount his war deeds to a group of Crow Indians incapable of understanding one word of his speech. A Shoshone once explained to the author how the folk tale of a giant bird that snatched and ate people could be told wholly by signs; and the Kiowa correspondingly gave General Hugh Lenox Scott an account of their complex Sun Dance ceremonial.

Plains Culture

These tribes share a sufficiently large number of cultural traits to be classed together as representing a distinctive mode of life. Inasmuch as they inhabit a continuous territory, it is proper to speak of a "Plains" culture area, using the geographical term in its wider sense. In characterizing such an area we must keep in mind neighboring areas, for only by comparison can a type of culture stand out clearly. This means that lacks as well as positive occurrences must be noted. The Plains peoples, then, were typically large-game hunters, dependent for a considerable part of their diet on buffalo and using buffalo hides and deerskins for clothing and receptacles. Unlike the Basin and Plateau tribes to the west, they made little or no use of fish and of such small game as rabbits. Houses of stone or adobe, such as are still inhabited by the Pueblos of New Mexico and Arizona, were wholly absent. During at least part of the year the Plains Indians lived in conical skin-covered tents (tipis); these were larger than the similarly shaped tents of the Mackenzie River region to the north and further differed from them and from the occasionally skin-covered Eastern Woodland tents in having a special arrangement for a smoke vent. Characteristic was the seasonal grouping of tipis in a large circle.

The only aboriginal domestic animal was the dog, eaten by a few of the tribes, more generally used for packing and traction. The Spaniards introduced horses, which vitally altered hunting and transport methods, secondarily also affecting other aspects of life. The Plains Indians, favored by their environment, turned into equestrian nomads, sharply contrasting with Pueblo, Woodland, and Basin peoples. However, this transformation does not antedate the eighteenth century. The Spanish settlements in present New Mexico were the source of supply, and the new feature spread slowly toward the north (see page 42). Equestrian culture and its derivatives are therefore typical of the whole area only from well into the eighteenth century. Travel before and after the introduction of the horse was by land, the Woodland bark or dugout canoe being conspicuously absent among all but the easternmost tribes of the area.

As regards crafts, Plains Indians were good skin dressers and extensively used hides and dressed skins. In glaring contrast to their western and southwestern neighbors they displayed next to no aptitude for weaving and basketry. Woodwork likewise was not developed. However, the women made a good deal of fine porcupine-quill embroidery, and some skill was displayed in the attachment of feathers for decoration.

Several nonmaterial traits require mention at this point. Like the Eastern Indians, the Plains tribes were very warlike, thus again differing sharply from the natives of the Basin and the Plateau. A periodically functioning police force is another characteristic of the area, and clublike organizations promoting the military spirit as part of their functions were widespread. The number and complexity of ceremonials again distinguishes the Plains from the Basin and Plateau, the climax being attained in the usually annual festival of the Sun Dance. Decorative art in painting, quillwork, and beadwork emphasized straight-lined geometrical designs, the style of painted figures on rawhide containers being highly distinctive. Except near the eastern border of the area, the absence of floral patterns until recent times separated Plains from Woodland art.

The foregoing diagnostic traits suffice to set off the Plains from other areas. However, some supplementary statements are required. In the first place, a few of the outlying tribes, such as the Ute and Shoshone, share the external features rather than the religious and social traits, which tend to be at best attenuated among them. Secondly, the Southern Siouans together with the Pawnee, Mandan, Hidatsa, and Arikara unquestionably represent a distinct subculture. That is, while displaying most or all of the Plains criteria, they show additional traits, notably agriculture and a semisedentary existence with pottery-making and part-time residence in fixed villages of earthlodges.

Finally, any classification on cultural and geographical lines has an element of arbitrariness in borderline cases. Whether to include certain peripheral groups is optional. Thus, the Upper Kutenai, recently living in the extreme north of Idaho and Montana as well as in British Columbia, but once living east of the Rockies, were buffalo hunters and adopted a few traits, such as the Sun Dance, from the Blackfoot or Cree. They have been regarded both as a stock by themselves and as another Algonkian group. Several other Plateau groups—Flathead, Nez Percé, Yakima, Spokane—also periodically invaded the Plains to hunt, but apart from dress and certain decorative art designs, they took over very little from the Plains tribes.

Two additional Uto-Aztecan tribes, the Bannock and the Northern Shoshone of Idaho, likewise exhibited a few Plains features. Finally, the Jicarilla Apache (Athabaskan) of northern New Mexico and southern Colorado similarly shared some Plains Indian traits. In all these instances, however, the similarities are of comparatively recent date and relate to superficial features. Thus, though the Jicarilla hunted buffalo in the Plains, they never felt comfortable there and promptly hurried out of the unfamiliar territory. According to Professor Morris Opler, who has made a comparative study of most Apache groups, "psychologically they are anything but a Plains people." Corresponding remarks hold for the other dubious cases. For example, the Northern Shoshone (Idaho) discovered by Lewis and Clark in 1805 largely depended on a fish diet and sometimes resorted to their ancient grass lodges for dwellings; their social and ceremonial life was always extremely meager, and their myths conformed to the Basin rather than the Plains pattern. Other borderline cases include members of the inadequately known Caddoan stock, encountered by the Spaniards as early as 1541 and 1542, and the Quapaw or Arkansas Indians. However, both are properly put into the Southeastern culture area, though linguistically the Quapaw are one with the Omaha subdivision of the Siouan family.

Political, Linguistic, Cultural Units

The term "tribe" may be used in a political sense, corresponding to the "nation" of civilized peoples. This is unobjectionable *provided* we remember that linguistic and political groups need not coincide. As the use of the same language did not prevent the American colonists from founding a new nation, so Omaha and Ponca Indians separated and at times even fought each other. In other words, linguistically they remained one, politically they became two tribes. The Piegan, Blood, and Northern Blackfoot differ only in minutiae of speech, but politically they were independent. The Dakota, popularly known as "Sioux," fall into three dialectic groups, roughly distinguishable by the use of *d*, *n*, or *l*: the Eastern dialect has "Dakota" for the tribal name of the speaker, the Central dialect (of which Assiniboin is a subvariety) substitutes "Nakota," the Western dialect "Lakota." So close are these variants that when missionaries reduced the language to writing in the Santee (Eastern) form the Teton (Western) groups read it without trouble, merely pronouncing the words after their own fashion—precisely as an American reads "clerk" in a British book though the author pronounced it "clark." Politically, however, there were many distinct Dakota groups.

In short, it is necessary to be clear whether the term "tribe" is to be understood politically or linguistically.

If two groups are identical, or nearly so, in speech, it seems a fair assumption that their separation took place a relatively short time ago, that accordingly both have preserved essentially the same mode of life. However, there is no regularity about this; a change of environment may bring with it new adaptations or the loss of adaptations to an earlier habitat. The Teton could not have split off from other Dakota many centuries ago, but by 1700 they were neither gathering wild rice nor paddling canoes after the Santee fashion. Of great importance in this connection are the alien contacts experienced, which may profoundly alter a people's culture. The Sarsi language differs very slightly from that of the Beaver Indians but moving southward, possibly about 1700, they soon attached themselves to the Blackfoot and assimilated the essentials of their culture, so that they are in historic times incomparably closer to the natives of the northern Plains than to their linguistic congeners. Naturally a complete transformation is rarely achieved within a short space of time; the Cree clung to snowshoes even in the Far West, and the Uto-Aztecan buffalo hunters preserved the Basin type of mythology.

Population

to consider the size of the several
inal times. For the earlier contact
es are available; hence, we must
he estimates of travelers and trad-
conjectures of different observers
approximately the same date; in
there were sometimes discrepan-
figures of the United States Cen-
hose furnished by Indian agents.
asons for such disagreement can

be guessed; *e.g.*, in a matrilineal group a person whose maternal grandmother was Mandan would be reckoned as Mandan by the Indians even if his patrilineal kin and his mother's father belonged to other tribes. Apart from the influence of rules of descent, intertribal marriage would obscure the picture. A son of the Shoshone chief Washakie would naturally be classed as Shoshone, but he himself was half Flathead and had married one Crow and one Ute woman.

POPULATION OF PLAINS INDIANS

Tribe	Population	Tribe	Population
Northern Blackfoot	2,400 (1855)	Kiowa Apache	300 (1805)
Blood	2,000 (1855)		184 (1930)
Piegan	3,200 (1855)		
All Blackfoot	7,600 (1855)	Pawnee	10,000 (1780)
	15,000 (1780)		4,686 (1856)
	9,000 (1801)		1,440 (1879)
	4,600 (1932)		959 (1937)
Cheyenne	3,500 (1780)	Arikara	3,800 (1780)
	3,055 (1910)		2,600 (1804)
	2,695 (1930)		616 (1937)
Arapaho	3,000 (1780)	Wichita	3,200 (1780)
	1,419 (1910)		385 (1937)
	1,241 (1930)		
		Kiowa	2,000 (1780)
Gros Ventre	3,000 (1780)		1,126 (1910)
	510 (1910)		1,050 (1930)
	809 (1937)		
		Mandan	3,600 (1780)
Plains Cree	4,000 (1835)		1,600 (1837)
	1,000 (1858)		271 (1930)
Sarsi	700 (1670)	Hidatsa	2,500 (1780)
	160 (1924)		2,100 (1804)
			528 (1930)
Crow	4,000 (1780)	Ponca	800 (1780)
	1,674 (1930)		939 (1930)
	2,173 (1937)		

INTRODUCTION

Theoretically, we ought to compare the data for all groups at the same point of time, but our earliest information for the several tribes does not synchronize. The late James Mooney of the Bureau of American Ethnology made reasonable guesses for the year 1780, *i.e.*, before White influence had profoundly affected most of the western tribes; and his work forms the basis of A. L. Kroeber's estimate in his *Cultural Areas of Native North America* and J. R. Swanton's later studies for the Bureau. The table summarizes findings for a relatively early date and one or more recent dates.

POPULATION OF PLAINS INDIANS

Eastern and Central Dakota	15,000 (1780)	Osage	6,200 (1780) 3,649 (1937)
Western Dakota	10,000 (1780)	Kansa	3,300 (1780) 1,850 (1822) 515 (1937)
All Dakota	25,000 (1780) 27,175 (1904) 25,934 (1930)	Wind River Shoshone	1,500 (1820) 1,250 (1878)
Assiniboin	10,000 (1780) 8,000 (1829) 2,800 (1920)	Comanche	7,000 (1690) 1,423 (1930) 2,213 (1937)
Iowa	1,100 (1760) 800 (1804) 112 (1937)	Ute (incl. non-Plains Ute)	4,500 (1845)
Oto	900 (1780) 500 (1805)	Jicarilla Apache	800 (1845) 714 (1937)
Oto-Missouri	931 (1843) 332 (1910) 627 (1930)	Kutenai	1,200 (1780) 1,087 (1905)
Omaha	2,800 (1780) 300 (1802) 1,103 (1930)	Nez Percé	4,000 (1780) 3,000 (1849) 1,415 (1937)

Compared with African Negro tribes, which commonly numbered tens of thousands of individuals and occasionally over a million, the Plains Indian tribes were numerically weak. In addition, we must remember that, where the figures in the table rise to 10,000 and above, they refer merely to linguistic, not to the much smaller political units. The Pawnee, for example, politically comprised at least four independent groups.

The apparently always inconsiderable size of the Sarsi and the Kiowa Apache explains their attaching themselves to larger tribes. In other instances, there has been a marked decrease since the earlier notices in consequence of devastating diseases. In 1837 the Mandan were so greatly reduced by smallpox that, instead of the 1,600 estimated just before an epidemic, only 150 remained in 1850. Since then they have increased only slightly. In other cases, too, spectacular decline due to sickness and warfare was followed by partial restoration. Because of the hazards of fighting and hunting, adult females preponderated over males in prereservation times, at least in the Northern Plains, but since then there has been a tendency toward sex equality. The birth rate has been high, while the death rate, as a result of the elimination of warfare and improved hygienic conditions, has decreased.

2 MATERIAL CULTURE

Food and Stimulants

HUNTING

Large game—elk, deer, antelope, and especially buffalo (bison)—formed the greatest part of the nomads' diet and contributed significantly to the villagers' food supply. An individual hunter would skillfully sneak up to his quarry, often disguised in a wolfskin covering his head and back, until close enough to shoot. In the winter Arapaho or Assiniboin hunters pursued buffalo and antelope on snowshoes, killing the game with ease as they became embedded in the snow. Sometimes a pair or a few men would combine in the chase.

Far more important, however, was the collective hunt in which the entire tribe participated. Even villagers like the Omaha abandoned the settlements after planting their crops and went on their big summer hunt, pitching tipis in a circle on the open prairie, which the cold prevented them from doing in the late fall or winter. Four methods of collective hunting may be distinguished—the "surround," driving game down a cliff, impounding, and encircling the victims with fire. The first of these became increasingly popular with the use of horses: the mounted hunters surrounded the herd, got the animals to mill around, and shot them down, usually with bows and arrows. The remaining methods, though not excluding horsemanship, did not require it. Grass firing by itself implied hemming in the herd by setting fire on all sides except for the hunters' ambush, thus driving the buffalo to the only opening, where they were promptly killed. This was a Prairie technique reported for the Santee, Miami, and other tribes of the Upper Mississippi country.

The more distinctive aboriginal Plains methods, then, were impounding and driving down a cliff; they could be combined with each other, *i.e.*, a corral could be built below the cutbank down which the beasts were stampeded, but if the height was considerable the enclosure below was unnecessary since the buffalo would be crippled or killed by the fall. Both methods could also be combined with either the use of horses or the firing of grass to force the animals into the required path. In either case, artifice was needed to start the herd in the proper direction, and great care had to be taken lest the beasts scent their enemies. Since the survival of the people might hinge on success in the chase, the directors of the undertaking issued orders that had to be implicitly obeyed, on pain of severe punishment by the police. Also rituals were performed to promote success.

The drive down a cliff requires no explanation, but impounding does. It involved the construction of a corral with an opening approached between two converging lines. These were formed by a solid fence in the vicinity of the entrance, but farther away there would be merely rock piles or bundles of brush at intervals; indeed, men and women sentries would string out for miles, screaming and waving robes (or in later times blankets) to frighten any animals that might try to escape outside the lines. First of all, scouts had to locate the herds,

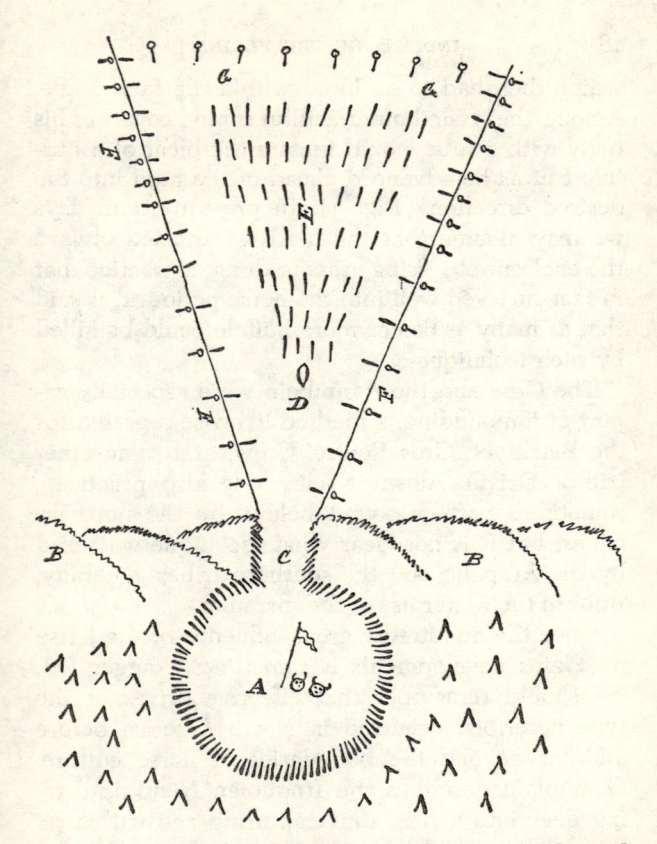

Fig. 3. *An Assiniboin buffalo pound. Key: A) The park below the cliffs; B) High range of hills; C) Gap or opening through the hills and descent to the park; D) A person on horseback leading in the buffalo; E) Buffalo on the level prairie behind the bluffs and enclosed within the lines; F) Dirt and stones thrown up about 3 feet high (straight lines) and men (straight lines with small circles) lying down concealed behind them; G) The buffalo having passed the stations of these, they close in behind them. The upside-down V's are Indian camps in the valley below the cliffs.* Courtesy of Bureau of American Ethnology, The Smithsonian Institution.

which then had to be lured within the fatal angle. Among the Assiniboin a skillful mimic covering his body with a robe would imitate the bleat of a buffalo calf as he advanced ahead of the herd into the desired direction (Fig. 3). In pre-equestrian days we may assume that the herd was started toward the enclosure by firing grass or dung, a practice that in fact survived well into the horse period. It is said that as many as 600 or more buffalo could be killed by such techniques.

The Cree and the Assiniboin were especially expert at impounding, a method likewise reported for the Blackfoot, Gros Ventre, Crow, and some other tribes. Driving down a cliff was also practiced, sometimes with a pound below, by the northern tribes, but it is not clear what technique was used by the Arapaho and the southern tribes generally, prior to their later use of the surround.

Since the admittedly great influence of the horse on Plains developments is sometimes exaggerated, we should remember that effective drives of the type described occurred in North America before and far beyond the boundaries of horse culture. Champlain describes the Iroquoian Neutrals driving deer into a pen, thus capturing 120 within 38 days; and grass firing netted 200 buffalo a day for the Miami. In California the unmounted Maidu drove deer down cliffs, the Yokuts surrounded antelope in collective drives, the Washo charmed antelope into corrals. According to Tornaeus, a Swedish missionary of the period, horseless seventeenth-century Lapps drove reindeer between converging lines down an artificial "five-stepped slope, at the foot of which there is a lofty and strong enclosure, well protected like a stockade or blind alley, so that no creature could escape from it." Collective drives of the two aboriginal Plains types are thus widespread among the preliterate peoples, and there is no reason to assume that the horse was prerequisite to make them economically possible or effective. Its advent did, of course, make the hunt considerably less arduous and more profitable.

FISHING

Nowhere in the area were fish the staple, but sundry tribes caught fish at least when other food was scarce. Thus, if short of meat, the Cree caught river fish with the aid of weirs (Plates 1, 2), scooped them up, and clubbed them; in the winter, they speared fish at open places in the ice. The Blackfoot, in times of need, trapped fish in crude basketry traps (Fig. 4). The Omaha speared fish with sharpened wooden sticks or shot them with special headless arrows. Mandan and Hidatsa village sites contain considerable numbers of catfish bones, suggesting that these villagers attached rather more value to such fare than most people in the area. This is likewise indicated by the ritualistic aspect of catfish capture, the right to make a trap being regarded as a purchasable ceremonial privilege. The

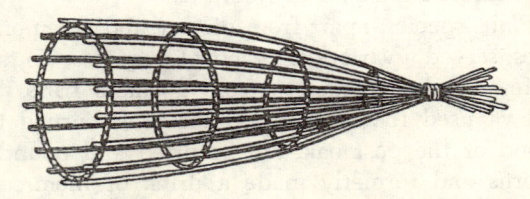

Fig. 4. A crudely woven willow fish trap used by the Blackfoot.

fisherman set up a weir of 6-foot poles in deep quiet water and used a basketry trap. Modern Iowa deny that their ancestors took fish in any other way than by spearing. The Eastern Dakota, who are of course not geographically Plains people, consumed quantities of turtle and fish, but did not like to have them to the exclusion of meat. They hooked, speared, and shot fish with arrows. Whether the hooks were of native make remains questionable. The absence of reference to nets and the denial of the use of narcotics for drugging fish are noteworthy.

WILD PLANTS

Both farming and pure hunting tribes of the Plains made use of berries, chokecherries, wild turnips, and the like. The wild turnip (*Psoralea esculenta*) ranked as a prized subsidiary food, large quantities of the root being dug up in early summer to be peeled and dried for winter use. It grew in hard ground with the root extending some inches below the surface; consequently, women dug it up with some difficulty. The Eastern Dakota, like the Menomini and Ojibwa, harvested considerable quantities of wild "rice," one of two canoers paddling while his partner beat the seeds off into the canoe with a stick. To a lesser extent it was gathered in the Sand Hills of Nebraska.

Plant species, apart from dietary and ceremonial uses, served a variety of practical purposes. To take a few random instances from a single tribe, the Kiowa used the cottonwood for fuel; burned the wood of the post oak, ate its dried and pounded acorns and formerly made a drink of them; and manufactured points for bird arrows from the thorns of the prickly pear.

AGRICULTURE

The part of agriculture in Plains economy has often been underestimated, both by minimizing its place among the villagers and by ignoring that even the nomads obtained farm products from the semisedentary tribes in exchange for peltry, horses, and sometimes European trade goods. As early as 1541 the members of Coronado's expedition found Plains tribes bartering their "cloaks" against the corn (maize) of agricultural Indians. In 1736 a Jesuit missionary spoke of the Assiniboin visiting the Mandan in quest of corn as though this was part of the annual routine. Two years later La Vérendrye, the earliest explorer in these regions to record his experiences there, witnessed an exchange between these tribes, the nomads offering muskets, axes, kettles, powder, knives, and awls for grain, tobacco, etc. In Lewis and Clark's day the Cheyenne bartered buffalo meat and robes against Arikara corn and beans.

Although such exchange implies a surplus of maize among the Plains Indian farmers, we must not make the opposite mistake of exaggerating dependence on maize. Even among the Pawnee, who represent the acme of development within the area, the two staples—corn and buffalo meat—were very nearly equally stressed; there was not the intense agriculturalism of the Pueblos. Archaeologists find plenty of buffalo bones in Pawnee village sites; and "the dire straits into which the tribe was thrown by failure to find the herds shows very clearly how heavily the Pawnee leaned upon the bison economically, even with their fields of maize" (Wedel). What holds for the Pawnee holds still more strongly for the farmers of the Upper Missouri. About 1800 the trader Tabeau records that the Arikara very often lacked maize and were hard put to it when buffalo likewise failed them. In 1834 the Mandan suffered from the same cause. Probably the Eastern Dakota were the least productive of the farming groups; except near Lake Traverse (between Minnesota and South Dakota) most of their villagers planted so little corn that according to the Rev. Samuel William Pond, who spent many years among these people, they "probably did not raise enough annually . . . to feed the whole population more than a week or two." Nevertheless, according to George F. Will, who, with George E. Hyde, has given special attention to the practical aspects of the question, in 1878, a good year, the Santee are credited with having raised 25$\frac{5}{7}$ bushels per acre, and in a fair season the villagers of the Upper Missouri produced 20 bushels.

Maize, beans, squashes or pumpkins, and sunflowers were the principal crops, the first overshadowing the others in importance. As usual in North America, except where agriculture was absolutely predominant, women did most or all of the cultivating. They had to struggle with the same difficulties that confronted subsequent White settlers—drought and grasshoppers. They lacked plows, draft animals, and fertilizers, and did not know about rotating crops. But considering the crudeness of their techniques and implements (Plate 3)—a hoe made from the shoulder blade of a buffalo or elk, a digging stick, and a rake—they obtained creditable results. The plots varied in size from about one-half to three acres. Since the tools were unsuitable for heavy turf, the land sought for cultivation might be 5 to 8 miles from the village, in the soft Missouri or Platte bottom lands. Pawnee women cultivating at such a distance were exposed to the attacks of hostile raiders; so they sometimes had bodyguards of armed warriors. Enemies of a different sort were the birds threatening the maturing plants; women erected stages from which they and their children frightened away the intruders. According to an expert estimate, the Kansa and Osage probably cultivated one-third of an acre for each person in the tribe, while for the Mandan and other more intensive agriculturists the figure was one acre.

There were generally two harvests. The earlier one, lasting a week to ten days, occurred in the first half of August, when part of the green corn was gathered, boiled or roasted, shelled, dried, put into bags, and stored for future use. Though the corn thus processed is often referred to as "sweet," it was not the true sweet or sugar corn, but the common species of soft flour or starch corn. On the Upper Missouri, the real sugar corn was ripened and made into corn balls. During later historic times in Nebraska, the natives used sugar corn both in green and mature form, but had probably followed the northern practice previously.

The second and main harvest occurred in September or the beginning of October. The Hidatsa harvesters plucked the ripe ears and carried them home in distinctive baskets (Plate 4). Subsequently, amidst merrymaking and feasting, the maize was husked with the assistance of young men, braided, hung from a scaffold for drying (Plate 5), and threshed with flails of ash or cottonwood in a booth under the scaffold. After winnowing, the women deposited the corn, as well as other

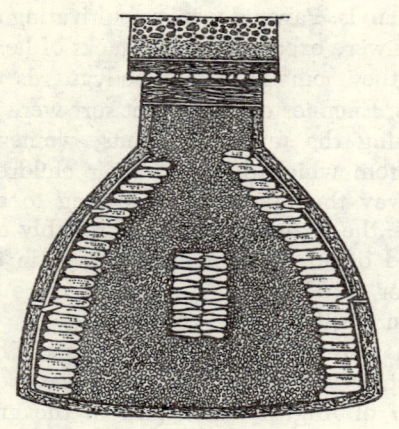

Fig. 5. A diagram of a Hidatsa cache pit, based on a native sketch. Ears of corn are stored around the outside of the pit; in the center, shelled corn and squash. The pit is covered, from the top down, with ashes and refuse, then a layer of dirt, a layer of grass, and finally a circular skin cover. At the "throat," this pit is a little over 2 feet wide. After a drawing by F. N. Wilson.

vegetables, in jug-shaped pits (Fig. 5), sometimes 8 feet deep, that were entered by a ladder. Since the mouths of these "caches" were 2 to 3 feet wide, people had to be careful in walking about at night. The Indians also stowed meat and various valuables in the pits when going off on a big hunt.

The Plains Indian farmers did not grow the dent corn preferred by White men, but had flour, flint, and sweet corns, which developed much variety of color within the area and differed in size according to latitude and soil. In the south, Pawnee corn grew up to 10 feet tall, but the stalks and ears diminished in size northward, so that in a poor year Mandan plants were dwarfed to 2 feet, with 4-inch ears. Yet the same plants attain a height of 5 to 6 feet under favorable conditions, the ears growing from 7 to 11 inches. The three native forms are very hardy, drought- and frost-resisting, requiring only 50 to 70 days to mature. In 1881, Oscar H. Will recognized the superior quality of aboriginal varieties under northwestern conditions and by experimentally improving the native types conferred a blessing on White farmers in the area, where a purely Mandan variety, Dakota White Flint, yields 40 bushels and more in eastern Montana and sections of North Dakota. In fact, on a model farm a yield of 70 bushels was achieved in 1914. Thus, as George F. Will and George E. Hyde have pointed out, the agricultural activities of Indian women have stimulated important development of Caucasian regional agriculture.

PREPARATION OF FOOD

The White man's flint-and-steel strike-a-light was adopted soon after contact, but the aboriginal firedrill lingered in memory (Fig. 6). For tinder, the Crow used rotten bark or buffalo droppings, the latter serving very widely as a substitute for fuel in timberless country. The drill was revolved between the palms, the bow not being apparently employed for this purpose in the area.

Among the northern agricultural tribes, wooden mortars and pestles (Plate 6) served to reduce corn to flour; even Pawnee sites noticeably lack the familiar Southwestern stone metate or hand mill, which is however common in prehistoric sites of Kansas and southern Nebraska. The semisedentary

Fig. 6. Drawing of a model of a Crow firedrill, about 15 inches long.

tribes made crude earthenware pots for boiling, while some of the nomads practiced "stone boiling," *i.e.*, they lined a pit with a hide, filled it with water, and dropped red-hot rocks into it. The same effect was obtained by suspending a hide or paunch from four sticks driven into the ground. The Blackfoot and some other nomads, however, have traditions of ancient pottery vessels. Besides boiling, cookery techniques included roasting meat on a spit or broiling it on coals. The prairie turnip was often baked in hot ashes. For camas roots the Blackfoot dug a pit, placed very hot stones over the bottom, and covered them with wet willow foliage and branches, on which the roots were laid. Then they put willow brush on top, heaped earth over it, built a fire on the earth, and tended it for 36 hours at least, until the odor indicated that the camas was cooked. Raking away the fire, the women uncovered the food amidst a cloud of steam and took the roots out of the earth oven. Roots not eaten at the time were stored in bags. This technique is clearly borrowed from the Plateau, of which the camas is typical.

Pemmican, *i.e.*, preserved meat, merits special attention as probably all the tribes used it, since buffalo meat and venison were often not available fresh. Sun-dried slices of meat, pounded fine with a maul (Fig. 7), were mixed with melted fat, marrow, and the dry paste from wild cherries that had been crushed, pits and all.

TOBACCO

Though probably all tribes smoked tobacco, by no means all grew it. The Cree in the north obtained theirs from traders and mixed it with dried bearberry leaves; the Comanche were dependent for their supply on the Mexicans. In their agricultural state the Cheyenne raised the plant as late as 1802, but later they relied on the Arikara and White traders. About a hundred years ago Denig knew only the villagers of the Upper Missouri and the Crow to be cultivators of tobacco in the northern section of our area. Certainly neither the Arapaho nor the Gros Ventre have any tradition of raising the plant themselves. On the other hand, three nomadic tribes —the Blackfoot, the Sarsi, and the Crow—planted tobacco ceremonially as their only crop, first burning

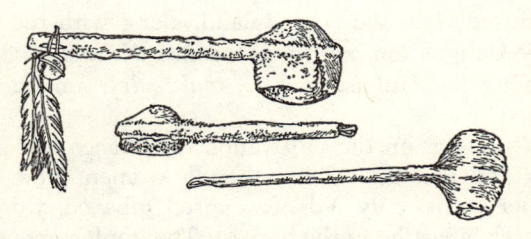

Fig. 7. Blackfoot rawhide-encased stone mauls. The example at the top is about 12 inches long.

over the ground chosen as the site. Interestingly, the Crow smoked not the ceremonial tobacco they cultivated, but another species or variety obtained from the Hidatsa.

The species grown east of the Mississippi and to some extent west of it was *Nicotiana rustica*. The Blackfoot, judging from a somewhat defective specimen, planted *N. attenuata*, which was undoubtedly the species of the Thompson River Indians west of them and also of the Ute, Navaho, Zuñi, the Washo of westernmost Nevada, and some groups in southeastern California. The Hidatsa, Mandan, and Arikara cultivated *N. quadrivalvis*, the Crow *N. multivalvis*. Botanically, both these varieties are related to *N. bigelovii*, which appears wild as well as cultivated in California and Oregon; and they are conceived as having originated from this Pacific form by simple mutations. It is a suggestive fact that the word used by the Crow and Hidatsa for tobacco is *ōp, ōpe*, which is virtually identical with the terms applied to it by the Diegueño of southern California, the Shasta in the northern part of that state, and the Takelma of Oregon. Since the majority of Siouan tribes have other words for tobacco, it seems reasonable to suppose that *N. bigelovii* was diffused from the coast inland, along with the native designation, and mutated into *N. quadrivalvis* among the Hidatsa and *N. multivalvis* among the Crow.

Our data on the cultivation of tobacco are best for the Hidatsa. There, though women grew the other crops, only old men raised tobacco, women merely assisting in the harvest. The implements employed included a hoe and a rake, respectively, for softening and leveling the soil, and a buffalo rib for hilling up the earth around each plant. The seeds were inserted early in the spring, at the same time as sunflower seeds, but in separate fenced gardens averaging about 21 by 18 feet. About the middle of June the blossoms were picked and dried indoors; they were prized more highly than the stems and leaves, which were plucked just before the frosts, the stems furnishing the greater part of the tobacco smoked. Both crops were oiled with buffalo fat before being stowed away in a pouch for future use. Seeds were set aside, but without selection.

Tobacco was as a rule reserved for ceremonies and other solemn occasions, and its use was subjected to restrictions. Pipes (Figs. 8, 9), not cigars or cigarettes, were prevalent in the area. Mostly only the men smoked, though small pipes were used by Blackfoot and Cree women; among the Hidatsa only elderly men indulged to any extent, juniors being warned that smoking would make poor runners of them. The Pawnee prohibited all but a few old women from smoking, and these were doctors. Even of the men, only those relatively few who met special qualifications were allowed to smoke.

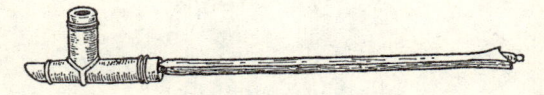

Fig. 8. A man's pipe, from the Comanche, with a carved red pipestone bowl and wooden stem, about 24 inches long.

Pipes were handled and passed according to definite tribal rules. A Blackfoot host handed a pipe to his vis-à-vis or to his left-hand neighbor, who puffed it several times, then passed it on to the left, and this continued till the end of the line was reached. Then the end man either returned the pipe to the host or, more generally, sent it back toward the right, no one who passed it taking a puff until the last man got it and returned it to the host, who smoked and sent it on a second round as before. Many tribes offered a pipe to the cardinal directions before smoking. In addition to such stereotyped tribal rules there was an infinitude of individual usages. Shoshone doctors removed their moccasins when smoking while treating a patient, and Lewis and Clark were requested to take off theirs among these people before accepting a pipe. Some Blackfoot would not smoke while an old pair of mocca-

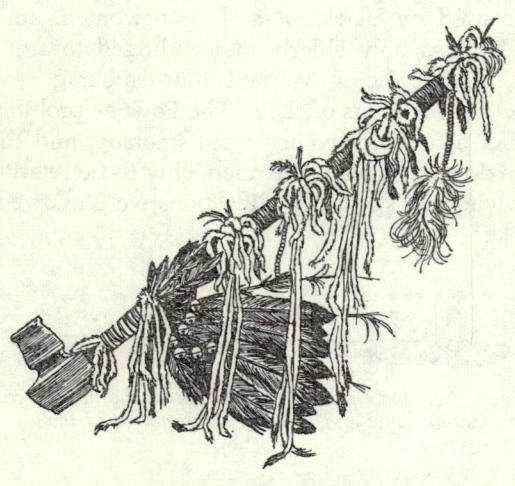

Fig. 9. A Blackfoot medicine pipe, the principle ritual object in one of their sacred bundles. This particular example is a little over 3 feet long, trimmed with strips of white ermine and feathers.

sins was hanging up; others had to put the pipe on a slice of meat or a buffalo tongue. Presumably such taboos were those imposed by supernatural beings.

Spirituous liquor was completely lacking in aboriginal times.

Settlement and Dwellings

Whereas the nomads lived throughout the year in portable dwellings, *viz.*, the skin-covered tipis, the semisedentary tribes used tipis only when on the move, otherwise occupying fixed earthlodges in permanent villages. Seasonal migrations were typical of both groups. In the winter the Cree, for example, were able to subsist only if they divided into very small bodies, and the whole tribe would reunite in the spring, resume full social activity, and hold the Sun Dance. The Pawnee, after a second hoeing of the maize about mid-June, left their villages for the summer hunt and returned to harvest in September; after storing the crops, toward the end of October, they would set out for the winter hunt, returning to plant early in April. When the cold set in, the Omaha scattered to sheltered spots; similarly the Mandan and Hidatsa sought protection in forest land with access to fuel, erecting earthlodges similar to those of the permanent village but smaller and of cruder construction. When on the tribal hunt, these tribes also pitched skin tipis.

The permanent settlements were fortified, and advantage was taken of natural features, such as ravines, that would serve for protection. The Pawnee did not use palisades, but erected a 3- to 4-foot embankment, in front of which was a ditch 3 feet deep and 5 feet wide. On the Upper Missouri these features were supplemented by palisades.

Naturally sites were chosen with an eye to the water supply. In the disposal of the available space, differences developed. The Omaha did not arrange their lodges according to any regular plan, though on the hunt they put up their tipis in a circle and allotted definite areas to each clan. But the Mandan kept an open central plaza for ceremonial performances.

Among the purely hunting peoples a camp circle was formed for major gatherings, notably at Sun Dance time. Some tribes, among them the Cheyenne (Fig. 29) and Dakota, fitted their tribal subgroups into the circle according to a definite plan, while such a scheme was not clearly in evidence among the Blackfoot. Important gatherings of a political or ceremonial nature took place in a special lodge set up at or near the center.

THE TIPI

The tipi (Dakota word) was an approximately conical tent, originally covered with buffalo skins, later with canvas. Women put up and took care of the tipis and were generally considered their owners. The size and number of poles used varied a good deal. An Eastern Dakota tipi measured by Prof. Wilson D. Wallis of the University of Minnesota had sixteen supporting poles, was 14 feet high, and had a ground diameter of 14 feet; for the cover the tribe is said to have used only seven or eight buffalo skins. This would be small, indeed, for Crow tipis, which averaged fourteen, the normal maximum being eighteen and for a medicine lodge twenty or twenty-two skins. The Blackfoot, Cheyenne, Arapaho, and Dakota all used more poles. Favored by the proximity of the Bighorn Mountains, the Crow have kept up the erection of substantial tipis of extra height, some of the poles being 30 feet or even 40 feet long and towering so far above the cover as to suggest the shape of an hourglass for the tipi.

Basic and correlated with other differences is the use of either three or four poles as a foundation for the rest. The Cheyenne, Arapaho, Teton, Assiniboin, Kiowa, Gros Ventre, Cree, Mandan, Arikara, Ponca, Oto, and Wichita use three poles, whereas the Crow, Hidatsa, Blackfoot, Sarsi, Ute, Shoshone, Omaha, and Comanche use four. From observation and experience, Prof. W. S. Campbell finds that the three-pole type is the stauncher, offering greater resistance to winds, the Cheyenne form being the most serviceable of all; the Crow variety is the most elegant in shape, though inferior in painted decoration to that of the Blackfoot, Dakota, Arapaho (Plate 9), and Kiowa.

All the Plains tipis are far more impressive than the similarly shaped tipis found among North Canadian tribes, Siberians, and Lapps. In pre-equestrian days the humbler form must have been prevalent since only shorter, lighter poles could have been readily transported. Quite probably this simpler variety, covered with bark or mats, was the original one and spread over a large area in North America and Eurasia.

Distinctive of the Plains tipi as compared with similar structures elsewhere was the regulation of the smoke vent. The fireplace was in the center; as an outlet for the smoke a hole was left at the top and the tent cover was provided with flaps ("ears") attached to two poles outside the general framework. By moving these extra poles it was possible to close the opening in bad weather.

The entrance, a narrow opening in the cover, generally faced east, and the place of honor was in the rear. A skin curtain with two parallel sticks above and below shielded the opening and was lifted by a person entering and allowed to drop back into position after he had gained admittance. The Blackfoot and Crow, though like all Plains Indians without chairs and stools, had backrests made of parallel willow sticks united with sinew threads and hung from a tripod. These tribes slept on robes placed on the ground, but the Arapaho had a veritable bed, combining a backrest at the head and at the foot with a platform a foot above the ground. Apart from ceremonial objects in the rear, the bedding, and the backrests, the tipi held mainly rawhide containers and such utensils as wooden dishes, horn spoons, weapons, and implements. Several tribes used a skin lining at the back wall to keep out the draft.

THE EARTHLODGE

The earthlodge of the semisedentary peoples was a circular, dome-shaped structure roofed with earth, entered by a covered passage, and accommodating up to forty inmates or more. The heavy posts had to be fitted into place by men, and altogether the erection of the house was a communal enterprise, the owners compensating their fellow villagers with a feast.

Variations occurred, sometimes even within one tribe. Whereas the Omaha tied the wooden elements of the structure with cords, the Hidatsa depended on skillfully fitting the posts, beams, and rafters by appropriate joinery; no nails or pegs were used. The Hidatsa roofs were either conical or had the extreme top flattened. The Omaha used from

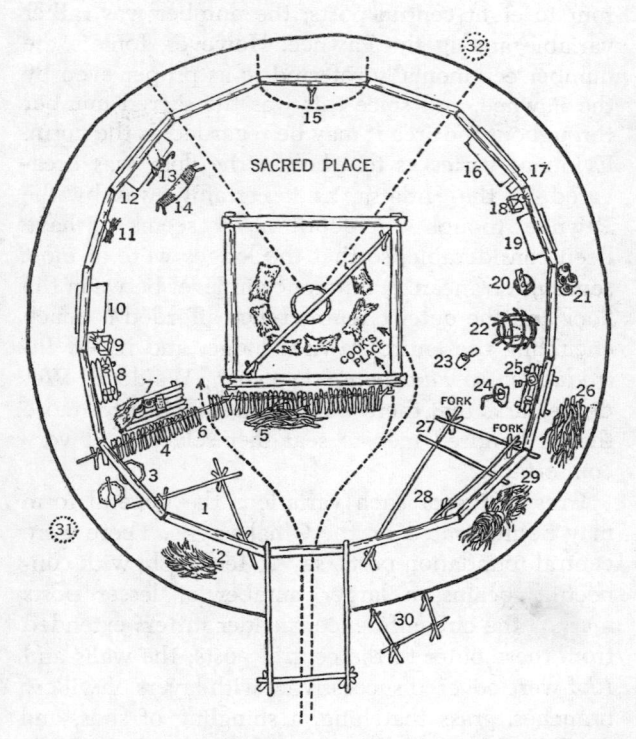

Fig. 10. *Diagram of the interior arrangement and equipment of Hairy-coat's father's Hidatsa earthlodge at Old Fort Berthold. Seats for the family are arranged around the central fireplace;* 1, *corral for stud horse;* 2, 29, *feed for the horse;* 3, *bull-boats;* 4, *partition;* 5, 26, *firewood;* 6, *door;* 7, *food platform;* 8, 25, *saddle platforms;* 9, 18, *clothing;* 10, 12, 16, 19, *beds;* 11, *arrowshafts and feathers;* 13, *lance;* 14, *backrest;* 15, *shrines;* 17, *arrow-making tools;* 20, 31, 32, *cache pits;* 21, *cooking utensils;* 22, *sweatlodge;* 23, *mortar;* 24, *stone hammers;* 27, *stall, for mean horse;* 28, 30, *corrals.*

four to eight central posts; the number was rather variable among the Pawnee. However, four is the number ceremonially referred to as proper even by the Pawnee, and since this was the sacred number throughout the area it may be regarded as the norm. Evidence varies as to whether the floor was excavated by the Hidatsa, as it certainly was by the Pawnee, though the depth never seems to have been considerable, so that the lodges were at most semisubterranean. A difference in level between the floor and the outer circumference afforded a bench encircling the entire Pawnee lodge, and in *An Introduction to Pawnee Archaeology*, Waldo R. Wedel remarks that there was "room sufficient for more than a hundred men to seat themselves on it very comfortably."

Irrespective of such variations the general form may be illustrated by the Omaha type. There were central foundation posts, say 10 feet high, with connecting beams; a larger number of lesser posts marked the circumference; slender rafters extended from these outer to the central posts; the walls and roof were covered successively with layers of willow branches, grass thatching, a shingling of sods, and finally earth. The entranceway was similarly built, 6 to 10 feet long, and had a skin curtain at either end. The fireplace was in the middle of the earthlodge, and an opening was left for the smoke vent; on the Upper Missouri a bull-boat, a hemispherical wooden skin-covered frame, was inverted over this hole to shut out rain.

The Hidatsa estimate the duration of an earthlodge at 7 to 10 years. By actual measurement some of their lodges extant in 1912 varied from nearly 11 to 13 feet in height and from 42 to 50 feet in outer

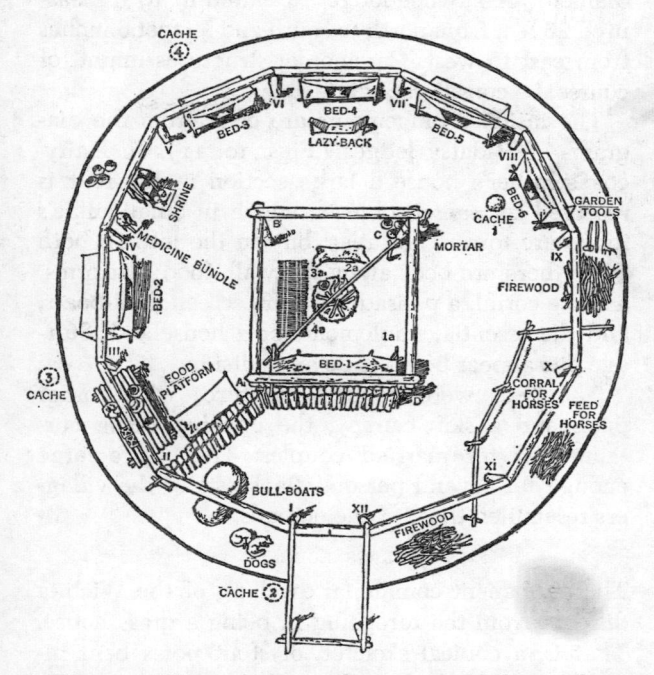

Fig. 11. Diagram of a twelve-post earthlodge, Hidatsa. The equipment and interior arrangement are shown in relation to the posts (I-XII). At the center of the earthlodge, between the interior posts A and D and in front of the fire, is a bed customarily occupied by the older people; across the fire from this is a cowskin seat; 1a is the cook's place; 2a is a good seating place with no special distinction; 3a and 4a are places of honor for distinguished guests. Extended diagonally across the fireplace is the pole from which the cooking kettle was suspended. Pottery vessels, used as containers for water, were generally kept near the mortar and pestle at interior post C.

diameter. A Pawnee lodge excavated in 1930 measured 46 feet from north to south and 44 feet 6 inches from east to west. Ceremonial structures might, of course, be considerably larger.

The inside arrangements are clear from the diagrams of Hidatsa lodges (Figs. 10, 11). In Hairycoat's father's house a large section in the rear is reserved for sacred objects, which in Small-ankle's lodge are toward the rear, but on the left. In both cases there are beds along the wall, food platforms, a horse corral, a palisade as a fire screen, bull-boats, and the essential implements of a household. Storage pits appear both inside and outside.

The beds were boxlike structures with corner posts and a skin canopy, the opening being curtained off for married couples. They were large enough for several persons. Backrests of the villagers resembled those of the nomads.

GRASS LODGES

The permanent communal dwelling of the Wichita differed from the foregoing in being a grass house. That is, a conical skeleton of stout poles bent inward was overlaid with grass thatch, the whole simulating the appearance of a haystack (Plate 8). The heavy thatching was tied with slender rods, and decorative tufts of grass were fastened at the junctures of the rods. Roof and walls were thus continuous and carried to the ground. A relationship to the earthlodge is indicated. The grass house is characteristic of the Caddo and other Southeastern tribes linguistically related to the Wichita and Pawnee, and archaeologists find remains of earthlodges of Pawnee type in Caddo territory. In what probably corresponds to present-day Kansas, Coronado discovered a type of habitation differing alike from the stone or adobe structures of the Pueblos and from the skin-covered tipis of the nomads he had encountered. "The houses which these Indians have," wrote one of Coronado's Spanish captains, "were of straw, and most of them round, and the straw reached down to the ground like a wall." It is generally assumed that he was writing of the Wichita or a related group.

OSAGE HOUSE

The Osage (and possibly also the Missouri) houses were oval or oblong in ground plan. Upright poles were arched to overlap on top where they were tied together, the lower poles being at the ends, the higher near the center. These vertical poles were interlaced with tiers of horizontal saplings. The domelike structure, not unlike a sweatlodge, was covered with mats or skins; it might be 30 and even 100 feet in length, 15 to 20 feet wide, and 10 feet high. Bell-shaped pits indoors served for storage or refuse containers.

When hunting, the Osage used the skin-covered tipi.

Domestic Animals and Transportation

The only domestic animal in precontact times was the dog, which in this area existed in a larger wolflike and a smaller coyotelike variety. The Comanche are said to have kept dogs solely as pets. Several tribes liked dog flesh—the Arapaho so much so that neighboring groups called them "Dog-eaters." The Dakota attached special importance to the eating of dog flesh at various ceremonies and the custom seems to have spread widely with a particular festival, the Grass Dance. Some tribes, however, never ate dogs, and the Blackfoot and Crow had a strong disinclination to do so. In any case, even among the dog eaters, there was no question of depending on the animal for subsistence. Nor were the dogs used in the chase by the typical tribes except for carrying the game; some of the marginal tribes of Plateau affiliation (Kutenai, some Shoshone) did find dogs a help in chasing deer and elk. Transport was, indeed, the general economic motive for keeping the animal in our area, particularly in the days before the Indians obtained the horse. Since the Indian dogs fiercely attacked strangers, they also had some value as sentries.

Dogs either carried loads on their backs or were trained to draw a crude vehicle, the "travois." Crow and Cree raiders packed extra moccasins on dogs' backs when setting out on an expedition. The true travois, prevalent north of the Platte and in later times adapted in larger form to horse transportation, consisted of two long poles whose front tips converged for attachment to the dogs' shoulders while the butt ends dragged along the ground; midway was attached a frame either in ladder form or made of a hoop with a netting of thongs (Fig. 12), and to this frame the load, sometimes 60 pounds and more, was tied. An important use for the dog travois was to relieve women in the transportation of firewood. A Hidatsa declared that women "with fifteen or twenty dogs could bring in enough wood to last the family a month"—presumably in the summer. The Indians similarly loaded meat secured in hunting, a quarter of a buffalo being considered a proper load among the Hidatsa. On the Missouri, bull-boats were sometimes lashed to

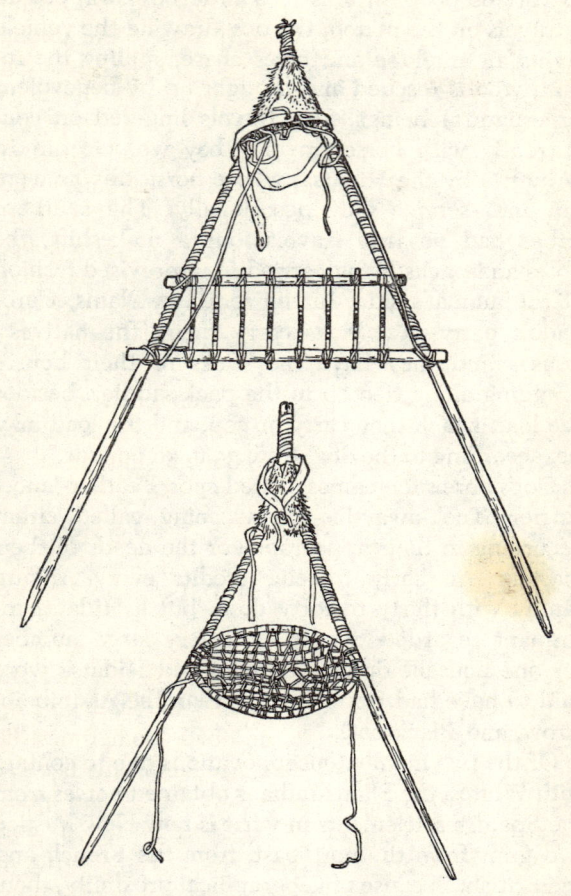

Fig. 12. *Blackfoot travois: at the top, for a horse; below, for a dog.*

the travois. A popular Plains Indian tale, known to various peoples, tells of a little boy strapped to a travois on the march; the dog drawing the vehicle sights an antelope and gives chase, spilling the infant, who is rescued and brought up by benevolent supernatural beings. Dog travois lingered on concurrently with horse travois; they were in almost daily use by the Hidatsa, whose horse travois were put into service only occasionally. The southern tribes had no true travois, but a makeshift, the poles and packs being carried in improvised fashion at the animal's side. In the southern Plains, Coronado's party saw "dogs carry their [the natives'] houses and they have the sticks of their houses dragging along tied on to the pack-saddles, besides the load which they carry on top, and the load may be, according to the dog, from 35 to 50 pounds."

Dogs bore such names as Red-spot, Feather-lance-carrier, Took-away-his-shield, being called either according to their appearance or the deeds of their masters. An early traveler credits every Arikara family with thirty to forty dogs, but a Hidatsa informant regarded twenty as a very large number for one household. The Mandan and Hidatsa were said to have had fewer in 1833 than the Assiniboin, Crow, and Blackfoot.

Of the two momentous innovations due to contact with Whites, the Plains Indians obtained horses from the Spanish settlements in what is now New Mexico and guns from the northeast, from the French and the British. Because of geographical proximity, then, the southern tribes had horses earlier than the northern tribes. We must assume that southern Indians impressed into Spanish service around Santa Fé learned to ride and to tend horses from their masters

MATERIAL CULTURE 43

and that some herders abducted animals in their care and passed them on with the acquired knowledge to other tribes. This development presumably did not set in until after 1630, for in that year a group of nomadic Apache are known to have traveled exclusively with dog travois and to have hunted buffalo unmounted. Later the keeping of horses spread by barter and theft, but at first diffusion was slow. By 1690 the Hasinai (Caddoan) of Texas had four or five horses to a household, but along the Red River the Caddo had altogether only about thirty head. In 1719 two Pawnee villages on the Arkansas owned a total of 300—less than one horse to a man—while by 1800 probably every Pawnee village on the Platte and Loup rivers had several thousand. In 1724 a body of 1,100 Kansa traveled with dogs exclusively, and another group of the same tribe had only a few horses. Prior to 1735 there were no horses north and east of the Missouri; in 1766 the Dakota of central Minnesota were still traveling in canoes rather than on horseback, but by 1772 horses had become common, and by 1796 their canoes had been replaced by horses. Farther west the Shoshone, Flathead, and Nez Percé preceded the Blackfoot and Crow as equestrians and may be taken as the source of supply for them. The Blackfoot probably did not obtain horses before 1730. Paradoxical though it may seem, the essentially nonequestrian Indians of the Southwest and the region marginal to the Plains Area on the west had horses before the Plains tribes who became the chief representatives of equestrian culture in North America; and the typical horse Indians stole horses largely from tribes with an essentially nonequestrian pattern of culture.

Though the horse became integrated with daily life, it did not evoke much originality except in a minor way. Without creating new forms the Indians did make their own riding gear—saddles, bridles, stirrups, quirts, ropes, cruppers—and in this way they made their horse culture independent, whereas guns, axes, knives, cloth always had to be acquired from Whites.

The travois was adapted to the new animal, which could carry much heavier loads; even the Crow, who made sparse use of the horse travois, transported disabled tribesmen on it. As explained, dog and horse travois were used simultaneously: on a communal Hidatsa hunt in about 1870, one family made its two ponies drag only tipi poles, while two mules and three dogs each pulled a travois.

Concerning the saddles it is worth noting that in most parts of the area a high-pommeled and cantled form was mainly reserved for women; men generally used a pad saddle or a frame of elkhorn tree and cantle with wooden side bars. Stirrups were of wood, bound with rawhide.

Horses were pastured on the prairie grasses, often under the care of young boys and men, who watered and otherwise tended them. In the winter the animals fed on cottonwood bark and branches. Particularly valuable animals were tethered to the tipi pegs or, among the villagers, put inside the earthlodge. Gelding was practiced, but possibly it was merely copied from Whites.

The introduction of horses revolutionized the natives' economic conceptions. It created great differences in wealth and correlatively in prestige. Paupers in a settlement, and those who had no more than one or two head, would trudge afoot when a camp moved, while favored tribesmen owned herds of 70 or 100. In 1870 or thereabouts one Hidatsa family owned about a dozen, which included one stallion and two swift runners reserved for chasing buffalo and enemies.

In course of time a horse came to be the preferred standard of value. Men paid for a ceremonial privilege with a horse, and a suitor might offer ten horses for a virtuous girl. Social standing could be enhanced by giving away property; hence, a man who had horses to present or lend to those less favored enjoyed an opportunity to rise in prestige.

In order to see Plains Indian horse culture in proper world perspective, however, we must remember that it lacked significant features associated with Mongol and Turkic horse breeders. The Asiatic nomads gained subsistence directly from their herds —by eating the flesh of their animals and milking their mares. Few of the Plains Indian tribes ate horse flesh except in times of famine—even the Comanche used it as a distinctly subsidiary food— and no American natives ever dreamed of milking mares. The economic utility of horses in our area, then, lay in enabling riders to kill large numbers of big game animals more rapidly and efficiently than was otherwise possible and in facilitating transport.

It is hardly superfluous to explain that, as Prof. Julian H. Steward of the University of Illinois points out, the horse was not everywhere an unmixed blessing. In Nevada it could not be kept easily because of grass shortage. "It would in fact have eaten the very plants upon which people depended." Its utility for transport did not compensate for the cost of its keep where large game herds were lacking, so that horses acquired by the Western Shoshone were eaten. Dr. D. B. Shimkin (Federal Bureau of the Census) argues that even in Wyoming the economic improvement due to the horse can be questioned. The density of population in the Wind River area was no greater in horse days than in the nonequestrian Great Basin. The Shoshone of that region were tempted to slaughter buffalo merely for skins and tongues, and the need of providing fodder for their mounts proved a liability, making long stops in one locality impossible. More horses did mean more buffalo killed, greater transport facility, and improved military position, but also less fodder for each animal, frequent migrations, and the attraction of alien raiders.

As pedestrians, the Plains Indians had several auxiliary devices apart from the dog travois. Among these was the cradleboard, for, unlike its Pima equivalent, the Plains Indian cradle was not primarily a sleeping place for the infant but a means of transportation. While a Pueblo woman carried her child's cradle in her arms, a Plains Indian mother transported it on her back by means of a buckskin band across her chest and upper arms. On the march the baby in its cradle might be put into a willow basket attached to a travois; a horsewoman slung the cradle from her saddle. The Kiowa, Comanche, and Dakota put the baby into a skin pocket elaborately beaded and attached to a "lattice" frame of two tapering flat sticks converging toward the bottom. The Arapaho placed a U-shaped framework inside the buckskin cover for the child, the U being made by bending a willow branch and fixing the position by means of a transverse stick. The Blackfoot, Kutenai, Crow, Nez Percé, Shoshone, and

MATERIAL CULTURE 47

Ute substitute for this type of frame was a board U-shaped at the top and tapering toward the bottom. The Southern Siouan form of frame is exemplified by a board 34½ inches long and uniformly 11¾ inches wide with a plain bow and two decorative zones at the head end, each carved and painted with an X-shaped figure enclosing triangles after the fashion of parfleche decoration (Fig. 13). In many cases the cradle was profusely ornamented.

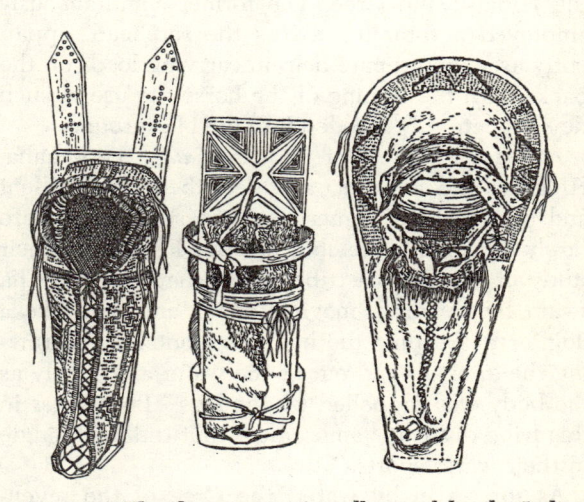

Fig. 13. The three types of cradles used by the Indians of the Plains area. On the left, the most typical, a bead-covered case attached to two pieces of wood which form a modified V, from the Kiowa. Center, a decorated flat wooden board from the Pawnee; the baby was wrapped in fur or fleece and tied onto the board with buckskin lacing. This type of cradle was used mostly by the eastern tribes. Right, decorated skin covering a wooden or basketry board; these cradles were used primarily in the western area, this example being from the Ute. The largest cradle, that from the Kiowa, is about 45 inches high.

The Cree and Assiniboin seem to have made little or no use of cradleboards in early days.

Dog sleds, though reported from the Mandan in 1833, are quite probably of alien derivation. On the other hand, the Cree used the snowshoe constantly in the wintertime, finding it very serviceable in the hunt and in fighting the Blackfoot, who lacked the device. Farther south, the Arapaho when in the Rockies pursued buffalo on oval snowshoes.

A carrying strap across the chest is recorded for the Hidatsa and Cree. The former simultaneously employed a tumpline across the forehead, apparently as a subordinate help in carrying loads on the back. With the coming of the horse the use of such devices naturally receded into the background.

At least a number of the tribes, *e.g.*, the Omaha, Hidatsa, and Arikara, are described as excellent and passionate swimmers, but the strokes used are rarely described. Fletcher and La Flesche in their study of the Omaha tribe report that "The Omaha swam by treading, moving hands and legs like a dog, or by keeping the body horizontal and throwing the arms up and out of the water alternately as the body was propelled by the legs." Both sexes in this tribe dived for amusement, but did not mingle in their water sports.

As for travel by water, the Cree of the seventeenth century are known to have made canoe trips and continued to do so in the following century. But as they turned more and more into buffalo hunters they, like their Blackfoot neighbors, knew only crude temporary hide rafts for ferrying across a deep stream. Blackfoot rafts, says Wissler in his paper on the material culture of this tribe, "were towed by the able-bodied men and women, usually the latter, swimming out and holding the lines with their teeth."

On the Missouri River, ferrying was done in a "bull-boat"; in later years cowskins replaced the buffalo hides originally employed (Plate 10). This tub was paddled; it was so light that a woman could easily carry it by means of a chest strap. Quite similar boats were used by the ancient Britons and are known from modern Wales, Ireland, Tibet, and elsewhere. The invention is so simple and distributed so spottily that it must have been achieved independently a number of times.

Dress and Personal Decoration

CLOTHING

Essential clothing was made of dressed skins. Because of the ease of obtaining cloth from the traders, it is difficult to give a comparative picture of tribal dress before White contact, for early travelers' accounts are much less ample for certain groups than for others. To indicate the kind of change brought about, we note that Omaha women came to wear skirts and to shorten their tunics, and quite commonly calico displaced skin shirts. Breechcloths were general in recent times, but there is doubt whether they are aboriginal; since ceremonial dress tends to preserve traditional forms, the ancient equivalent possibly was a deerskin apron or pair of aprons similar to those of Arapaho dancers.

The Crow costume (Plate 11) probably was typical of the northern Plains. It included a shirt, leggings reaching to the hip instead of trousers, moccasins, and a buffalo robe. Women wore a long dress of deer or mountain-sheep skin extending from the chin to the feet, knee-high leggings, and moccasins. The gala dress of Crow women was remarkable for its decoration—300 elk teeth—since no single hunter was likely to kill many elk and only two of the teeth of any one animal were acceptable for the purpose, rarity made such garments very pre-

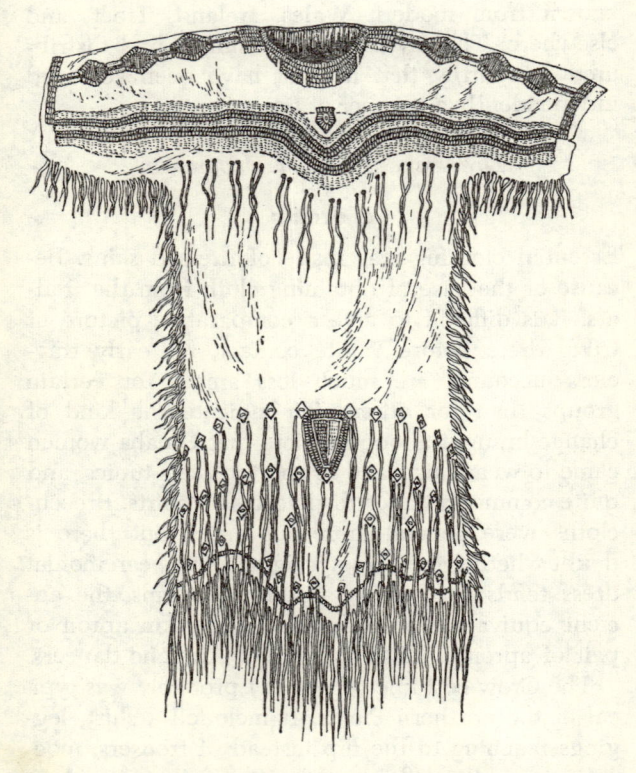

Fig. 14. A Blackfoot woman's dress, dating to the first half of the nineteenth century.

cious. A hundred years ago, a hundred elk teeth were rated of equal value with ten ermine skins (another decorative feature) or with one horse. Crow women wore similar dresses with bone imitations of elk teeth. The Crow were also conspicuous for the beauty of their buffalo robes.

Shirts are reported as originally lacking among the villagers and several southern hunting tribes. Indeed irrespective of the Canadian winter climate the Cree never covered the upper part of the body with anything but a robe, except ceremonially. The widespread use of the ornamental shirt seems to be a modern development in the Plains. The most usual feminine dress (Fig. 14) was in one piece and lacked sleeves; a two-piece garment is described for the Cheyenne, Osage, and Pawnee, who are said to have worn a skirt and a cape after the Eastern fashion. The ancient Omaha tunic was fringed at the sides, with the arms free.

Heelless skin shoes, in other words moccasins, were the general footgear (Fig. 15). Hard rawhide

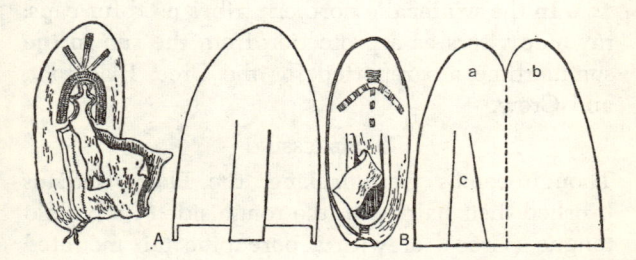

Fig. 15. Patterns for Plains Indian moccasins. In the two-piece pattern (A), the soles are of rawhide, the uppers in one piece, the tongue may or may not be separate, the ankle flap is separate. On the right is a one-piece pattern (B) for the upper (a), the sole (b), and the tongue (c).

soles distinct from the soft uppers were common, but this may have been due to Southwestern influence, for one-piece soft-leather moccasins have been collected or seen among the Blackfoot, Sarsi, Crow, Cree, Assiniboin, Gros Ventre, Shoshone, Omaha, Pawnee, and Dakota. For winter wear, buffalo skin was used with the hair inside.

The essential clothing was made by women, who sewed with buffalo sinew for thread, punching holes with a bone awl. Very general were fringes, pendants, and ornamental strips, which served aesthetic purposes and often also symbolically indicated the wearer's military accomplishments.

HEADGEAR

In the sign language, a White man is indicated by drawing the right hand across the forehead to suggest a hat, a fact that implies the absence of native headgear in ordinary circumstances. The familiar war bonnet and buffalo-horn caps were reserved for festive occasions, and various headdresses in museum collections are ceremonial regalia (Plate 12). In the winter the northern tribes used fur caps; rawhide visors as a protection from the sun in the summertime are reported for the Cree, Blackfoot, and Crow.

HAIRDRESSING

Though combs were lacking, the Plains Indians brushed their hair—with the rough side of a buffalo tongue (Cree), or with a porcupine tail mounted on a stick, or with porcupine bristles tied to a stick with rawhide (Fig. 16) or, as among the Omaha, with stiff grass, one end being tightly wound about to provide a handle.

MATERIAL CULTURE

Coiffures were modified in the course of time by imitation of alien fashions and there were considerable individual preferences, at least among the men. A common feminine style was to part the hair in the middle, from the forehead to the nape of the neck, and to paint the parting line red. Omaha women arranged the hair in two braids, which were tied together at the ends and allowed to fall behind the ears. Blackfoot girls and young matrons used two braids or let the hair hang loose, tying it with a forehead band.

The Crow consider braids a departure from ancient usage for either sex. Their men in earlier times divided the hair roughly into two parts, they say, and let it flow loosely down the back and the sides of the face. Doubtless there were different fashions even then; one of Bodmer's subjects has his hair coiled in a bulky foretop. The Crow were conspicuous for artificial additions to their hair in the back.

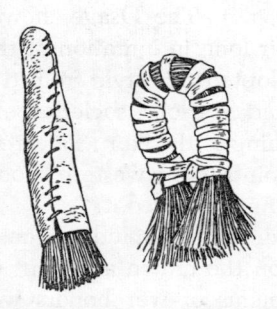

Fig. 16. Blackfoot hairbrushes: left, porcupine bristles on a stick, bound with rawhide (about 4 inches high); right, horsehair, also bound with rawhide.

Horse hair ... is arranged in 8 or 10 strands, each about as thick as a finger, and laid parallel with spaces between them of the width of a single strand. Fine gum is then mixed with red ocher, or vermilion ... and by means of other hair, or fibers of any kind laid cross-wise, the strands are secured, and around each intersection of hair a ball of gum is plastered to hold it in place. About 4 inches further down, a similar row of gum balls and cross strings are placed, and so on down to the end. The top of the tail ornament is then secured to the hair on the back of the head. The Indians frequently incorporate the false hair with their own so as to lengthen the latter without any marked evidence of deception [Mallery].

A pompadour effect worn by Crow men was sufficiently common to be used as a tribal mark in Dakota pictographs (Plate 13).

Highly distinctive of the Pawnee and Southern Siouans was the practice of closely cropping the hair so as to have only a central ridge across the crown (Plate 14). The Osage, however, came to wear their hair long in imitation of the Ponca, who themselves adopted this style from the Dakota. On the other hand, various societies of other tribes adopted roaching of the hair as a ceremonial badge. The custom points to the western Woodlands, where the Sauk and Fox observed it.

A number of tribes, including the Omaha, separated a lock on the crown and kept it distinct and braided. Emblems of war honors were tied to it, and it was cut from the head of a slain warrior for use in triumphal processions.

ADORNMENT AND MUTILATION

There were innumerable minor decorative devices, some of them native, others obtained from alien tribes and, in historical times, from White traders. The Plains Indians wore bear-claw necklaces, earrings, shell earrings and drops, shell gorgets, and a variety of other articles, some indicative of status. Body and face paint were usual, red pigments being perhaps most frequent. Pigments were derived from animals and plants. Men plucked out their facial hair with the fingers or tweezers, and the Comanche removed their eyebrows even so recently as a generation ago.

Tattooing, though not so highly developed as in Polynesia or aboriginally in our Southeastern states, was far from rare. The Wichita indulged conspicuously in the practice, and so did the Southern Siouans. An eminent Omaha could get prestige for himself and a daughter recently come of age by having her tattooed in the center of the forehead with a black circle representing the sun and with a four-pointed star on her chest to symbolize the night.

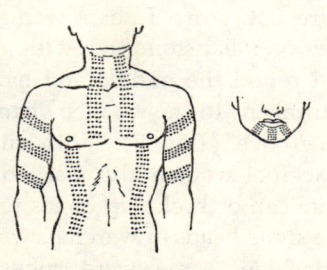

Fig. 17. Plains Cree tattoo designs: left, on a man's body; right, on a woman's face.

The Osage tattooed both sexes, a warrior gaining the privilege by deeds of valor both for himself, his wife or a daughter. However, the practice was not limited to the southern part of the area. The author has seen an old Hidatsa tattooed on one half of his chest; the Crow sometimes tattooed both sexes; and with the Cree, tattooing was common for men and women (Fig. 17), the former marking arms and chests, the women only as a rule the space between lips and chin. The custom evidently had ritualistic and social aspects apart from the aesthetic.

Tools and Artifacts

TOOLS

The obvious superiority of metal tools soon led the Indians to abandon their earlier equivalents of bone, stone, etc. It is accordingly difficult to reconstruct their aboriginal tool kit. Nevertheless some ancient implements have survived into the present or recent past, some have been described by early travelers, still others are revealed by archaeological excavation.

Even in recent years Indian women pounded chokecherries on a flat stone slab with a stone hammer grooved round the middle and hafted by wet rawhide shrunken to a wooden handle passed around the groove (Fig. 7). With such mauls a Crow or Blackfoot woman also mashed chokecherries for pemmican or broke up bones to extract the marrow. The stone heads of warclubs were mounted in similar fashion; some were spherical, others pointed at both ends (Fig. 18), still others ax-

MATERIAL CULTURE 57

Fig. 18. A Crow stone-headed war club, about 42 inches long.

shaped. Such clubs were sometimes used for killing a wounded buffalo in the corral.

Water-worn pebbles and slabs struck from their outer surfaces served as scrapers. Arrow shafts were smoothed between two grooved stones. Knives were of stone or bone (Fig. 19). Coronado saw buffalo-hunting nomads cut off mouthfuls of meat with

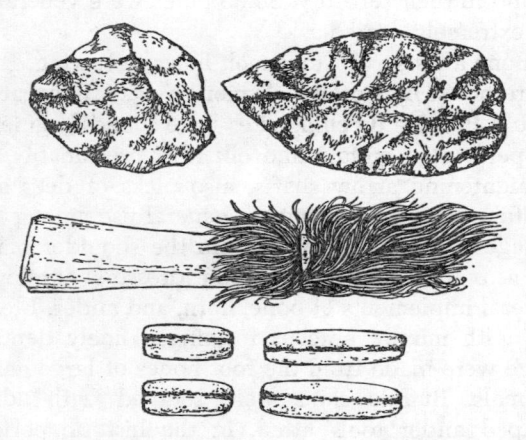

Fig. 19. At the top, chipped stone knives from the Blackfoot. Center, a model of a Blackfoot bone knife, decorated with fur, about a foot long. Bottom, Pawnee arrow-smoothers used for arrow shafts, 2 to 3 inches long.

flint knives. Blackfoot arrowheads are said to have been more frequently of bone, deer, and buffalo horn; the Omaha used flint or other stone points in big-game hunting and warfare. In early historic Pawnee sites the predominance of small, thin, triangular stone points is noteworthy, being suggestive of Iroquoian connections. Pressure flaking with an elk horn is reported as an Omaha technique in stonework.

Pipes were commonly of stone, especially catlinite. The quarry for this red stone lies in southwestern Minnesota, which is in Eastern Dakota tribal territory, but catlinite pipes were diffused to distant tribes, such as the Arapaho and Crow. However, other materials also were used; the Arapaho had black stone pipes as well, and the Blackfoot shaped their pipe bowls from a dark greenish stone found in their territory. Some pipes were venerated as extremely sacred.

Bone awls served to punch holes in sewing; they were noted by Coronado's men in 1541. Excavators of old Pawnee dwelling sites have found fragments of perforated buffalo and elk ribs, presumably for straightening arrow shafts, also picks of deer and buffalo bone for digging. In general use among the villagers was a hoe made from the shoulder blade of a buffalo (Plate 3). Skin dressers employed several implements of bone, horn, and antler. Fleshers with minute notches forming a finely dentate edge were made from the foot bones of large game animals. Buffalo skins were scraped with adze-shaped antler tools fitted, in the historic period, with iron blades, whose antecedents are unknown since archaeological stone scraper blades do not jibe with the handle. In dressing a deerskin the

MATERIAL CULTURE 59

hide was thrown over a log and cleared of hair with a rib or leg bone (Fig. 20).

CRAFTS

Throughout the area the textile crafts were poorly developed. Cotton was unknown. Thread for sewing was of sinew. The Blackfoot twisted the tough bark of some shrub into rope; the Omaha pounded the fibers of a nettle free from the woody part and braided it into rope, aboriginally probably weaving buffalo hair into lariats, scarfs, belts, and forehead bands. The women of this tribe doubled broad, short scarfs and sewed them together at the sides, using the resulting bags for practical purposes while men stowed away ceremonial articles in them. The

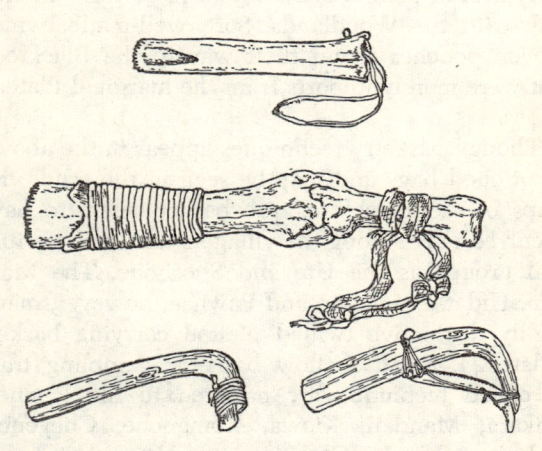

Fig. 20. At the top, two kinds of tooth-edged fleshing tools: above, shaft from tibia, Ute; center, shaft from tibia with part of femur attached and iron blade, Gros Ventre. This tool is about 15 inches long. At the bottom, adze-shaped tools used for scraping hides, with antler handles and iron blades. These are about 12 inches long.

Iowa wove floor mats of reeds over a bark-cord foundation, employing the same technique as the Winnebago and Central Algonkians. The same tribe made loosely twined rectangular storage bags, the fiber being basswood or nettle. Floor mats are definitely reported from the Pawnee, who also made them do service as bedding, bed curtains, and wrapping for corpses. The last-mentioned use is indicated likewise in a Pawnee burial site, where remnants of matting show a simple twining technique with narrow-leaved grass or rush fibers. The same excavation revealed bits of buffalo-hair cloth, the same piece being sometimes in different weaving techniques. Spindle whorls were lacking.

Soft twilled buffalo-hair wallets may be regarded as typical of the Southern Siouans and form another link with the Woodlands. Soft, well-made twined woven pouches found their way to the Blackfoot, but were merely imports from the marginal Plateau tribes.

Though basketry techniques appear in the above-mentioned bags and may be seen in the crude fish traps of the Blackfoot, true baskets seem to have occurred only among the villagers and such peripheral groups as the Ute and Shoshone. The Mandan, Hidatsa, Arikara, and Pawnee, however, made highly distinctive twilled plaited carrying baskets (Plate 4). Small shallow basketry gambling trays of coiled technique are credited to the Pawnee, Arikara, Mandan, Kiowa, Comanche, Cheyenne, and Arapaho. In Cass County, Nebraska, a site excavated by Prof. W. D. Strong of Columbia University harbored clay fragments with impressions of coiled basketry.

Pottery is not impossible for peoples without ag-

1. A Plains Cree fish weir, located near the bend in the river.

2. A close-up, showing the construction of the entrance in the center of the weir.

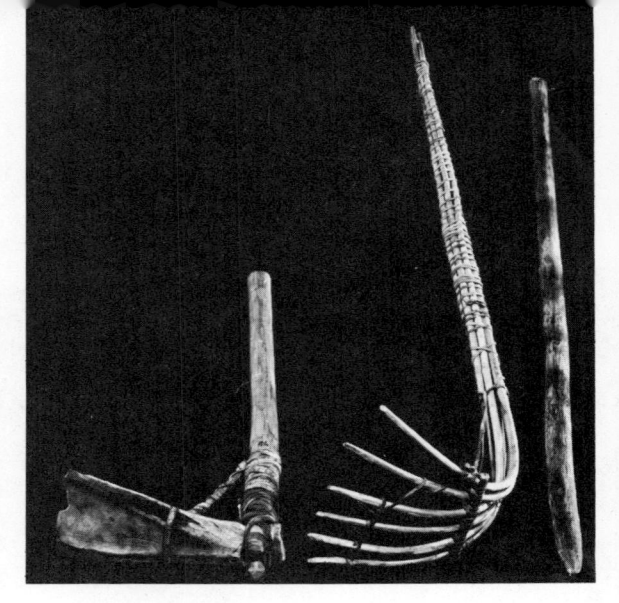

3. Hidatsa agricultural implements: left to right, a bone hoe, a rake, and a digging stick.

4. Hidatsa burden baskets. At the left, a basket made of skin, used for carrying off debris when building an earthlodge; at the right, a willow bark harvest basket.

5. *A scaffold with surrounding rack used by the Hidatsa for drying corn.* Photograph by F. N. Wilson.

6. *A Hidatsa woman pounding corn into meal with a wooden pestle and mortar.* Photograph by F. N. Wilson.

7. *Hidatsa agriculture: raking with a horn rake (left) and hoeing squashes with a bone hoe (right). Photographs by F. N. Wilson.*

8. A grass-covered lodge and shade built by the Wichita.

9. *A painted tipi used by the keeper of the sacred pipe in 1900, from the Arapaho.*

10. *A Hidatsa woman paddles a bullboat on the Missouri River.*

11. *Crow couple in costume, about 1915.*

12. The Sun Dance headdress and hair-lock necklace of the Blackfoot.

MATERIAL CULTURE 61

riculture, but if they are obliged to move constantly, as did the Plains Indian hunting tribes in search of buffalo, the maintenance of earthenware becomes extremely difficult. Accordingly, though the modern Blackfoot, Cree, Arapaho, and other nomads have occasionally referred to ceramics as a lost art practiced by their ancestors, the evidence on this point is contradictory; however, recent archaeological findings lend some support to such statements. The villagers of the Upper Missouri have been observed manufacturing pots (Plate 15), and the proof is perfect for demonstrably Pawnee sites. Accordingly, there is no reason to doubt relevant statements by the Omaha and other cultivators within the area who lost the art soon after access to metal substitutes.

Compared with the ceramic ware of other areas, Plains earthenware seems crude. However, this has been plausibly explained by assuming that the villagers lost interest in the craft when the trader's utensils became available and the Indians intensified their hunting. From unquestionably prehistoric Pawnee settlements, archaeologists have unearthed pottery of a much better quality than from later sites, and certainly much better than the earthenware observable in the recent period.

Technologically, Plains pottery, unlike that of most North American natives, was not coiled, *i.e.*, not built up spirally from little sausages of clay, but hand-molded. It largely comprised globular cooking vessels, but clay pipes as well as stone ones occurred among the Mandan. A noteworthy Pawnee feature is the collarlike rim of the pots with its incised ornamentation largely consisting of isosceles triangles enclosing chevrons or lines parallel to one of the sides. The importance of the phenomenon lies in the resemblance to the ware of the Iroquois of New York State.

Woodwork is another craft that is quite undistinguished among Plains Indians, though the skill shown in fitting the posts and beams of earthlodges commands respect. Such Arapaho carvings as the three-dimensional representation of a supernatural patron (Fig. 21) were rather unusual. The men did manufacture a number of utilitarian articles, of which mortars among the villagers and bowls more generally were important. The Omaha shaped a mortar from a section of a tree trunk about 1 foot in diameter and 3 feet long, chipping one end to a point for insertion into the ground and hollowing out the opposite end. They put coals on the surface, fanning them till they burned into the wood to an adequate extent, finally smoothing the mortar with sandstone and water. The pestle, 3 to 4 feet long, was much larger at the top than at the tapering end used for pounding; this held also for the Hidatsa equivalent (Plate 6).

The Omaha made their bowls from black walnut burrs, the excavating process being the same as for the mortars. Ladles were made so that the handle could be hooked over the rim of the bowl. Spoons were sometimes of wood instead of horn. Not all bowls were for food. The Crow had some for mixing tobacco seeds or paint or for throwing dice. Aboriginal ladders were notched logs; a Hidatsa woman reached her corn-drying stages by a notched cottonwood trunk pointed for security at the butt end.

If the Plains Indians achieved little as carvers, potters, and textile workers, their women were conspicuous for their craftsmanship as skin dressers,

Fig. 21. An Arapaho wood carving (about 24 inches high), decorated with fur and feathers, representing a supernatural patron.

making not only clothes but also most of their containers from the hides of buffalo and other large game animals. Skin objects were either of rawhide or of leather. For both, the hide was first staked out on the ground, with the hairy side down, then the worker hacked away fat, muscle, and connective tissue with the toothed flesher. After several days' bleaching in the sun, the woman scraped the skin down to an even thickness with the antler adze; if she desired to remove the hair, the hide was turned over and treated with the adze. With this dehairing the rawhide process ended.

Rawhide served for binding or for the manufacture of receptacles. The handle of a stone cherry pounder or maul (Fig. 7) was attached to the head by a covering of green or wet rawhide, which dried and shrank, thus firmly holding the parts together. The containers include women's square bags of envelope shape; similar but heavily fringed bags, usually for storing ceremonial articles; roughly cylindrical medicine cases, similarly fringed and closed at either end by a rawhide disk; and the "parfleches," mainly for storage of pemmican and other edibles (Figs. 22, 23). The decoration of these receptacles is dealt with in the chapter on Art; here only a few structural details will be mentioned. For the fringe on the sides of the envelope bag and the cylindrical container, an oblong piece of hide was cut into strips without completely severing them from one edge and inserted between the edges of the bag and sewed to them. The parfleche, as defined by Clark Wissler, is "a sheet of hide folded up into a package after the usual manner of the powders prepared by a physician." In order

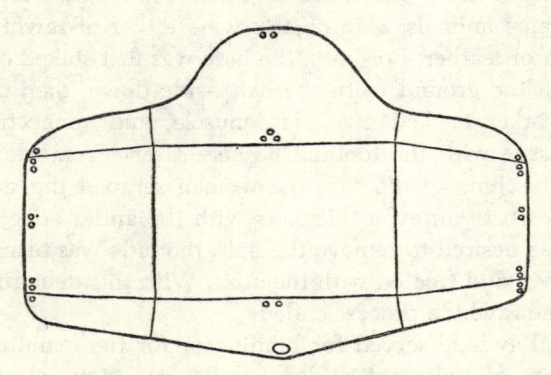

Fig. 22. A pattern for a parfleche. To close, first the long flaps and then the short ends are folded over and laced with thong (see top illustration in Figure 23).

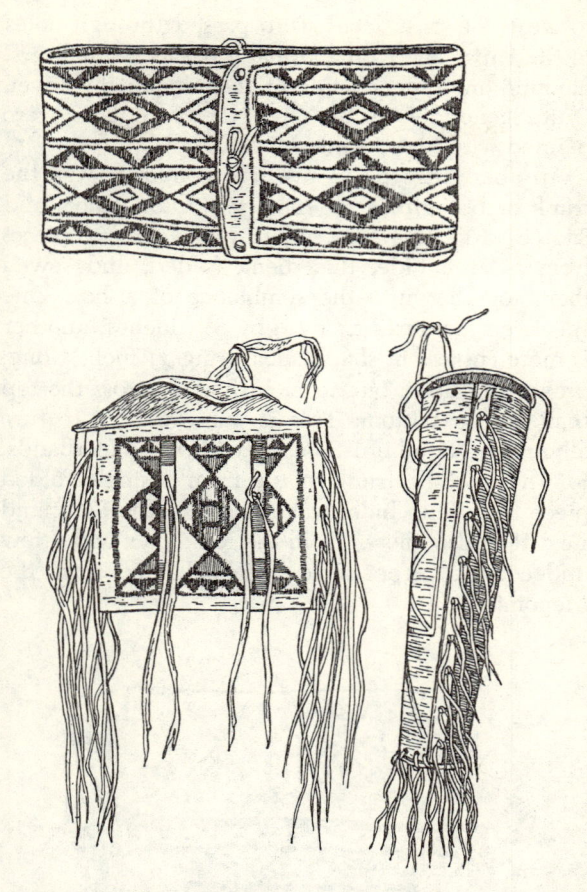

Fig. 23. Above, a painted rawhide parfleche (26 inches long, 13 inches high) from the Blackfoot. Lower left, a painted rawhide bag decorated with buckskin fringe. Lower right, a rawhide container for ritual objects (about 14 inches high). All these are from the Blackfoot.

to close the case, laces were passed through holes in the flaps. The Arapaho made parfleches in pairs, hanging one on each side of their mount in travel. Quite generally in the area the two flaps were painted with identical designs.

An aberrant type of rawhide container was the trunk or box typical of the Iowa, Oto, Ponca, and Santee (Fig. 24). The Iowa and Oto cut pieces from a large hide, then bent, folded, and sewed them together into the semblance of a box. One specimen measures 14 by 9 by 8½ inches; another is more cubical in shape, measuring 11 inches long, broad, and deep, but an inch shorter across the top than at the bottom. This is once more a feature allying the Southern Siouans with the Woodlands, for the rawhide trunk, made from a single folded piece of buffalo hide, was typical of the Sauk and Fox. It is also known from the Kickapoo, and a few undecorated pieces have been collected from the Menomini.

Fig. 24. A painted rawhide trunk from the Hidatsa, about 15 inches from side to side and 10 inches high.

MATERIAL CULTURE

Leather was required for clothing and soft pouches. In order to produce it the skin dresser had to subject the fleshed and scraped rawhide to a kind of tanning. She thoroughly rubbed into the surface an oily mixture of fat with buffalo or other brains, first with her hands, then with a smooth stone. Then the hide was dried in the sun and rolled up into a bundle. At this point it would shrink and had to be stretched back to its proper size. Next a rough-edged stone was rubbed over the surface, and the skin was run back and forth through a loop of sinew attached to a pole. This process dried and softened the skin, which thus became pliable. For some robes the hair was left on. Unlike buffalo skins, those of deer had the hairy surface rubbed down with a rib as a "beaming" tool before being rubbed over a cord. Some skins were browned by smoking: a smoldering fire was built in a small pit, and over it the skin was wrapped around a set of poles put up in the form of a cone. According to Catlin this operation made the skin capable of remaining soft and flexible irrespective of exposure to moisture. The Omaha made a practice of smoking skins to be cut up into moccasins.

Apart from articles of dress, which have been dealt with separately, leather was used in manufacturing a variety of soft pouches, including receptacles for smoking appurtenances, paint bags, women's workbags, knife cases, and toilet bags (Fig. 25).

Probably none of these articles, either of rawhide or of leather, was universal, but they were very widely diffused, partly through friendly visits associated with gifts and trading. For instance, the Cree did not make parfleches, but occasionally

Fig. 25. A bead-decorated soft skin pouch used for paint by the Arapaho. Note that the design differs slightly from the front to the back.

acquired them from other groups. However, parfleches are known from such borderline Plains peoples as the Nez Percé and Kutenai, while the peripheral Shoshoneans even developed a distinctive style of decoration for these containers.

Skin dressing was deeply influenced by the introduction of iron blades and the fur trade. Also robes and other skin manufactures spread widely from their centers of origin through gifts and trading among the tribes. The fur trade deeply affected native life. Whereas formerly the Indians had killed game for their own needs, they now hunted for gain on a much larger scale than before. One consequence was the rapid killing off of buffalo, another the increased duties of women in supplying the White men's demand for abundant dressed skins. Since, in addition, buffalo became virtually extinct and deer and elk scarce, it has not been possible to reconstruct in complete detail the aboriginal way of dealing with hides. Nevertheless early accounts and observation of processes preserved even recently on reservations, though mostly with the substitution of cattle skins, give a fair idea of this important native industry.

One of the feminine crafts highly developed in the area was porcupine-quill embroidery. It was best among the Dakota, Cheyenne, and Arapaho but lacking in the south among the Kiowa, Comanche, Apache, and Wichita. This absence is not wholly explained by that of the porcupine since quills could have been traded in. In the practice of this industry, too, White contacts brought changes in the use of new dyes for the quills and in providing glass beads as a replacement of quill embroidery.

Though the Omaha did not equal the skill of more northern tribes in this craft, relatively full information is available concerning their operations and will accordingly be drawn upon. The men killed the animals, from which the quills had to be promptly plucked to prevent breakage; these were sorted as to size and put into bladder bags. The largest quills, from the tail, served to decorate workbags and comb cases, while the hair of the animal was used for extra-fine ornamentation. The Omaha used fine quills for moccasin designs but were less given than other tribes to ornament other articles of clothing. The quills were not split, but put into the mouth to render them more pliable and flattened with the fingernails. With an awl the embroiderer punched holes for the sinew and quills.

> A stitch was taken but not through the skin and the sinew was passed through and pulled tight. Then another stitch was taken in the same way but the sinew was not pulled tight. A little loop was left and through this loop the blunt ends of the quills were put. If, for exam-

ple, four quills were to be used, they were placed one on the other through the loop, which was then tightened. A quarter of an inch from the first stitch of sinew a similar stitch was taken and in the loop four quills were fastened in the same way. Then the first quill was bent toward the second loop and the first quill of the second loop was bent toward the first loop, and the braiding went on, back and forth, until all four quills were in place, the last quill being doubled under and the sinew used in a stitch to hold it in place. In this way little by little the pattern progressed.

The Omaha prepared a black dye by roasting yellow earth and tallow, constantly stirring them, and adding the blackened result to a boiling mixture of maple bast and leaves. In the very black liquid thus procured the quills were steeped overnight. For red dye the root of an unidentified plant was boiled, the quills being added for a short time. Yellow was obtained by boiling either early cottonwood buds or the roots of a vine. In other districts of the area, corresponding results were attained from other sources. Northern Plains tribes boiled a moss growing near pine or balsam fir trees for a yellow dye; and Denig credits the Crow with using "several coloring herbs and mineral substances unknown to other tribes, which produce much better colors." Interestingly enough, Crow, Omaha, and Dakota deny the aboriginal use of blue, though this figured in considerable measure after the introduction of aniline colors.

The embroiderer's outfit included only awls,

sinew, a bone marker for tracing designs, and the container for these articles. The Dakota and Arapaho also had quill flatteners made of bone or antler (Fig. 26).

Fig. 26. An Arapaho bone tool used for flattening quills and painting skins (about 9 inches long).

The Plains Indians generally employed the "two-thread" sewing technique in which the threads ran parallel, say one-quarter inch apart, and were caught under the skin at intervals; one or more quills were folded around the threads, passing back and forth between them. The resulting bands are usually straight and stiff. More rarely, as a rule only for rosettes, the Plains embroiderer caught a single thread under the surface of the skin and wrapped quills round it, singly, as she proceeded with the stitching. This produced a finer line, capable of curving in any direction, as explained by Frederic Douglas of the Denver Art Museum in the occasional publications of his institution.

In beadwork either the "lazy" or the "overlay" stitch was used. In the former, beads were strung on threads, which were fastened to the surface at the ends of short parallel rows. The result resembles some types of quillwork and suggests adaptation of the earlier technique to the new material. In the overlay stitch "strings of beads are tightly attached to the surface, in close-set rows, with other threads, thus producing a smooth finish." Whereas the lazy

WEAPONS

Bows and arrows, clubs, spears, and shields were the weapons used in warfare and on the hunt.

Bows were either of wood or of horn and were comparatively short, though according to the Omaha they were longer before the horse was introduced, the greater length proving inconvenient for a mounted warrior (Fig. 27). A Blackfoot specimen collected in 1870 is 3 feet 5 inches, and Catlin, whose observations date back to the early 1830s, gives 3 feet as the standard length among Crow and Blackfoot. Ash and ironwood were preferred by the Omaha, the Osage orange (*bois d'arc*) by the Comanche, chokecherry wood by the Cree. The material would vary according to geographical conditions and even in the same tribe according to facilities of access at any given time. Thus the Crow tales refer to cedar as the material, and the Chicago Natural History Museum has several Crow hickory bows and one of ash.

Wooden bows were either simple (self-bows) or strengthened with sinews glued on the back. Simple bows were typical of the United States Indians east of the Missouri and occurred to the west as toys, whereas sinew-backed bows characterized the Far West. Accordingly, sinew backing was found among the Ute, Crow, Blackfoot, Plains Cree, Cheyenne, and Hidatsa, but not among the Omaha. It is highly probable that sinew backing was brought into the western part of the Plains through contact with Plateau and Basin tribes. The Blackfoot speci-

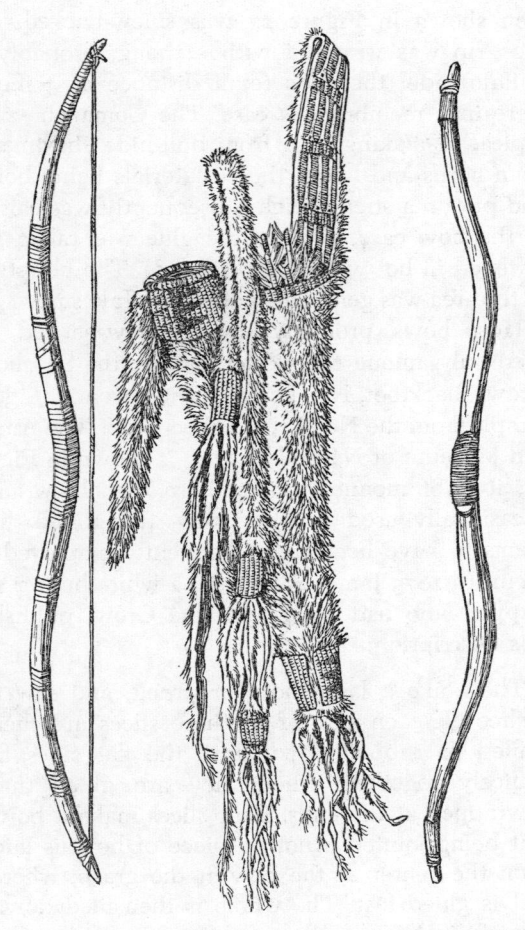

Fig. 27. A sinew-backed bow (45 inches in length), and combined otterskin quiver (with arrows) and bow case, Blackfoot; at the right, a mountain-sheep horn bow from the Nez Percé.

men shown in Figure 27 was sinew-backed, and the grip was wrapped with a thong, probably of buffalo hide; the ends for a distance of 4 inches were in a membranous case. The Comanche were typical in making glue from bull-hide shavings or from horns and hoofs, these materials being boiled and put on a stick, which subsequently was carried in the bow case, whence the glue was taken and softened in hot water for ready use. The bowstring of the area was generally made of buffalo sinew.

Horn bows, probably always sinew-backed, figured only among the western tribes, the Shoshone, Crow, Blackfoot, Nez Percé, and Cheyenne. A good sample from the Nez Percé collection of The American Museum of Natural History is shown in Figure 27; it is of mountain-sheep horn, which was also occasionally used by the Crow, though elk horn seems to have been more frequently employed by them. In 1875 James S. Belden, a white hunter and trapper who had lived with the Crow, published this description:

> They take a large horn or prong, and saw a slice off each side of it; these slices are then filed or rubbed down until the flat sides fit nicely together, when they are glued and wrapped at the ends. Four slices make a bow, it being jointed. Another piece of horn is laid on the center of the bow at the grasp, where it is glued fast. The whole is then filed down until it is perfectly proportioned, when the white bone is ornamented, carved, and painted. Nothing can exceed the beauty of these bows, and it takes an Indian about three months to make one.

Compound bows existed in ancient Babylonia at least as early as 2500 B.C. They appear among various Asiatic civilizations, composed of picked wood, sinews, and horn. Their origin is sought in steppe regions where long staves of wood could not be obtained. Scholars assume that the invention, in simplified form, was brought to North America, where the composite type consists either of wood and sinew or of horn and sinew, but not of all three materials joined. This view is supported by the complete lack of anything but simple bows either in the higher civilizations of the New World or in the eastern half of the United States. The Crow, Blackfoot, and Gros Ventre were likely to cover their horn bows with the skin of a rattlesnake.

Arrow shafts were proportionate in length to the bows. Blackfoot arrows in The American Museum of Natural History average 25½ inches, approximately the same as Sarsi, Dakota, and Cheyenne shafts. A shoot of the favored wood was straightened and rounded by passing it through a hole drilled in a piece of horn and by rubbing it between two grooved stones (Fig. 19). To increase the accuracy and carriage of the projectile, three feathers were generally attached to the butt end of the common shaft which was usually notched. Arrows for shooting birds, small game, or at a target did not require heads. For more serious purposes the Indians used sinew to fasten the stone, bone, horn or, in later times, metal points.

The bow was retained long after the introduction of firearms, not from sheer conservatism, but because old-fashioned muskets were difficult to load on horseback and could not be fired with equal rapidity.

As a protection against the rebound of the bowstring, Crow and Cree archers wore a wrist guard of hide, the Omaha and Iowa a leather band. A Blackfoot quiver with bow case attached, both of otter-skin, is shown in Figure 27. The combination is widespread, being found among the Omaha and Iowa, but not in the Woodland Area.

Most Plains Indians released the arrow by holding the nock between the ends of the index and middle fingers, while the first three fingers are hooked on the string. The Plains Cree, however, are said to have shared the Eskimo technique of drawing the string with the first, second, and third fingers, the nock being lightly held between the first and second fingers.

Clubs were of several forms. The Cree favored a stone in a hide bag attached to the end of a 2-foot stick, the hide not fitting tightly round the stone. In the Assiniboin equivalent the stone weighed about two pounds, was sewed in leather, and was whirled round the handle, to which a wrist loop was attached. A Crow warclub with double-pointed stone head is shown in Figure 18.

Spears (lances), invariably thrust, not hurled, served in the chase as well as in fighting. Mounted Comanche often charged buffalo with this weapon; in warfare only brave members of this tribe were privileged to carry spears. Straight, hooked, or at the end of a bow (Plate 16), the spear played a considerable part in the military societies of many tribes.

Shields were circular and made of buffalo hide. The Blackfoot generally decorated the shield itself,

MATERIAL CULTURE 77

whereas the Dakota and Crow tended to put designs revealed in visions and other ornamental features on the buckskin cover that normally enclosed the shield proper (Fig. 28). Sometimes the painted cover was itself put into another case.

Fig. 28. Two painted and feather-decorated shields used by the Crow (about 20 inches in diameter).

3 SOCIAL ORGANIZATION

Marriage and the Family

Though some Plains Indian customs connected with sex depart widely from our norms, they adhered as a rule strictly to their own. As in many civilized societies, there was a double standard: elders carefully watched over the behavior of young women, while a young man was rather expected to philander. Feminine chastity was highly prized; it was only a virtuous girl for whom a suitor was likely to offer many horses, and certain honorific tasks at sacred ceremonies could be executed only by a woman of irreproachable purity.

Romance was by no means lacking in the sex life of these Indians. Lovers would court a girl when she was fetching firewood or water, or they tried to attract attention at night by playing a flageolet. There is an affecting tradition of a young Hidatsa woman who heard that her sweetheart had been crippled and at his own request abandoned by his companions on a raid. She at once set forth, braving all dangers, traversed hostile territory, reached him, and with her brother-in-law, who had stayed with the deserted man, managed to rescue him.

All the Indians had definite rules barring marriage with the closest relatives and in some tribes even with distant relatives and with unrelated clansfolk (see page 95). On the other hand, there were also some positive prescriptions. An extremely widespread primitive view treats siblings (a sibling is either a brother or a sister) of the same sex as socially equivalent and looks upon marriage as a bond primarily between families rather than between individuals. In consequence, by way of maintaining the family tie, a widower would marry his dead wife's sister and a widow her husband's brother. The former custom is known as the "sororate," the latter as the "levirate." Although not always binding, these unions were regarded as desirable, so that an Omaha has been known to marry his brother's widow though she was many years his senior. Among the same people a man might also marry the daughter of his wife's brother or his wife's father's sister.

Although elopements were far from rare and might be accepted by society if the union proved stable, the most generally approved form of marriage was by purchase. There was nothing at all derogatory to a girl in being paid for, quite the contrary. It must be emphasized that she did not thereby become a chattel. In fact, in certain cases, as among the Mandan, there was actually no purchase, but rather an exchange of gifts between the two families, each furnishing precisely the same number to the other. In other instances there was clearly the conception of a payment by the groom's side, or its equivalent in the form of services rendered by the groom, who acted somewhat like a hired man during a year or two. This was of course most easily done by his taking up residence with the bride's family (matrilocal residence). On the Plains there was no universal rule concerning the place where the newlyweds were to live; Cheyenne and Arapaho marriages were generally matrilocal, while the Blackfoot had the reverse custom (patrilocal), and the Crow seem to have been indifferent on the subject.

Temporarily a Pawnee youth was allowed access to his maternal uncle's wife and an elder brother might share conjugal rights with a junior brother, but these practices were not characteristic of the area. Full-fledged polyandry (marriage of one woman with two or more husbands) was not a Plains institution, though polygyny (marriage with two or more wives) was commonly allowed. Among these warlike Indians many men would fall in fighting, a situation which created a surplus of marriageable women. However, polygyny never reached the excessive degree found in some African kingdoms, where the ruler would appropriate several hundred women for his service. A prominent Plains Indian might have several wives, but rarely more than four or five, and most marriages were monogamous. It was by no means degrading for a woman to be one of several wives. As a matter of fact, a man of distinction who married the eldest daughter in a family established a preemptive claim to her younger sisters as they reached maturity. Small-ankle, an eminent Hidatsa, married Yellow-head and subsequently three of her junior blood-sisters and a fourth girl classed as a sister because she was adopted by the wife's mother. Polygyny was not restricted to the "sororal" form, but this was the most common; with astonishing unanimity the tribes declare that sisters in a polygynous household were less likely to quarrel than unrelated co-wives. One reason for taking two or more wives was that a man of distinction owed it to his status to entertain, which in the absence of domestics involved considerable work for a single mate. "I must take another wife," said an Omaha; "my old wife is not strong enough now to do all her work alone." Not infrequently an additional wife was captured from a hostile tribe.

In the absence of religious sanctions for marriage, it could be dissolved without much ado and often was. But a faithful, industrious woman was not likely to be deserted.

The division of labor between the sexes followed a general primitive pattern in so far as the husband hunted while the wife supplied the vegetable fare. This meant that among the semisedentary tribes she did the cultivating and among the nomads dug up wild roots and collected berries. In all cases she prepared the meals, brought fuel and water, put up and took down the tipi, dressed skins, and made all the clothing. Men butchered game, cleared the plots for planting, and also cut and transported the large posts for an earthlodge among the villagers. The manufacture of weapons, stone implements, and all woodwork everywhere devolved on men. In art, the men painted realistic designs on robes, shields, and tipis, the women painted geometrical figures on hide and were responsible for all beadwork and quilling.

The position of women was decidedly higher than is often assumed. An adulterous wife was liable to severe punishment and, as in all societies, instances of wanton abuse are on record, but these were definitely disapproved by public opinion. In cases of matrilocal residence the wife's relatives would protect her from arbitrary cruelty. A good woman enjoyed the esteem of her husband and of the community at large. As there was at times romantic devotion in youth, so there was probably more frequently a deep attachment between old partners in matrimony. Institutional recognition of the wife's status is shown by the fact that among the Crow she took part jointly with her husband in sacred rituals. Altogether there was nothing like the Melanesian or Australian native's social segregation and exclusion of women from ceremonial life.

Indians had a generic love for children, touchingly illustrated in a Blackfoot story. A scout sent out to detect the enemy discovers a lonely tipi inhabited by a couple from the hostile tribe. Their baby, just able to walk, was dipping up soup from a kettle and detected the stranger peeping in by a hole. Toddling over, it fed the man again and again, unnoticed by the parents. The scout left and was assailed by qualms. It was his duty to announce the discovery, but he could not bring himself to bring death to the infant and its parents. Sentiment overcomes his sense of duty, he returns and warns the couple so that they and the baby are able to escape.

As might be expected, then, parents deeply loved their own offspring and were inconsolable over their loss. In such cases they generally adopted some youngster who seemed to resemble their deceased child. Informally a parent would give instruction to the children of his or her own sex, who were thus initiated into the skills necessary in life. Discipline was not lacking but was mild compared to what was, until recently, customary in Western civilization. Often it was applied not by either parent but by, say, an elder brother. Very rarely was a child beaten; an unruly youngster of two or three might have water dashed on him or be frightened by a bogy, the owl or coyote especially being often chosen for the role. For praiseworthy conduct an Arapaho youngster might be rewarded by words of commendation or some delicious tidbit. When a Crow lad had shot his first deer or done well on his first raid, a father's kinsman would advertise the fact by singing a song of praise.

It was a foregone conclusion that siblings should aid one another in every way possible. An elder brother loomed as his junior's natural protector; horses offered by a girl's suitor were rightfully appropriated by her brothers; sisters made moccasins and finery for brothers. This genuine affection and mutual helpfulness did not prevent a rigid taboo: as soon as a boy and his sister attained maturity, they no longer played or chatted together but had to avoid each other. Only a few years ago a ninety-year old Arapaho woman declared that she had never spoken to her brother. In case of absolute necessity a message might be delivered curtly, with averted eyes. The mutual avoidance of adult brothers and sisters falls under the head of what are known as "respect relationships." Siblings being regarded as socially equivalent, the Indians generally extended relationship terms far beyond what seems reasonable to us (see page 103).

Contrary to our own notions, primitive tribes attached very specific duties or privileges to relatives outside the immediate family circle. For example, the paternal aunt of an Arapaho girl would take it upon herself to instruct her niece, and a maternal uncle did the same for his nephews. This uncle, like a young woman's brother, might receive horses from a suitor and have the right to marry her off. An Omaha uncle of this category had more power to dispose of his nieces than their own father. Among the Crow a father's brothers and sisters were entitled not only to great respect but also to gifts, especially whenever a nephew returned with loot from a raid.

Marriage created a series of new bonds with one's relatives-in-law, and most Plains tribes prescribed definite rules of conduct between a person and his (her) mate's kin, though the details varied in the different tribes. Extremely widespread was the mutual avoidance of a person and his (her) parents-in-law, especially if not of the husband's (wife's) sex. In accordance with the principle that brothers (sisters) are equivalent, the siblings of the persons involved were included in the prohibition. A Crow never spoke to his wife's mother; if he had to convey a message to her, it was relayed through his wife. He even refrained in conversation with anyone from uttering a Crow word that happened to be part of her name, being obliged to paraphrase his meaning. The underlying sentiment was not one of hostility, but of supreme reverence. An Arapaho wife might not speak to or look at her husband's father; even quite recently an interpreter could not question her father-in-law's brothers and an informant refused to answer questions with her son-in-law sitting 15 feet away from her. An attempt at conversation by either of two individuals subject to the taboo was viewed by the other as a lack of respect.

Considering the intensity of feeling on this point, it seems strange that a few tribes in the area, such as the Pawnee and Arikara, completely lacked the taboo. It is also odd that where it did hold it could be overcome by a man's presenting his parents-in-law with a scalp or a substantial gift. Again, the Crow and the Blackfoot, who insisted on the taboo between a man and his mother-in-law, had no parallel to the Arapaho rule for the wife and her father-in-law.

A particularly friendly relationship obtained between Crow or Hidatsa brothers-in-law. However, the Crow did not permit a man to indulge in obscene talk in his brother-in-law's presence. Considering this circumspect behavior between two connections of the same sex, it is remarkable that the Crow permitted the utmost license between a man and his sister-in-law; they romped together, might expose each other's nakedness, and addressed each other in vile language. In "The Social Life among the Blackfoot Indians," Wissler reports that among the Blackfoot "this is often carried to a degree beyond belief. . . . There is not only the same freedom here as between man and wife, but the conventional necessity for license." The Arapaho also favored mutual obscenity and teasing, such as pouring water on the in-law. In this context, we must recall that the marriage customs of the Plains would make of these connections possible spouses.

The Life Cycle

Because of the numerous folkways associated with marriage and family life, these have received treatment separately from other stages in individual existence. These phases did not receive uniform emphasis throughout the area. It will be best to treat the consecutive periods for a single tribe, the Plains Cree, and then supplement with an account of noteworthy deviations elsewhere.

During childbirth a Cree woman knelt, attended

by midwives, one of whom cut the navel cord. The afterbirth, wrapped in a piece of hide, was hung on a tree in the woods. The cord was subsequently put in a decorated skin bag worn by the child round its neck. The infant was not bathed but dried with dry wood or moss and after several days was placed in a hide bag stuffed with moss. Cradleboards were not typical of these people until relatively recent times.

Soon after birth a child received a name, formally bestowed at a feast by a person of the same sex and credited with supernatural power, who prayed to a spirit on behalf of his godchild, took the infant into his arms, and pronounced a name derived from an episode or character in the name-giver's vision. More rarely great warriors named a child after one of their exploits, *e.g.*, one chief called a baby Dragging-him, because he had once dragged an enemy out of a trench. Informally a person might gain a name in commemoration of a war experience of his own. If a child got sick, another medicineman would be asked to give him a new name. Sometimes a nickname given to an individual would stick to him for life. It was reckoned impolite to ask anyone for his name if it referred to a supernatural experience; and the names of the dead, unless they had been outstanding braves, were not mentioned. Fine-day, Bear, Fringe, Many-birds, Red-dog, Star-blanket, Upturned-nose, Rattlesnake, Wolf are some typical Cree names.

The nursing period often lasted much longer than with Whites; sometimes a child of four would seek the breast. Much time was spent with grandparents, who displayed a great deal of affection for their descendants. Two unrelated boys often became comrades in the preadolescent period, lived in each other's households, and subsequently went on the warpath together, joining in the same risks so that both might be killed at the same time.

At puberty a girl was secluded for four nights in a small tipi under the guardianship of an old woman. A married woman also had to withdraw while menstruating, as did the unmarried daughters of the owner of sacred objects, which otherwise were supposed to become polluted. To return to the pubescent, she had to chop wood, sew, dress hides in her retreat, and listen at night to tales related by her mentor. She got little food to eat, cried a good deal, and when necessary scratched her head with a pointed stick. This four-day period was the most likely for a female to acquire a vision, which otherwise might be experienced at any time. On the fourth night the women of the camp went to the shelter; four of them controlling spirit power prayed for the girl, piled up the wood she had chopped, and pushed it over, whereupon each woman carried off some of it. The girl was led to her home ceremonially and was once more prayed for. A feast followed, and then the parents distributed presents among the guests. No comparable ritual was celebrated for boys, but they were usually told by their elders to fast and try to gain a vision (see page 170).

At death the corpse was disposed of in any one of several ways, interment at a depth of about 5 feet being commonest. In the winter, when the ground was frozen too hard for excavation, the body was either put into a log chamber with brush heaped over it or wrapped up and placed on a platform of poles laid across the forks of a big tree.

At the special request of a dying man he might be placed against a willow backrest inside a tipi set up on a hill, a low stone wall being built indoors round the corpse.

Before disposal the corpse was painted and dressed in the dead person's best garments; the legs were bound together for a while, with knees somewhat flexed and hands folded over the chest. In the grave were placed a filled pipe and a container of grease—according to one authority, all his personal possessions. The corpse was pulled out of the side, not the door, of the tipi by a famous brave and carried to the grave amidst general lamentation. A warrior cut off a braid from the hair of the deceased. Close relatives gashed their forearms and legs and wore their hair loose, remaining in mourning until a man of eminence declared the period terminated. On the fourth night after the death there was a feast with ceremonial pipe and food offerings to the spirits. The braid was put into a sacred bundle with braids of other dead members of the family. Such bundles were highly regarded and carried by the women when camp moved. Whenever subsequently the bereaved got near the grave, they would give a feast and tidy the site. The dead person's personal property was given away lest their sight arouse sad memories; his tipi was abandoned or, more frequently, exchanged for another; the horses were distributed among sons and daughters with one reserved for the widow.

Several of the usages described for the Cree were widely shared. Delayed weaning, for example, was a common primitive practice; Assiniboin children were never weaned under two or three years old, and among the Arapaho a child was conventionally nursed until it was four years old. Widespread, too, were the change of name of an ailing infant and the reluctance to inquire after a person's name or to mention that of a dead person. Probably quite general in the area was the notion of comradeship, especially between boys, that suggests the blood-brotherhood of other continents. Arapaho girls as well as boys formed these bonds in preadolescence and maintained them for life.

The dread of menstrual blood and of its contaminating sacred objects by contact or proximity extended far beyond the bounds of the Plains, sometimes attaining a morbid degree, considering the freedom with which natives often discussed sexual matters. Even ten years ago Arapaho women displayed the utmost disinclination to speak of the subject to a woman investigator, Sister M. I. Hilger. "Very few give instructions to their daughters about it. . . . You know if a menstruating woman enters a sickroom, it will kill the sick person." Yet though some restrictions were usually imposed on a girl when coming of age and at subsequent periods, neither the retreat to a special shelter nor the puberty ceremonial for a girl, as described for the Cree, was general in the Plains; the Blackfoot, for example, lacked both, as did the Arapaho—notwithstanding their intense feelings about menstruation. As for adolescent boys, the Plains Indians had nothing comparable to the *tribal* initiation of African or Australian indigenes, though initiation into ceremonial organizations was a familiar practice.

The rule that a corpse should not be taken out by the regular entrance occurs in various tribes, the Crow reason being that otherwise some other inmate of the lodge would die soon after. The practice has been reported from Woodland natives (Ojibwa, Menomini, Saulteaux) and even from the Greenland Eskimo and the Lapps. Disposal of the body never seems to have been by cremation in our area, but both interment and tree burial after the Cree fashion were typical of the Plains, where the body was also often put on a four-pole scaffold. After decomposition the bones might be deposited in rock crevices. Quite general in the area were demonstrative mourning with laceration of the body and mutilation of a finger, the distribution of the deceased person's property, the abandonment of the tipi. Economic conditions wrought some significant modifications. In the Basin the destruction of a man's property wrought no great loss, but when the Comanche as Plains people acquired large herds of horses there was a revulsion against sacrificing a large number, and Professor Ralph Linton tells us a compromise solution was found by killing only one favorite horse and distributing the remainder among the survivors. Again, it was much easier for nomads to abandon a tipi than for semisedentary folk to leave their earthlodge after a death, which the Hidatsa do not seem to have ever done, presumably because of the material sacrifice involved.

Bands, Clans, Phratries, Moieties

In the very simplest societies the family or a union of a few families, often related to one another, coincided with the local group or "community." West of our area, the Shoshoneans of Nevada had so difficult a time existing at all in their habitat that during much of the year they had to live in minute nomadic bands rarely much larger than a single family. Only for brief periods, when provisions were ample, could several of these small groups unite into a larger body to hold a dance. The Plains tribes developed greater complexity of organization, but it should be noted that during the winter economic reasons caused them also to split up into very small units. D. G. Mandelbaum, who has studied the Plains Cree, has written that in January and February these people, sometimes on the verge of starvation, "scattered in small family units into the more densely wooded country." One year, about 1837, the Cheyenne departed from ancient custom by sticking together during the cold season, but they very nearly perished in consequence. Economic factors, then, normally enabled the Plains tribes to carry on their more complex social activities only from the beginning of spring until the beginning of winter. This applies perhaps particularly to the nomads, but even a semisedentary people like the Mandan took up special and less pretentious dwellings in the cold season.

LOCAL UNITS

A "band" is a local group of people jointly wandering in search of sustenance. Its size varied considerably in our area, as did its make-up. The Kiowa, numbering altogether about 1,600, embraced ten to twenty bands, each formed by the inmates of twelve to fifty tipis. A new band came into being when a leader separated from the parent group with a following of brothers and sisters with their spouses and offspring. The Comanche at one time had thirteen bands, four of which were especially important. They bore such names as Burnt Meat, Making Bags While Moving, Those Who Move

SOCIAL ORGANIZATION 93

Often—*i.e.*, nicknames. The Plains Cree bands each claimed a range of territory that, however, was ill defined. In the nineteenth century at least eight of these units were recognized, most of them bearing a geographical designation, such as Upstream, Calling River, Touchwood Hills People. The Crow comprised two politically independent major subdivisions, the Mountain and the River Crow, the former roaming mainly over southern Montana and northern Wyoming, the latter along the lower Yellowstone. Bands, called by such names as Ugly People and Red Willow Men, jointly formed the Arapaho and occupied distinct positions in the

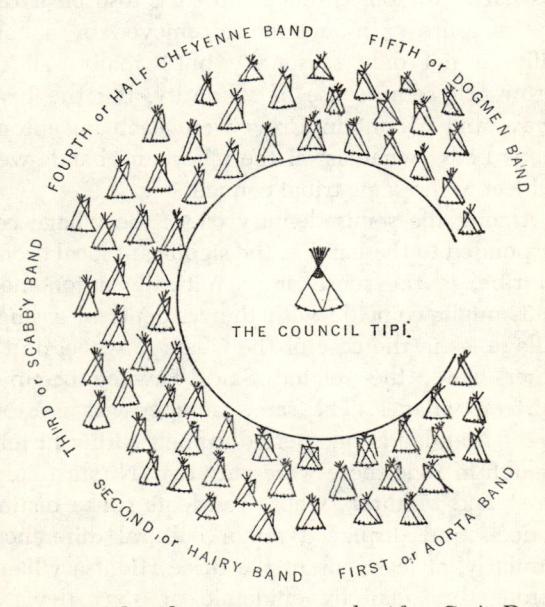

Fig. 29. The Cheyenne camp circle. After G. A. Dorsey.

camp circle when the entire tribe was united. Eleven comparable subdivisions have been noted for the Cheyenne (Fig. 29); characteristic sobriquets were Small Windpipes, Hair Men, Shy People, Eaters.

It should be noted that, though bands were consistent with another and more rigid type of grouping (as among the Crow), the band itself was a unit of shifting constitution. A Plains Cree could freely pass from one to another; among the Arapaho a husband usually lived with his wife's family so that the children came to be identified with her band rather than with the father's, but there was nothing to prevent his taking wife and offspring to his native or some other band. It is also clear that the measure of independence enjoyed by a band differed not only seasonally but tribally: all the Crow felt some sense of solidarity, but the River Crow and Mountain Crow were each an autonomous body, whereas all the Cheyenne bands were subject to the same tribal council.

Among the semisedentary tribes the village corresponded to the band as the significant local group. A tribe, in the sense of a politically autonomous unit, might coincide with the residents of a single village, as in the case of the Chaui Pawnee; on the other hand, the related Skidi Pawnee occupied thirteen villages. The same number was ascribed to the Mandan at one period in their earlier history, though in 1833 there were only two, Núpta (Puhptare) and Mi'tutak, whose residents spoke distinct dialects and displayed minor cultural differences. Similarly, at least one of the three Hidatsa villages before the smallpox epidemic of 1837 deviated somewhat in speech from the others and had some ceremonial peculiarities.

KINSHIP UNITS

In contrast to local groups, where membership rested on the accident of residence, were the units in which membership was fixed by heredity. This might be done by consistently ignoring one side of the family and stressing the other. If children were all reckoned as of the father's unit, the principle of "patriliny" held; if they belonged to the mother's unit, we are dealing with "matriliny." All persons of either sex descended from the same ancestor, through males only, form a "patrilineage," all those descended from one ancestress, through females only, form a "matrilineage." Actually it often happens that primitive folk regard themselves as sharing the same ancestor or ancestress without being able to trace the genealogical blood relationship, either because they have lost track of the links or because the connection was once established by legal fiction. In this case we speak of patrilineal or matrilineal clans.

The clan, then, differed from a band in absolutely fixing membership. Whereas an Arapaho child shifted its affiliation when taken out of the Ugly band to settle in the Red Willow band, the situation would be different for a Crow youngster. If his Mountain Crow parents decided to join the River band and he remained there, he would indeed belong to the River Crow, but he could never change his clan affiliation; once a Sore-lip, always a Sore-lip.

Further, the clan differed from the family in being a unilateral group; whereas the family takes cognizance of both parents, a clan system one-sidedly ignored either in favor of the other. It must be remembered, however, that though the *clan* neglected either patrilineal or matrilineal kindred, this does not mean that the people as a whole did so. For since family ties are universal, both parents had a definite place with reference to the child. What is meant, then, is simply that for *certain* specific purposes only one half of one's relatives counted, while in respect to other matters the half excluded from one's clan might be quite as important. For instance, the Omaha had patrilineal clans, so that a mother's brother was never in his sister's daughter's clan; yet he had to be consulted when his niece was to be married (page 84). On the other hand, while the Crow clans were matrilineal, the father's relatives were nevertheless entitled to respect and to gifts from their brother's children.

Even the most remotely related, or only fictitiously related, fellow clansfolk were morally obligated to help and shield one another, and in case of intratribal murder the bereaved clan might try to punish the offender or, on the principle of collective responsibility, even a clansman of his. Such a situation might precipitate a feud between the two clans involved. Another general function of clans was the regulation of marriage: because fellow members of a clan were related by blood or were considered relatives, they were not permitted to marry one another, *i.e.*, the clans are "exogamous" (Greek *exo*, outside; *gam*, marriage).

Of the Plains Indians, the Crow, Hidatsa, and Mandan are known to have had matrilineal clan systems. The same is reported of the Oto and Missouri by Lewis H. Morgan in his *Ancient Society*, but our information on these tribes is fragmentary, hence not quite satisfactory. One authority believes that the Cheyenne once had matrilineal clans that degenerated into the recent band system, but other observers reject his conclusion. The Pawnee were unquestionably matrilineal in the sense that an individual permanently belonged to his mother's village, and since a woman never left the settlement she was born into, she with her mother, mother's sisters, daughters, and daughters' daughters formed what elsewhere would be the permanent core of a matrilineal clan. A Pawnee village, however, was not a clan; by permission a man might marry into another village, but this was very rarely granted, so that the settlement was not exogamous, but the reverse—"endogamous."

The Omaha, Ponca, Iowa, Kansa, and Osage all had patrilineal clans. As to the Blackfoot and Gros Ventre, there is a disagreement on the part of authorities. The decision hinges on the fixity of the tie between an individual and his tribal subdivision. Wissler's evidence, published in papers of The American Museum of Natural History, indicates that a Blackfoot was free to select his subdivision and that marriages within it were frowned upon simply because of "the suspicion that some close blood relationship may have been overlooked"; hence, he prefers to speak of Blackfoot bands. It must be conceded, however, that they represent a borderline case, for on Wissler's evidence the general feeling assigned a child to his father's group and migrants were often reminded of their original membership. "Thus, it seems that the bands are in part, at least, gentes [clans]." There is also doubt concerning the Dakota and the Assiniboin. In 1767 a visitor to the Eastern Dakota recorded names of tribal subdivisions that certainly resemble the clan names of other Woodland tribes. It is therefore probable, though not certain, that the subdivisions mentioned were clans.

The Southern Siouan clans were generally subdivided into what may be called "subclans." Frequently the name of the smaller unit was a variation of the clan's: the Iowa Elk clan embraced a Big Elk, a White Elk, a Bull Elk subclan.

Sometimes two or more clans within a tribe regarded themselves as related to one another more closely than to other clans. Such a union was called a "phratry." The Kansa had seven larger units, which they called "those who sing together"; three comprised two clans, three were made up of three each. The sixteenth clan was reckoned co-ordinate with the phratries, possibly because it had formerly been linked with another clan that died out. Often the phratries had no important function beyond assembling friendly clans. They might be nameless (Crow) or bear such names as Fire and Earth (Ponca).

More significant was the "dual organization" by which a whole tribe was split into two complementary units or "moieties" (French *moitié*, half). These tribal halves, if exogamous, may be considered the equivalent of major clans; but it is possible that their origin is historically different from that of a multiple-clan system. Among North American Indians we find both undivided moieties and moieties subdivided into clans. In the latter case the moiety might still regulate marriage, which inevitably made the clans exogamous; or it might have nothing to do with marriage; or there may have been a disinclination to marrying inside the moiety without a strict rule to that effect. In the last of these possibilities, realized among the Omaha, we may reasonably suspect that the moieties were formerly exogamous. The Pawnee, though devoid of clans and exogamy, nevertheless had a strong sense for a dual division. Whenever they played important games or seated themselves for ceremonial performances, the Winter people sat in the north half of the circle, the Summer people in the south half. Membership was hereditary, every individual permanently belonging to his mother's moiety. The Southern Siouans similarly expressed the complementary nature of the moieties in spatial terms when camping on the march or on a hunting expedition. Among the Omaha one moiety was associated with the sky, the other with the earth; the Osage halves represented, respectively, peace and war. Such linkage of moieties with opposite concepts occurs in various parts of the world, including Brazil and Australia. It is also a widespread feature for moieties to render each other services. When an Osage child was sick, the parents asked members of the other moiety for food.

Apparently the Mandan and Hidatsa moieties were less striking phenomena than those of the Southern Siouans. Designated as Three-Clans and Four-Clans, respectively, each comprised the corresponding number of clans. They did not regulate marriage and functioned as distinct units mainly when political issues, such as treaties, were at stake. In the old days each had its own territory for eagle hunting.

Clans, phratries, and moieties were variously combined. The Pawnee had moieties without clans;

the Crow lacked moieties but grouped their thirteen clans in six phratries, five pairs of clans and one trio; among the Omaha each moiety embraced five clans, divided into subclans; the Ponca moieties were divided into four clans each, paired into phratries; the phratry grouping of the Kansa partly crisscrossed the moiety division, so that the Earth and the Elk clan, though of opposite halves, formed one phratry.

The designations of the clans present variations of historical significance. The Crow clans bore fairly uniformly such names as Treacherous, Filth-eaters, Sore-lip, Greasy-inside-their-mouths. This type of nomenclature was shared by the problematic tribal subdivisions of the Blackfoot and Gros Ventre, who had such groups as Ugly-ones, Those-who-do-not-give-away, Fighting-alone, Fish-eaters, Liars, Bad-guns. Obviously the same type held for the band names of the Arapaho and Cheyenne quoted above. The Dakota equivalents were as a rule similarly labeled, witness Wears-a-dogskin-round-the-neck, Breakers-of-the-law, Not-encumbered-with-much-baggage. In short, over a wide region in the western Plains nicknames were common.

In sharp contrast to this system was that of the Southern Siouans. Here the nomenclature is preponderantly derived from the animal kingdom or some cosmic phenomenon, the particular species or natural feature being, in technical language, the "totem" of the tribal subdivision. Among the Omaha, even when the clan is not actually named after an animal, it is in some way conceived to be associated with the species or natural phenomenon. The Omaha have an Elk, Black [Buffalo] Shoulder, Wind, Deer clan; and even when a name is of a

13. *Costume and hairdress from the Crow.* Courtesy of Bureau of American Ethnology, Smithsonian Institution.

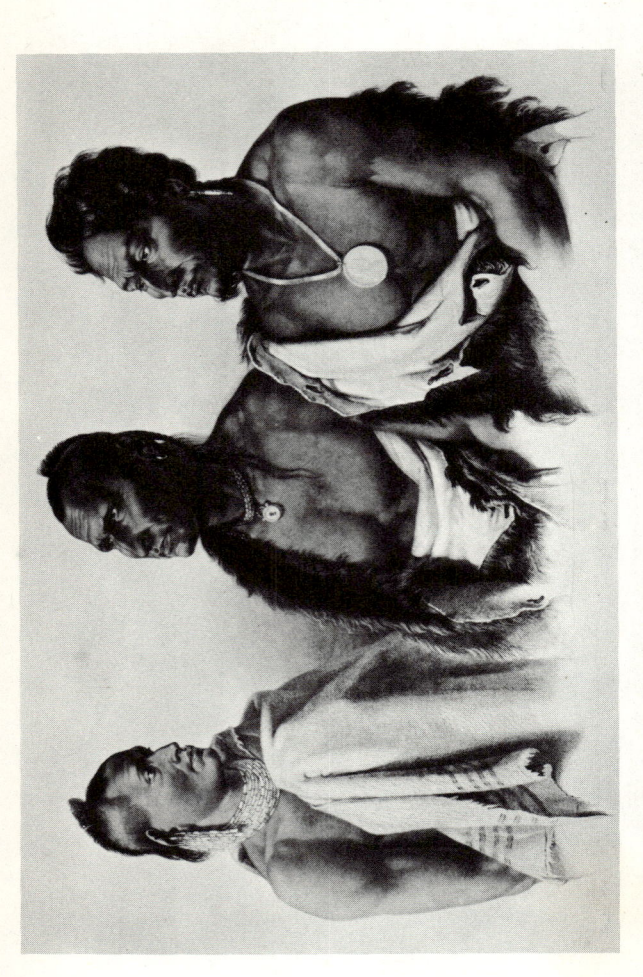

14. *The hair roach, as worn by the Missouri and Oto Indians (left and center), and a Ponca chief. Carl Bodmer engraving in Maximilian.*

15. Mandan pottery vessels.

16. An Assiniboin warrior with shield and bow spear. After Carl Bodmer in Maximilian.

17. *A Hidatsa Dog dancer.* Carl Bodmer engraving in Maximilian.

different character, its bearers are connected with a totem. Thus, the Earthlodge-makers are also expressly referred to as Wolf and Coyote people, the Gray-eyes as Thunder and Reptile people. The names of subclans may refer to taboos imposed on the members, *e.g.*, Do-not-touch-buffalo-heads or Do-not-eat-buffalo-tongues. Among the Crow there is no suggestion of such a clan nomenclature; and though a Prairie-chicken clan is common to the Mandan and Hidatsa and the former also have an Eagle clan, there is no evidence of any deeper meaning to these designations.

Further, the clans of the best-known Southern Siouans each owned a set of ordinal birth names. An Omaha Elk man's eldest son was called Softhorn; the second, Yellow-horn; the third, Branching-horns; the fourth, Four-horns. No trace of such a custom has been reported from the three matrilineal Siouan tribes.

Apart from names, the Southern Siouan system had another feature not encountered in the north— the holding of distinctive ceremonial and political functions by particular clans. Among the Omaha the Black [Buffalo] Shoulder people kept the peace pipes, one of the Buffalo clans was in charge of two sacred tents, and only the Pipe subclan of the Deerhead clan had the privilege of wearing down in their hair. Osage policemen were always recruited from particular clans.

A remarkable point about all this is that, while the Southern Siouans of the Plains differed so markedly in their clan system from their northern fellow Siouans in the area, they closely resembled the pattern of patrilineal Woodland peoples, including the Algonkian Menomini and the Siouan Winnebago, both residents of Wisconsin. The Menomini clans all bore animal names, a fair number coinciding with those of the Southern Siouan divisions, *e.g.*, Bear, Wolf, Eagle, Beaver, Elk. The clans also owned distinctive personal names, bestowed on children according to the order of their birth; and governmental functions belonged to the Bear clan. Furthermore, though less explicitly than the Omaha and their closest tribal relatives, the Menomini recognized a dual division suggestive of moieties: in playing lacrosse the clans with bird totems were regularly pitted against those with animal totems. As might be expected, the correspondence was still closer with the Siouan Winnebago: here there were not only totemic nomenclature, ordinal birth names peculiar to each clan, and specific functions, political and ceremonial, of particular clans, but also explicit moieties, associated with sky and earth, and in the old villages the dwellings of men of these halves are said to have been divided by an imaginary northwest-southeast line.

In short, if we mapped culture areas exclusively on the basis of social structure, the traditional Plains Area would have to be split up so as to unite the Southern Siouans with the more westerly Woodland tribes. Knowing that the Southern Siouans came from the East, what happened is simply that they brought an Eastern clan pattern with them into their new habitat. Altogether the historic Plains Area presents an extraordinary diversity in this respect: matrilineal and patrilineal descent, nontotemic and totemic clan systems, tribal subdivisions approximating but not quite attaining clan status, and completely loose band organizations are all found between the Rocky Mountains and the Mississippi.

Kinship Terms

In this connection another fact is significant. Most primitive tribes have a way of designating relatives by blood and marriage that differs markedly from ours. They draw distinctions we ignore and on the other hand fail to distinguish where we consider differences of the utmost importance. Thus, most of the Plains tribes have separate words for an older and a younger brother and also for an older and a younger sister. But nearly all of them call the father and the father's brother by a single word, while carefully separating the uncles on the father's from those on the mother's side. Correspondingly, they generally called a mother's sister "mother," but distinguished both the real mother and the maternal aunt from the paternal aunt. Since the natives were usually very logical in applying these terms, they also recognized a vast number of brothers and sisters; for persons who call the same individuals "father" or "mother" naturally regard one another as siblings.

Now this phenomenon is doubly interesting, both in its sociological and in its historical aspects. Sociologically it appears that the rule of descent has a good deal to do with the relationship system. Where the individual family and the local group are the only essential social divisions, people are as likely to distinguish uncles from the father and aunts from the mother as we do. But where a one-sided rule of descent prevails, it tends to go with the classification described above. That is, relatives are then considered with reference to whether they stem from the father's or the mother's side; accordingly, the paternal and the maternal uncle cannot be called by the same name, but father and paternal uncle can be, because interest centers on the lines of descent, not on the physiological relations of individuals. So we find that among the Dakota, whose eastern branches probably had patrilineal reckoning, a person had many fathers and mothers, for in addition to the uncles on the father's side all his cousins would be reckoned as "fathers" provided they were in the same clan as the father, and correspondingly for the mother's sisters and female cousins.

Certain Plains tribes emphasized the matrilineal or patrilineal side even more strongly, so as to ignore even differences of generation. Thus, in the Crow and Hidatsa languages the word we translate as "father" meant not only "begetter," "begetter's brother," and "clansman of begetter's generation," but also "father's sister's son." This is quite logical, for if a Crow was of the Sore-lip clan, his sister was likewise, and by matrilineal descent her children must have been the same. Hence, one cousin, the mother's brother's son, addressed the other, his father's sister's son, as "father" and logically was called "son" in return.

The same notion in reverse appears among the patrilineal Omaha and other Southern Siouans. Here a boy called his mother's brother's son by the same word he applied to his maternal uncle, while the mother's brother's daughter was a "mother," for patriliny united these relatives in one social subdivision.

Evidently the Dakota, Crow, and Omaha schemes are distinguished from one another by their treatment of cousins. A fourth possibility in this respect was realized by the Arapaho, Gros Ventre, and Sarsi, who drew no distinctions between any cousins and siblings. Interestingly enough, none of the three had a clan organization.

Historically, the noteworthy fact is that once more the Southern Siouans fall in line with western Woodland peoples. Their system shows virtual identity with the systems of the Winnebago, the Sauk and Fox, Menomini, and Kickapoo. In other words, the resemblance cuts across linguistic family lines. Some Siouans are much nearer certain Algonkians than to some other Siouans. The social structure and a kinship nomenclature in harmony with it has undoubtedly been diffused over a considerable number of tribes in the central states, irrespective of linguistic affinity. Whether the Algonkians or the Siouans were the originators, it is impossible to tell, for the features in question are not general in either stock.

Clubs and Societies

Apart from a person's social ties with his family, band, and clan, he was in most Plains tribes connected with organizations in which membership did not rest on kinship. These associations served a great variety of purposes, and those essentially religious in character are best considered under another head (page 191). However, since religion and magic penetrated every phase of life, even predominantly secular societies rarely lacked at least a tinge of supernaturalism. Also, in a set of organizations within the same tribe and obviously related to one another, it happened that particular societies had much more of a religious flavor than others. Because of the breakup of tribes into small fragments with the coming of the cold season, associational activity was largely suspended until early spring, when a formal reorganization occurred.

Societies were far more frequently masculine than feminine, but neither from this nor from other phases of life were women so sharply excluded as in Australia or Melanesia. As a matter of fact, women auxiliaries figured even in the military societies. Further, the village tribes of the Upper Missouri had exceedingly important women's organizations (page 113), and the Pawnee had a curious association of single women and widows who displayed obtrusively shabby regalia and tortured prisoners of war. Among the Kiowa a man starting out on a raid was likely to appeal to a body of possibly forty Old Women whom he feasted on his return in gratitude for their prayers. Guilds of skillful tipi cover makers and of expert quill workers are known from the Oglala Dakota.

However, on the whole, men's clubs doubtless loomed larger, and among them the category popularly known as Dog Soldiers, or otherwise as military, police, or age-societies, stands out. None of these designations is adequate, for only a few tribes graded their organizations by age and everywhere the functions tended to be manifold. Since The American Museum of Natural History specialized in a comparative study of these societies, their insignia are well represented in the exhibits, especially those of the Arapaho, Hidatsa, Mandan, Blackfoot, and Crow.

Although Indians originally never reckoned their age by years, five tribes—Mandan, Hidatsa, Blackfoot, Arapaho, Gros Ventre—are known to have had a system of age-societies. This resulted probably from two causes: youngsters, inevitably more or less of the same age, would imitate the activities of their seniors; and among these it was customary to buy the right to a certain set of regalia, dances, and songs, usually linked with privileges of other kinds. The buyers did not join the sellers as members, but displaced them. The sellers, however, remained a fixed group that jointly bought the corresponding emblems and privileges of an older group; and this process was repeated at intervals until the original group of boys had reached the highest existing grade. When they had sold that, they retired from the associational scheme altogether. Virtually if not literally all males of the five tribes entered the system and remained with it until old age. Because the initial gang of youngsters who mimicked their seniors could not vary greatly in age and since they always bought new memberships in a body, fellow members throughout the series continued to be roughly age-mates.

The procedure in these purchases had some quaint features. At least among the Hidatsa and Mandan the younger group was eager to advance and the next older, who were called their "fathers," made the most of their advantage, professing great reluctance to give up their beloved dances, badges, and correlated behavior patterns. Hence the prospective buyers came to the sellers' lodge with a heap of gifts and offered them a pipe, which would be accepted only as a token of agreement to sell. The seniors were likely to declare that this first installment was insufficient; so the buyers scurried around to cadge more property from their relatives. The older men still acted as if doing their juniors a great favor, but finally smoked the pipe, ordering the buyers to bring food to feast their "fathers" for four or more successive evenings. Kinsfolk again helped the purchasers to collect enough food to satisfy the higher group; then, on the evenings stipulated, the sellers enjoyed their feast and began teaching the buyers the songs and dances distinctive of the society in question. To some extent the buyers would participate in the songs and dances on these occasions. The owner of the lodge would exhort the "sons" to pay generously for the emblems they were to receive and to emulate the example of some distinguished "fathers" as warriors. After the final evening of instructions, the insignia were turned over to the new members, and there was a public procession and dance by them, advertising the fact that they were henceforth the representatives of the grade just entered.

A smallpox epidemic in 1837 and other disturbances prevented the system from being maintained in the traditional way, but the collapse revealed its true basis. In 1910 a Hidatsa ninety years old declared that he was still a member of the societies he had joined at twenty, twenty-seven, and forty-five years of age *because he had never had the chance to sell his memberships*. In other words, for the natives membership in any organization meant merely ownership gained by purchase—not as in some aboriginal associations elsewhere, where it meant some particular age or marriage status. Other facts support this conclusion. The associations called, respectively, Kit-foxes or Dogs in any one of the five tribes with supposed age-societies resemble namesakes in the other tribes so much that there must have been a single Kit-fox or Dog prototype for all of them (Plate 17). However, the status of both differed notably in different tribes. The Mandan Kit-foxes comprised only unmarried youths, forming the second of the eight to ten grades; in 1833 the Hidatsa counterpart stood fourth in a series of ten; the Arapaho affixed the name to a preliminary order of boys not as yet properly within the series; but its long extinct Piegan namesake ranked high and was credited with sacred functions. In all Blackfoot lists the Kit-foxes take precedence of the Dogs; yet elsewhere the Dogs definitely rank higher. Among the Arapaho their average age has been estimated at fifty as against eighteen or even twelve for the Kit-foxes; in one Mandan list the Dogs are the seventh, the Kit-foxes only the second society in order of purchase; the corresponding figures among the Hidatsa were six and four in 1833, subsequently, seven and four or even nine and two according to later informants. In short, the same society was not essentially connected with a particular age or matrimonial status, but varied in rank in different tribes, indeed, even in the same tribe at different periods. If a new society, *i.e.*, a new combination of privileges, was created or imported from without, it was naturally assimilated to the existing scheme by the innovating tribe. This automatically altered the sequence it had followed there, but need not have affected the position of the societies anywhere else.

The shifts that occurred during the nineteenth century in a single tribe are brought out by comparing Maximilian's Hidatsa list (1833) with that supplied as correct for the period of his youth by an old informant in 1910:

MAXIMILIAN	BUTTERFLY
1. Stone Hammers	1. Stone Hammers
2. Lumpwoods	2. Kit-foxes
3. Hērerōka (Crow Indians)	3. Lumpwoods
4. Kit-foxes	4. Little Dogs
5. Little Dogs	5. Half-shaved Heads
6. Dogs	6. Enemies (Black Mouths)
7. Half-shaved Heads	7. Crazy Dogs
8. Enemies (Black Mouths)	8. Ravens
9. Bulls	9. Dogs
10. Ravens	10. Bulls

In the course of, say, 30 or 40 years several notable transpositions had evidently taken place, proving that the grading of the societies could vary. This was bound to happen if one society sold its rights to a foreign group, as we know happened within the area.

Societies of similar type, but not graded, loomed large among the Dakota, Assiniboin, Cheyenne, Crow, Pawnee, and Arikara. In much attenuated form they were found among the Southern Siouans, where they were eclipsed by fraternities of a strictly sacred order, and among some marginal tribes such as the Sarsi and the Wind River Shoshone. The Plains Cree had distinctive features, each band having only a single Warrior society into which worthy young men were invited, but which might buy new dances from another band or an alien people. If they had sold their old dance to younger band fellows, the Warriors might have started something like the Mandan scheme, but this did not happen. The one society merely held two sets of insignia and ceremonial privileges.

Typical of the ungraded societies are the Crow and Cheyenne schemes. Membership was voluntary and not dependent on age but, though theoretically coordinate, particular societies might eclipse others at particular periods. Among the Crow the Lumpwoods and the Foxes and among the Cheyenne the Dogs were conspicuously important in historic times. An age-system rather precluded rivalry between societies, but where these ranked as equals competition could and did set in. Thus, the Lumpwoods and the Foxes both tried to outdo each other annually in striking the first blow against an enemy, and the same kind of rivalry obtained between some Dakota societies.

As regards the functions of the military societies of both the graded and the ungraded type, we may distinguish private and public functions. For the individual his society was a club, and at its lodge he would lounge, sleep, eat, dance, sing, and generally have a good time with his fellows. But there were also serious public duties that devolved on either a special society in the series, or on all of the societies, or on one after another. Foremost among such obligations was the policing of the people at crucial times, such as the collective hunt, the march, or the Sun Dance. Each spring the Crow chief would appoint one of the societies to act as police until the tribal breakup in the fall, whereas this task always belonged to the Black Mouths among the Mandan. Further, as the epithet "military" implies, the majority of these organizations fostered the warlike spirit so typical of the area. Songs, always an important feature, constantly stressed the ideal. Thus, a Kit-fox of the Oglala Dakota would sing:

> I am a Fox.
> I am supposed to die.
> If there is anything difficult,
> If there is anything dangerous,
> That is mine to do.

But while every man was expected to be brave, most of the societies chose a few especially valorous members as officers, distinguished by their regalia, who were deliberately to flout danger. Thus, the rank and file of the above-mentioned Oglala organization wore kit-fox skin necklaces, a forehead band decorated with kit-fox jawbones, and at the back of the head a bunch of crow tail feathers and two erect eagle feathers. But in a dance the officers painted their bodies yellow, and four of them, carrying lances, were under obligation to lead in battle and not to retreat. Such lances, straight or bent at the top, were very common regalia in Plains organizations, as in the Half-shaved Head society of the Mandan and in an Arapaho organization (Plate 18).

At an annual reorganization of the military societies in the spring, as well as on some other occasions, they offered public entertainment by marching in procession or performing a dance outdoors. Maximilian's artist, Carl Bodmer, has caught such a spectacle presented by the Mandan Bull society (Plate 19). The rank and file are seen wearing a piece of a buffalo head with horns, but the officers, pledged never to retreat from an enemy, are masked by a complete buffalo skull, provided with eye slits. Spectators, some brandishing or discharging guns, as do two dancers, are perched on the roof of an earthlodge.

Some of these organizations had virtually or literally no religious features; others were highly charged with them, the Pawnee and the Arapaho societies perhaps most of all. Pawnee social life was largely dominated by their scheme of sacred bundles, and to this they assimilated ten associations exercising the military, social, and recreational activities elsewhere largely or wholly secular. A number of other societies, unconnected with the bundles, nevertheless had a religious basis in that the founder derived his sanction for starting a new club from a supernatural inspiration.

A remarkable trait found as an essential part of behavior in some societies, military or otherwise, is the obligation to say the opposite of what is meant, do the opposite of what is demanded, and generally to act contrary to common sense. Typical is the Heyōka association of the Oglala. As an example Wissler says, "One of their most spectacular feats is that of plunging the arms into boiling water and splashing it about over each other complaining that it is cold."

The village tribes of the Upper Missouri had several women's societies, which followed the pattern of the age-societies as regards collective purchase, but naturally lacked military and constabulary features. The two highest of them were the Goose and the White Buffalo Cow society. The Goose women performed ceremonies in order to make the corn crop prosper and to attract buffalo herds. The White Buffalo Cow women were also called upon to lure buffalo. They wore a feathered headdress of albino buffalo skin in hussar fashion and danced in position, raising each foot alternately higher than the other and waddling from side to side.

Warfare

Plains Indian warfare, compared with the practice of civilized peoples, had many distinctive features. Prolonged wars, standing armies, and officers holding permanent rank were lacking. The objective was never to acquire new lands. Revenge, horse lifting, and the lust for glory were the chief motives and readily blended since a fleeing horse thief might come to kill his pursuer, a raid for revenge might incidentally result in the capture of horses, and honor could be gained in either type of expedition. Though it did happen that major tribal forces were pitted against each other, this rarely happened, the usual military adventure involving only a few warriors. It was considered of the utmost importance that a party return without the loss of a man; deliberately to incur losses for strategic ends was wholly repulsive to Indian ideas.

Strange from our point of view was the mingling of supernaturalism with warfare. Dakota shields were invested with protective power mainly because of the symbolic designs and trimmings on them. A bad omen sufficed to make men give up an intended raid. Only if inspired by a supernatural being did a Crow venture to go on the warpath: the spirit appearing in a dream or vision would specify where the party was to go; how many horses would be driven off; that the prize animal had a docked tail, was painted with zigzag lines, and would serve as mount for a thumbless Cheyenne. Because of his supernatural sanction the leader enjoyed absolute control and theoretically claimed all the loot. In practice he shared it with his companions in accordance with tribal ethics; otherwise he would find himself without a following on his next venture. A man who scored repeated successes as a leader came to be renowned for his war medicine, so that novices would beseech him to give them a replica, entitling them to a share in its blessings, and would pay him large fees for the favor.

The Indians distinguished between a party organized for killing enemies and one for capturing horses, the latter type being the more usual enterprise in historic times. Generally the would-be raiders started on foot, equipped with plenty of moccasins, which might be packed on dogs; and they hoped to return on the backs of stolen horses. Valuable beasts were likely to be tethered to their owners' tent pegs, and it was obviously dangerous to slink into a hostile camp in order to cut loose such an animal; accordingly some tribes attached special merit to the accomplishment of this task.

Chiefs did not always favor such expeditions and might order the police to prevent them on grounds of safety. Hence the organizer and his chum would steal away at night, to be subsequently joined by volunteers. Various details of procedure were widespread in the area. The leader carried his medicine, which supposedly would benumb the enemy at the time of the surprise attack or cause weather that frustrated the pursuit of the raiders. Scouts, carrying wolfskins and howling as they approached their party to report, kicked over a pile of buffalo droppings to symbolize the truth of their statements. When the whole party returned to their tribe, they signaled from a distance, waving blankets according to a code to indicate how they had fared. In case of success they dressed up and paraded round the camp with blackened faces (Plate 20), showing off their scalps and their booty. Scalps were attached to sticks and carried by women dancers to the accompaniment of drumbeats and songs (Plate 21).

Prisoners might be adopted into a tribe, but were often jeered, abused, and even tortured. It was not uncommon, however, to marry a captured woman.

Fortifications were used both for the protection of settlements and to ward off pursuers of horse thieves. The villagers of the Upper Missouri built palisades too high to be easily scaled, put loopholes into the fence, and dug a ditch inside the village. About a century ago a Ponca fort harboring many earthlodges had an embankment over 6 feet in height. Situated on a bluff with a ravine at the rear, it could be entered only from one side and by passing for over 200 yards along the ravine. Approximately contemporary with this fort was a structure 4 feet high which the Omaha erected round their camp on learning of an attack contemplated by the Dakota and Ponca. The embankment was topped with interlaced tipi poles covered as far as possible with tipi covers, through which loopholes were cut; trenches were dug for the women and children.

From infancy a Plains Indian boy had it dinned into his ears that bravery was the path to distinction, that old age was an evil, while it was a fine thing to die young in battle. He would hear famous warriors reciting and perhaps enacting their exploits on public occasions; he would see such men honored and likewise drawing material rewards, as when a great brave outfitted a would-be captain with part of his medicine or when he named a newborn child and was paid for his offices. Thus, every lad was conditioned to emulate the example of eminent warriors.

In accordance with what was said above, a captain who had never lost a follower rated higher than one who, however successful otherwise, had failed in this respect. The emphasis on this point explains why a small body, even a single resolute brave, could hold off a force at ridiculous odds, why the Cree gave up revenge parties after the spread of firearms.

Scalping was general, but with a marked tribal difference in attitude. Whereas in the Southeastern culture area, the capture of a scalp was a primary aim so that a Creek was a nobody unless he had at least taken seven scalps, such one-sided emphasis was lacking in the Plains, where only a few tribes, such as the Teton and the Cree, set a high value on scalping. "You will never hear a Crow boast of his scalps," it is said; a Blackfoot dwelt rather on the number of horses and guns he had captured; and elsewhere, with few exceptions, the "coup" proper greatly overshadowed scalping as a deed of merit.

Often loosely applied to all recognized war deeds, the term coup (French *coup*, a blow) correctly designates the touching of an enemy's body with the hand or with a special stick, striped like a barber's pole among the Cheyenne. On the same enemy the Cheyenne permitted three men to "count coup," the first toucher taking precedence; the Crow, the Assiniboin, and the Arapaho allowed four men to score in descending order of merit. Nearly everywhere the coup definitely outranked the killing of a man. "Killing an enemy counts nothing unless his person is touched or struck" (Assiniboin). A man who had killed an enemy from a distance and raced to count coup but was outrun and forestalled by a tribesman had to content himself with the second honor.

As indicated, tribes differed about the exploits worthy of public recital and also as to their relative merit. The Crow systematized their notions, recognizing four categories of exploit: carrying the pipe, *i.e.*, leading a successful party; the genuine coup; the theft of a picketed horse; and the snatching of a bow (or gun) in a hand-to-hand encounter. In order to rank as a "chief," *i.e.*, a distinguished warrior, a man had to have at least one deed of each type to his credit. However, there were some rare exploits, such as rescuing another Crow from imminent death, that rated especially high; and a series of lesser deeds might also be recited as evidence of valor, though not counted toward the chiefly status. Thus, a man did cite his capture of loose horses or his having been wounded in battle. The Iowa recognized three grades, the highest being that of victorious captaincy; next came the killing of a foeman; and the lowest type included as of equal value the coup, the cutting off of a head, scalping, and cutting off a lock of hair.

Some tribes specifically emphasized the element of danger in an exploit: a Cree who had shot an enemy while himself exposed outranked a killer from ambush; to use a club in slaying a man was worthier than to lay him low with firearms. However, many tribes regarded the killing of a woman or a child as a feat entitling to war honors. Altogether the actual sentiments of Plains Indians were a result of the tribal ideologies that impelled a man to defy death and the universal human urge to survive. In consequence, all sorts of contradictions occurred: a man normally tried to get as much glory as possible without risking his neck. There were, of course, sporadic daredevils and likewise men laboring under great grief or disillusionment who deliberately sought death.

Given the exaltation of a splendid war record, men naturally tried to exhibit their brave acts for general admiration. They achieved this end by reciting their deeds at any major gathering, by pictorial representations of them on a tipi cover or robe, and by details of personal decoration. The pictures were predominantly realistic (Figs. 30, 31), showing such episodes as the untethering of picketed horses, the capture of a gun, the seizure of an enemy's shield or bonnet. Sometimes, however, the representations merged into symbolism, as when a horseshoe stood for a horse. In the symbolic ornamentation of costume, styles varied. An Assiniboin who had killed enemies wore an eagle feather for each deed; feather heraldry was highly developed by the Dakota while barely known to the Blackfoot, who made corresponding use of white weasel skins. A Crow coup striker wore wolf tails at the heels of his moccasins, a gun snatcher put ermine skins on his shirt, a captain trimmed his shirt and moccasins with hair.

The introduction of the horse gave a great impetus to raiding, thus multiplying martial enterprises. This means that an economic motive was added that had not previously existed. However,

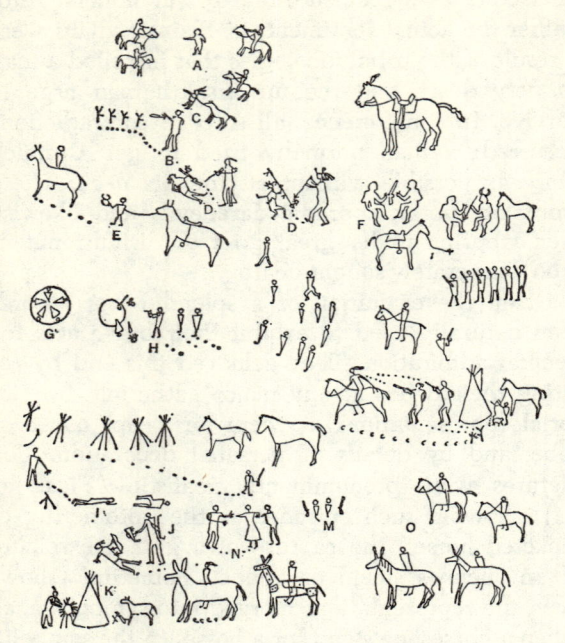

Fig. 30. War episodes as depicted on a tipi cover, Blackfoot. A, Bear-chief, afoot, escapes from Assiniboin Indians; B, Double-runner cuts loose from horses; C, he captures a Gros Ventre boy; D, he and a companion kill two Gros Ventre; E, he picks up a war bonnet dropped by a Gros Ventre, counting as a coup; F, he takes a gun from a Crow; G, he kills five Flathead; H, a Cree takes shelter in some brush, but Big-nose goes in for him; I, a Cree killed while running off Blackfoot horses; J, Double-runner with medicine-pipe takes a bow from a Gros Ventre and kills him; K, he takes a shield and horse from a Crow and is pursued; M, he kills two Gros Ventre and takes two guns; N, he captures a Gros Ventre woman and a boy; O, he takes four mules.

the strictly economic aspect of this phenomenon should not be exaggerated. The Plains Indians did not require herds of, say, 100 horses in order to supply their material wants. A few pack animals and a few for riding and hunting would have been quite adequate for that purpose. Since, unlike Mongols and Kirghiz, they neither milked mares nor as a rule ate horse flesh, anything beyond that limited number served purely social purposes of ostentation, like the several hundred wives of an African king. A Cree raider derived few direct benefits from his booty, for if he captured ten horses the tribal code would make him give away all but one or two to relatives and friends.

Certainly it is an error to assume that the desire for horses was responsible for the warlike spirit characteristic of the Plains. Apart from the overwhelming evidence for the craving of glory, it is clear that precisely the same eagerness for distinction prompted the tribes of the Southeast and of the western Woodlands, from which the majority of the historic Plains Indians emigrated into their subsequent habitat. In his report on the Indians

Fig. 31. The capture of horses as recorded on a Blackfoot tipi cover.

of the Creek Confederacy, J. R. Swanton says that Southeastern warfare "was a social institution and warlike exploits necessary means of social advancement"; its motive was not plunder, but scalping. Still more to the purpose is what we know about the tribes of Wisconsin and Illinois in the earlier days of Caucasian contact. According to W. Vernon Kinietz' study of the area from 1615 to 1760 "Indian [Miami] warfare was waged primarily for the glory of the participants. Acquisition of territory was not a motive, but the acquisition of scalps or tokens of the bravery and skill of the warriors was very important to them." And Paul Radin's research discloses that the Winnebago, linguistically close to the Omaha branch of the Siouan family, shared some of the most essential features of Plains militarism: "A man may go on the warpath for two reasons: either to revenge a slain relative or in a general way because he thinks he has received sufficient power and wishes to obtain glory." This tribe prized the coup and set it above mere killing; a headdress with a feather denoted a coup striker, killer, and scalper, while other decorations indicated other deeds conventionally recognized; a captain required spiritual sanction and was held responsible for the death of a follower (also true of the Illinois); a son was told that "it is good to die in war"; a warrior was expected to accompany his comrade on the warpath; oaths were sworn to attest the truth of one's military claims, perjury being punished with death. From Kinietz too, who quotes from the memoirs of Antoine Denis Raudot, we learn that in the very beginning of the eighteenth century the Illinois evidently counted coup with a stick or rock, thereby gaining the coveted right to claim a captive.

In other words, the typical Plains Indian war complex existed in a nonequestrian culture; and there, as in the Plains, the dominant motives were noneconomic.

Rank, Law, and Government

Aboriginal North American society was in the main democratic, and by and large the Plains Indians conformed to the prevailing pattern. Distinctions of rank occurred, but no *hereditary* classes, and to speak of "castes," as has been done occasionally, is preposterous since there was social mobility, and marriage was not legally restricted to one's own class. All that can be said in this respect is that, as everywhere, the children of distinguished men enjoyed certain advantages. As the son of a Rockefeller or Morgan has a better chance to become a great businessman than has a guttersnipe, so a Cree chief's son was more readily acclaimed as a brave man than an orphan would be. The tendency to stress such hereditary advantages was not uniform, on the whole probably increasing southward. Most of the tribes attached great importance to "incorporeal property"—immaterial privileges corresponding to our patents and copyrights. Naturally the owner of such prerogatives tried to bequeath them to his descendants, an urge that would foster the germ of hereditary privilege. Where specific public functions belonged to a particular clan, it might be regarded as socially superior, but since even the chiefly office implied little power, the practical significance of this phenomenon was slight. The essential point is that in the Indian's view a person of lowly origin could by supernatural favor gain wealth and standing; inevitably a boy with rich or eminent parents and many kinsmen had a better chance than an orphan. Characteristically, the worst Crow insult was to tell a man that he had no relatives, for it meant that he was a social nobody subject to abuse. To a spirited lad this taunt, however, was a challenge: he could court spiritual blessings, distinguish himself in fighting, gain wealth, and ultimately shame his detractors. The situation was utterly different from that of the Hindu or Tahitian social scheme that condemned the majority to an obscure social role.

A most important difference between the Plains Indians and Tahitians concerns material property. Whereas in Tahiti a monarch could appropriate the possessions of a lesser man, on the Plains any comparable act was unthinkable. On the contrary, a great man could maintain his status best by lavish generosity to the poor. Such liberality, next to a fine war record, was the basis for high standing. The Oglala had a society of chiefs enjoying superior prestige, but when a novice was admitted, he was urged to look after the poor, especially the widows and orphans. Among the Blackfoot a man aspiring to become a leader tried to outshine his competitors by his feasts and presents even at the cost of impoverishment, but not without thereby gaining the coveted status of a headman. J. O. Dorsey, in his study of the sociology of the Omaha, writes that the Omaha recognized two classes of meritorious tribesmen—"such as had given to the poor on many occasions, and had invited guests to many feasts," and those who, in addition, "had killed several of the foe and had brought home many horses." Rank is in fact so largely dependent on the military code that it has to some extent been considered under the head of Warfare.

As hinted above, the Plains Indian "chief" was by no means an autocrat. Autocratic chiefs did indeed exist in the Atlantic and Gulf regions, but not in our area, where the title was honorific and implied little authority for the bearer, though an exceptionally powerful personality could exert great influence. As a rule, the chiefs were titular, and any power exercised within the tribe was exercised by the total body of responsible men who had qualified for social eminence by their war record and their generosity. Until 1880 the Omaha had two principal chiefs, but they never made vital decisions without consulting the lesser titular chiefs, *i.e.*, without regard to public opinion. Coercive authority was exercised only indirectly through appointment of police for the hunt; when a quarrel occurred within the tribe, the chiefs did not quell the disturbance by force, but put sacred pipes between the combatants, "begging them to desist." This latter situation may be taken as typical of the area: in normal times the chief was not a supreme executive, but a peacemaker and an orator. So far as essentials go, it is therefore of no significance whether there was one chief, or a pair of chiefs or, as among the Cheyenne, a council of forty-four in a population of about 4,000, nor whether a man by virtue of his lineage could or could not ever qualify for the title of chief.

Nevertheless germs of governmental power existed in connection with special occasions. Especially during the collective hunt or a major festival a police force might exercise coercive authority.

Whereas normally the greatest chief would not dare lay hands on the meanest tribesman, the police appointed by him or, at some festivals, by the priest (page 179) did have the power to restrain a recalcitrant individual. The time of a great buffalo hunt, above all, required careful obedience to the leader's instructions lest the whole people suffer; hence the police would issue orders that no one must hunt by himself and thereby prematurely startle the herd. The Cheyenne police, more lenient than that of other tribes, nevertheless whipped even eminent offenders; among the Omaha, too, a highly esteemed man was once flogged so violently that he never fully recovered. Elsewhere the criminal's tipi might be destroyed and his goods confiscated; in extreme cases, if he resisted, he might be killed.

Such germs of strict government, however, never developed into a permanent oligarchy or monarchy because the spirit of Plains culture militated against it, as did also the splitting up of most tribes during a large part of the year.

Nevertheless, even apart from police activity, there were definite legal conceptions, though no courts in our sense. Sometimes religious ideas affected the attitude toward an undesirable action. Thus, the Cheyenne regarded murder of a tribesman as a sin and a crime; it polluted the Sacred Arrows, their holy of holies, and called for the penalty of possibly ten years' exile at the order of the forty-four councilors. But for the Crow a murder was a purely secular misdeed, though highly regrettable, since it might precipitate a feud between the clans involved. The camp chief and the police took cognizance, not as a punishing agency but as appeasers, trying to reconcile the parties by making the murderer's kin pay a substantial indemnity to the aggrieved family.

Crow and Cheyenne shared a form of oath or ordeal. If one Crow disputed another's claim to a meritorious war exploit, each contestant would take a knife, point it toward the Sun, and invoke the god to smite him with misfortune unless he spoke the truth. If one of the litigants soon after suffered death or misfortune, he was regarded as the perjurer.

A deterrent from reprehensible actions lay in the tremendous power of public opinion. The Indians were extremely sensitive to gossip that might affect their social standing. According to Clark Wissler, a Blackfoot who had made himself a nuisance would be "held up to general ridicule amid shrieks of laughter," and the mortification of the victim sometimes drove him into exile or upon the warpath. The Crow and Hidatsa recognized a definite relationship for exercising discipline of this order. It obtained between persons of either sex whose fathers were of the same clan. These "joking relatives" teased each other like certain true relatives by blood or marriage (page 86) but also had the serious duty of publicly upbraiding each other for deviations from proper conduct. A man thus exposed and jeered at for cowardice would feel like sinking into the ground with shame.

Trade; Economic Values

Within a particular local group there was little trading, for the necessities of life were freely shared and the crafts described elsewhere were not plied by professionals who devoted themselves exclusively to their practice. Nevertheless, some individuals excelled as bowyers, arrow makers, and skin dressers, and such persons were not as a rule inclined to exercise their skill gratuitously on behalf of unrelated tribesmen. If one of them did place his services at a stranger's disposal, the beneficiary understood that some compensation was expected. Good arrow makers were at least likely to be adequately feasted by prospective customers. With the development of equestrian life, the horse became a convenient unit of value; at an earlier period good arrows seem to have served the purpose, ten of them being subsequently reckoned the equivalent of a horse among the Crow.

Although reciprocal obligations were recognized, altruistic behavior was imposed in certain situations. A Blackfoot or Crow stumbling on a fellow tribesman butchering was sure to receive an ample portion of meat. Any self-respecting man gave presents to the poor, and no one could hope to rise to the position of a headman who failed to live up to his people's ideal of generosity.

The economic ideas attached to ceremonial privileges belong to a distinct category. Anything falling under this head commanded, from our point of view, exorbitant prices. Even the right to paint a simple design on one's face during a religious ritual might be worth a horse; and for so much as looking at the contents of a medicine bundle a man might have to pay the equivalent of $100. One Crow bought the prerogative of preparing a blanket, the modern substitute for a skin robe, as described in the seller's vision for a horse valued at $62; in addition the purchaser had to hire a draftsman to do the painting and to buy the proper feather trimmings. Another Crow paid ten horses to his sponsor in the Tobacco organization, and the novice's kin supplemented the fee with twenty-three more. Further, often even the closest kinship did not absolve the buyer of a privilege from making the usual payment. Thus, Hidatsa children inherited from a father who owned a medicine bundle merely the prerogative of buying it from him.

Why were people willing to give up valuable property in return for ceremonial privileges that seem to us quite worthless? To illustrate by Blackfoot data, the ownership of a bundle was supposed to ensure long life, success, happiness; in consequence, it also brought social prestige. To buy a bundle was a safe investment, for it was readily negotiable and the new buyer was under pressure of public opinion to offer at least the price exacted at one time from the seller. Apart from this, a onetime owner received perquisites in the form of fees whenever those conducting the pertinent ritual called upon him to participate because of his familiarity with the procedure. "While with us young men are exhorted to open a savings account, among the Blackfoot they are advised to become owners of medicine bundles" (Wissler).

Intertribal trade cannot be sharply separated from that between Indians and Whites. There was doubtless a fair amount of exchange of native commodities, as when visiting Crow Indians bartered fine robes against the corn grown on the Upper Missouri. Farther south, the corresponding phenomenon was observed by Coronado in 1541. But during the historic period the goods passed from one local group to another were largely those obtained from Whites. Broadly speaking, horses came from the Spanish settlements (page 42), hence first reached the southern Plains, while guns (as well as other wares) came mainly from the British and French in the northeast. This explains why, when the Cheyenne and the Kiowa-Comanche met amicably in 1840, the latter deprecated gifts of horses, of which they had plenty, but readily exchanged their surplus for guns, blankets, beads, calico, and metal kettles. Considerable relaying developed: in about 1820 the Arapaho are reported as holding "a kind of fair" on a tributary of the Platte, obtaining British goods from the Cheyenne, who in turn had got them from the Mandan.

The effects of White trade were far-reaching, as has already been pointed out in several connections. The acquisition of guns enabled the Cree to crowd out their western neighbors and helped to turn them from a Woodland into a rather typical Plains people. Quite generally, the Indians were for the first time tempted by fur traders to kill game for gain. They adopted totally new foods and stimulants—bread, sugar, coffee, spirituous liquor. Metal utensils superseded earthenware and wooden ones, strike-a-lights proved easier means of getting fire than the drill, cloth was made into clothing with less labor than skins, steel knives cut better than flint. Thus a large portion of aboriginal culture became obsolescent, fragments being retained only for ceremonial occasions.

4 RECREATION

The Plains Indians had a relatively wide range of amusements, including games, dances, attendance at major festivals, and storytelling.

Games

Children often played in imitation of their elders. Little girls would put up miniature tipis, and young boys would bring them rabbits or other food as though they were adult men returning from the hunt. Boys also imitated the performances of the military clubs and indulged in all sorts of pranks, including the snatching of meat from the racks set up in camp and then dashing off to a safe distance for a leisurely feast. In the winter, Dakota and Crow boys spun conical tops by whipping them on the ice. Adolescents and mature young people were allowed to go with their sweethearts berrypicking or bringing in the requisites for a major ceremony.

Adults were addicted to games of chance, at which a man might gamble away all his property —if legends are to be believed, even his wife and his own body. Conspicuous among most tribes were dice and the equivalent of our "Button, button, who's got the button?" Both extended far beyond the Plains area; in his report published by the Bureau of American Ethnology in 1907 Stewart

Culin found dice among 130 and the "button" game among 81 North American peoples.

The dice used were not cubical in shape, but sticks with different faces, plum stones, little pieces of bone, or similar objects (Fig. 32). One form of Pawnee dice sets consisted of cane slips. One cane was painted red on the concave side and had an incised line painted red on the convex side; the second was blue on the concave side and had featherlike marks on the reverse; and so forth. But instead of throwing sticks, Pawnee women might toss three large and three small plum stones from a flat twined basket. The smaller stones were burnt black on one side; the large ones, plain on one side, were marked with a curved band and seven dots on the other. The player held her basket near the ground, tossed the stones into the air, and moved the basket smartly against the ground, catching the stones in it. Tallies rested between opposing parties, and each woman laid bets against her vis-à-vis. Crow women also used either sticks or plum stones (or bone equivalents). Every combination of throws scored according to a definite system that seems arbitrary to the outsider. For example, the Blackfoot called one bone with thirteen pits the "chief," and this piece turning up with three blanks counted six points. A player continued so long as she scored; and in order to win, one side had to get all the tallies.

The "button" or hand game was played with pairs of small objects, one of them marked, say, by a string round the middle, the other plain; usually the guesser had to guess the hand holding the *un*-marked object. In case of more than two players, each bet against his vis-à-vis. The Blackfoot reck-

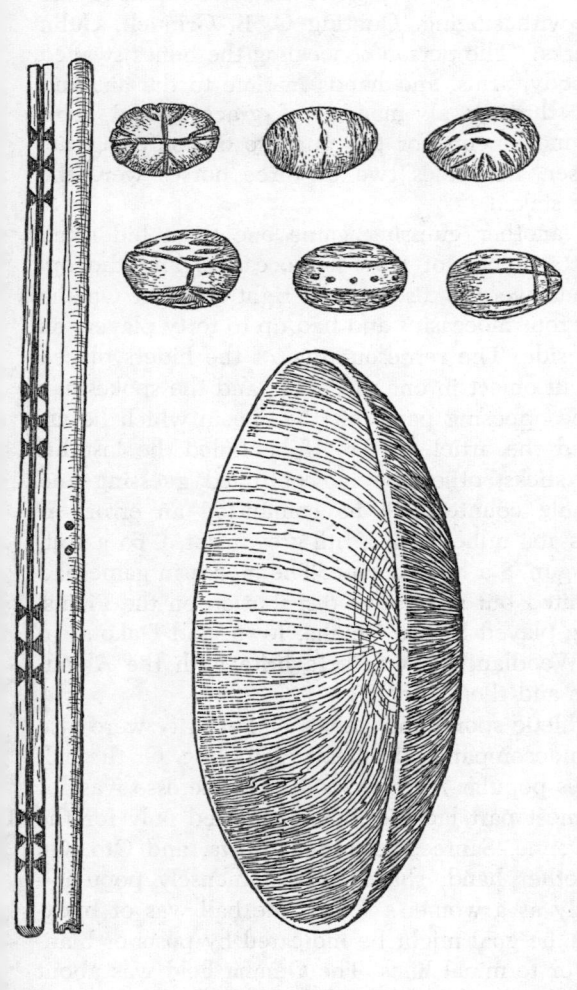

Fig. 32. Stick dice, decorated plum-stone dice, and a wooden bowl, all used in Crow games of chance. The stick dice is about 9 inches long, decorated on both sides with designs that were burned in; one side is flat, the other rounded.

oned ten points to a game and accompanied the play with singing. Quoting G. B. Grinnell, Culin remarks: "The person concealing the bones swayed his body, arms, and hands in time to the air, and went through all manner of graceful and intricate movements for the purpose of confusing the guesser." At times two or three horses were the prize staked.

In another guessing game one team hid small objects in one of several moccasins, and the opponents were to discover the right one. The Omaha used four moccasins and had up to forty players on each side. The representative of the hiders placed a small object in one moccasin, and the spokesman of the opposing party hit the one in which he assumed the article to be. If he failed, he lost his tally sticks; otherwise he continued guessing and winning counters till he committed an error. At times 100 tallies won a full-grown horse, 60 a colt, 10 a gun, 8 a buffalo robe. The moccasin game had a limited but suggestive distribution on the Plains, being played by the Omaha, Iowa, and Dakota. In the Woodlands it was a favorite with the Algonkians and the Winnebago.

Athletic sports and games of dexterity were also often accompanied by heavy gambling. Of the ball games popular in the Woodlands, lacrosse was for the most part lacking, being reported only for the Cheyenne, Santee, Assiniboin, Iowa, and Oto. On the other hand, shinny was immensely popular—mostly as a women's sport. The ball was of buckskin; the goal might be indicated by posts or blankets or terminal lines. The Omaha field was about three hundred yards in extent, and the moieties might be pitted against each other, while the Crow

RECREATION 135

sometimes had men play against women. A game with two balls joined was played by Cheyenne, Cree (Plate 22), Arikara, Pawnee, Santee, and Omaha women. The hoop-and-pole game, an exclusively masculine sport, was widely distributed. The players, generally two in number, rolled a hoop, either netted or plain, on a level course and threw darts at it, the precise way of striking the hoop or a portion of the net determining the count. The Pawnee used either a plain rawhide ring 4 to

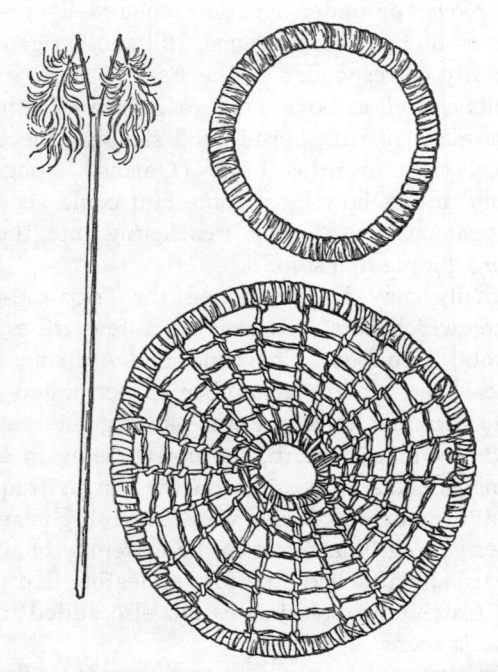

Fig. 33. Ring, hoop, and dart for the Crow hoop-and-pole game (see also Plate 23).

6 inches in diameter, to be pierced by a hooked dart, or a netted hoop up to 25 inches in diameter; they sometimes played the game as a magical performance for calling buffalo. As well as using a hoop the Hidatsa rolled small stone disks; the Comanche hoop, except for its smaller size, exactly resembles the Crow form (Fig. 33). Variations occurred tribally in the darts, which might be arrows, forked saplings, hooked sticks, or long poles. The Arapaho sticks were tied and thrown in pairs, the aim being to hit the hoop so that both sticks were either over or under a certain colored figure—one of four—on the circumference. Still another game of dexterity corresponded to the Eastern snow snake. Adults as well as boys slid sticks, arrows, feathered darts made of ribs, horn-tipped saplings, pieces of antler, even unstrung bows (Omaha) along the ground to see how far a contestant could send his projectile. Often it went ricocheting into the air before gliding to a stop.

Finally may be mentioned the "cup-and-ball" game, which was restricted to a few tribes, the Dakota, Assiniboin, Cheyenne, and Arapaho. In a typical Teton outfit a number of perforated deer hoofs attached to a pin were swung into the air by the connecting cord, the object being to catch as many hoofs as possible on the pin. A frequent substitute for the hoofs were several phalangeal bones, strung on a thong to the extremity of which was usually attached a perforated leather flap (Fig. 34). Catching a hole in this tab also added to the player's score.

Archery contests and foot and horse races figured among other forms of diversion. The public part

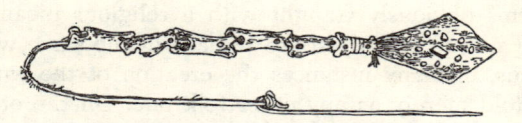

Fig. 34. Assiniboin cup-and-ball game.

of important ceremonials provided a great spectacle for the people at large and may be regarded as the equivalent of our theatrical shows. The "dances" during such religious festivals, however, generally were unimpressive and required a minimum of physical effort, such as alternately raising one's feet on tiptoes while standing still or alternately advancing the clenched fists while in position. An exception must be made on behalf of war dances and those associated with some military societies (Plate 18), which were executed with great vigor. Dances of men with women, though not unknown, did not represent an important or typical form of entertainment. Probably the commonest form was to have a group of men and women in alternation form a ring, each man putting his right arm around his partner's shoulders and both shuffling their feet slowly to the left, the entire group describing a circle.

Storytelling

Folk tales were told of a winter evening when the people had stretched out to rest for the night. A Crow narrator expected to get a periodic response from his auditors, failing which he assumed that they had fallen asleep and would stop talking.

Folk tales cannot always be distinguished from sacred myths; and we must remember that what seems obviously fraught with a religious meaning did not necessarily strike Indians in the same way. Thus, in many instances the creation of the world is told merely as any other folk tale. On the other hand, in certain tribes, such as the Blackfoot and the Hidatsa, the owners of medicine bundles often explained the origins of these sacred objects as the climax of a generally known story. There would thus be both an esoteric and a popular version, the former known only to the handful of bundle owners and differing mainly by its infinite dullness since the narrator was likely to graft on the plot a circumstantial statement of all the ceremonial details impressed on the original bundle owner by his spirit protector.

From a literary point of view the stories of the Plains show much greater affinity with the Woodlands than with the Basin Area. The Basin has a preponderance of tales revolving about the deeds and adventures of animals and a minimum of novelettes with distinctly human heroes, such as are very common in the Plains and the Woodlands. Of course, the animals of the Basin speak and act like human beings, and in view of the religious notions of the Plains tribes animal helpers automatically turn up in the novelettes, but they remain as a rule secondary characters.

A feature the Plains share with many other regions is the conception, though not so explicitly brought out by some tribes as by others, of a mythical era in which things were different from what they are now. The people at one time had to eat their food raw because fire was hoarded by some mean character, from whom some cunning Indian managed to steal it for the good of his fellows. Hunting was once unnecessary, for all the game animals were impounded in a corral where they could easily be shot at will. The ancestors of the race were not liable to death. The seasons were different from what they have been in recent times; the mole had good eyesight; the crow used to be white. The relevant myths explain what happenings led to the present state of the universe and man. Usually some one character of ancient times brings about many of the changes in question and may therefore be called a "transformer." Often the same person also teaches the ancestral Indians how to impound buffalo, chip arrowpoints, perform a victory dance, and so forth, in which case the transformer is at the same time his people's "culture hero." In Crow myth Old Man Coyote appears when the entire world is still covered with water and summons water birds to dive for mud from the depths. Three of the birds fail, the fourth fetches a little mud, from which Old Man Coyote molds the earth. Later he creates mankind, bids them multiply, and instructs them.

To us it seems paradoxical that the transformer and culture hero who is so definitely represented as a benefactor also frequently appears in the contradictory role of a "trickster." Thus, Old Man Coyote is forever greedily seeking food and resorts to all sorts of low wiles to gain his ends, *e.g.*, simulating friendship for a buffalo, whom he then lures to leap down a cutbank. He even covets his own daughter and in order to be able to marry her feigns death and returns in disguise to woo her, thus flouting the very strict Indian rules of incest. Even when he does not outrage custom, he is likely to play an undignified part, being outwitted by other characters or beaten in trials of strength. The inconsistency of these traits—creative power and impotence, philanthropy and unscrupulousness, establishment of social rules and deliberate flouting of them—does not seem to have disturbed the Indians.

Another frequent mythical conception is that of man-destroying monsters whom some conquering hero killed for the benefit of man. The Crow tell a long story about Old Woman's Grandchild, the offspring of the Sun and a Hidatsa woman. He tames a ferocious bear, allows himself to be sucked in by a huge buffalo that used to swallow Indians, in order to stab the beast, chops off the heads of snakes accustomed to crawl into human bodies, and so forth. Ultimately he ascends to the sky to turn into a star. Similar feats are often ascribed to twins.

Boy heroes are common in Plains stories of later times too. A favorite theme worked out in harmony with the ideology of the area is the rise to fame and fortune of a poor orphan who has been pitied by some supernatural being. Another popular subject is that of a proud beauty who spurns all suitors, only to fall prey to a Bluebeard from whose clutches she is rescued with difficulty. If the haughty maiden has insulted her admirer, he may seek a vision and obtain such power from an elk spirit that women become infatuated with him, so that he is now able to turn the tables on the girl who humiliated him.

Some highly specific motifs in these traditions have an amazing distribution far beyond our area. The conception of a primeval ocean and earth

18. *Mandan Half-shaved Head Dance.* Carl Bodmer engraving in Maximilian.

19 *Mandan Bull Society Dance.* Carl Bodmer engraving in Maximilian.

20. Two young warriors returning with their first scalps; their faces are blackened as a symbol of the attainment of a "coup." Courtesy of Bureau of American Ethnology, Smithsonian Institution.

21. An Assiniboin scalp dance. The legend reads "Scalp Dance. Drawn by an Assiniboine warrier. Fort Union. Nov. 10, 1853." Courtesy of Bureau of American Ethnology, Smithsonian Institution.

22. *The Cree double-ball shinny game.*

23. *The Hidatsa hoop-and-pole game as played in a winter earthlodge village.* Carl Bodmer engraving in Maximilian.

divers was found among Algonkian tribes on the Atlantic Coast in the early seventeenth century and was sometimes interpreted as a distorted fragment of the Biblical deluge story; it has been reported from California, Siberia, and even eastern Europe. Again, there is a frequent North American idea of a perennial conflict between the Thunderbird and a water dragon; in the Plains version the monster regularly rises from a lake to destroy his enemy's fledglings while the parents are gone. At last the distressed father seeks the aid of a skillful Indian hunter, who kills the dragon by throwing red-hot rocks into his mouth. The generic notion of conflicting air and water powers extends at least from Dakota to British Columbia. Several Plains episodes or conceptions have been reported from South America. A Cree story of an adulterous wife killed by her husband embodies the notion that her skull rolls after him and her children. This curious idea of a rolling skull occurs as far south as the Gran Chaco. The Assiniboin tell of a hunter who whittles one of his legs to a point and with it tries to impale his companion, and this odd conceit is likewise found in British Guiana. More amazing still, the trickster simulating death in order to attain an incestuous union with his daughters turns up in Tierra del Fuego, among the Ona and the Yahgan, the southernmost natives of the New World.

Where parallels are so specific and intrinsically strange, it is difficult to suppose that the motifs were independently invented. We may assume that early migrant tribes carried part of the ancient American lore with them as they traveled south. Theoretically, one might of course also guess that these details were diffused in comparatively late times, but this hypothesis suffers from the fact that the intervening territories have not so far yielded any evidence of the features in question.

A Plains Indian raconteur was not limited to the traditional body of fiction. He could also narrate ever-interesting tales of actual warfare or hunting adventures or, if he had a streak of the comedian, get up a topical story showing some well-known tribesman in a ridiculous light.

Clowns

Clownish behavior sometimes blended with serious and even sacred observances, as when those so instructed in a vision did the reverse of what they were asked by their tribesmen, pretended to freeze in the sweltering summer heat or to be overcome with the temperature on an icy winter day. But on some festive occasions buffoons might appear for the sheer purpose of amusing the crowds—dressed in the shabbiest of clothes, riding a miserable pony, and disporting themselves in the most absurd and at times most obscene fashion.

All in all, the natives evidently enjoyed a respectable number of entertainments and attached considerable importance to them.

5 ART

Among the Plains Indians, stone sculpture was absent and wood carving as a craft too little developed to foster artistry, as demonstrated by some ceremonial objects (Figs. 35, 36). On the other hand, there was a good deal of painting and of decorative art in quills and later in beadwork.

Painting on Skins

Painting was executed on buffalo robes, tipi covers, parfleches, and other hide or skin objects. The colors were derived largely from iron-containing clays, which yielded brown, red, and yellow, while a black earth or charcoal provided black. The aboriginal use of green and blue, though contested, seems established. Paints were pulverized in stone

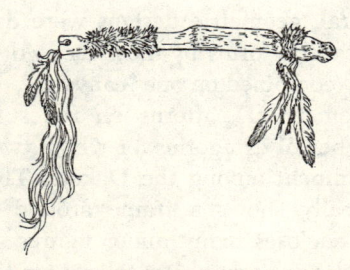

Fig. 35. A ceremonial carving carried by an officer of the Crow Lumpwood Society (about 2 feet high).

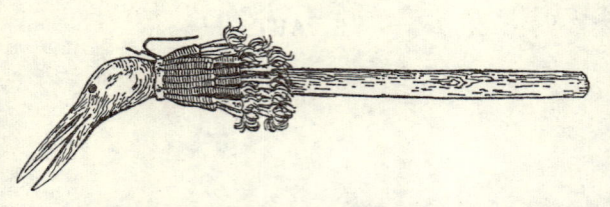

Fig. 36. A ceremonial carving surmounted by a crane head, used in the Crow Hot Dance (about 2 feet high).

mortars and mixed with a gluey material that made the colors stick. The artist, in action, held the paints in hollow stones, shells, or sherds. Brushes, one for each color, were of bone, horn, or wood; later a tuft of antelope hair was mounted on a stick. The Hidatsa first pressed the designs into the hide, then applied the paint over them, and finally set the paint with the glue. The glue outlined the patterns and could be used without colors on parts of a hide. The hide to be decorated was extended on the ground, the artist crouching over it, sometimes aided by a colleague, especially in pictographic work.

In general, geometric designs were done by the women, realistic forms by men; the two styles were very rarely combined on one "canvas."

The geometrical patterns on robes fall into a small number of categories, of which two are especially prominent among the Dakota. The women's robe typically shows a frame around an oblong field that encloses many minor figures and is in a characteristic position above the center (lower illustration on page 146). The characteristic men's robe bears the "black warbonnet" pattern, *i.e.*, concentric

ART

circles with numerous small radiating figures each composed of two isosceles triangles and designated by the Indians as "feathers" (illustration this page). Widely distributed, but common only among the Comanche and their neighbors, seems to have been a frame with a central hourglass pattern enclosing minor designs (top illustration on page 146). Red is the dominant color in the geometrically decorated specimens, but yellow and blue are also very popular.

Pictography might be regarded as a means of communication rather than as an expression of the artistic urge. It is certain that the realistic pictures on robes or tipi covers drawn by the Indians served

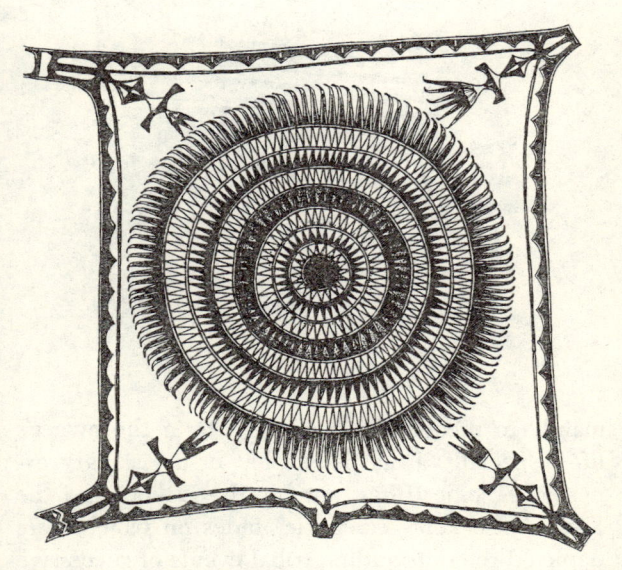

Fig. 37. Three examples of patterns often used on buffalo robes are shown on this and the following page.

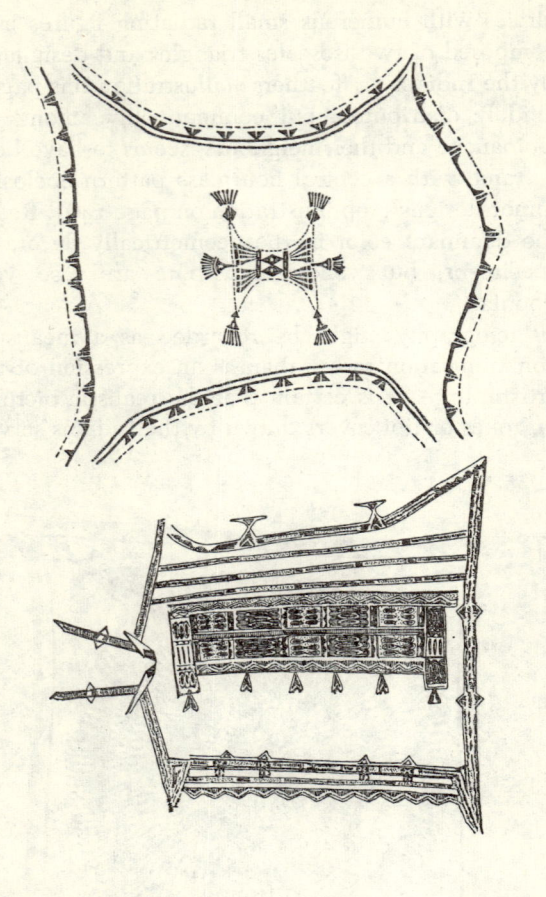

mainly to record significant events in the owner's life, especially a martial exploit or a visionary experience; some tribes, notably the Dakota and the Kiowa, also kept "calendric" hides on which were depicted the outstanding tribal events of successive years. Nevertheless all these representations can be viewed likewise from an aesthetic point of view. As hides became scarce, materials introduced by Whites were used. Even sacred events were recorded on cloth, and historic occurrences were sometimes depicted in notebooks with crayons furnished by the trader.

As for theme, the robes preponderantly represent scenes of battle and raiding. As John C. Ewers notes, in his book *Plains Indian Painting*, human and equine figures are by far most common, jointly appearing in 90 per cent of the specimens examined; even the buffalo is rare, the dog completely lacking. Perspective was absent; figures, both human and animal, generally appeared in profile; and though there was composition in the portrayal of hand-to-hand encounters of the looting of an enemy's horses, there was hardly any attempt to coordinate all the scenes of a hide into a unified painting. Individual figures are variously represented: hoofs may be either realistically drawn or provided with a hook; human legs and arms may be lifelike or merely suggested by straight lines; the head is often merely outlined, in other cases only an eye and the nose are indicated; manes may be omitted or emphasized; figures are either in solid color or merely in contour. Notwithstanding technical deficiencies a fair number of pictographs display an estimable dynamic quality.

We do not know how far back into the past Plains pictography extends. The fact that horses are so frequent on Museum specimens does not prove the art modern, for shields and their buckskin covers show a variety of animals—buffalo, deer, eagles—which could well have been drawn in precontact days (Fig. 28). That skins were painted in the southern Plains in 1540 appears from a letter by

Coronado, though he is reporting on hearsay and does not state whether the decoration was realistic. The oldest known piece, now in the Peabody Museum at Harvard University, was collected by Lewis and Clark among the Mandan in 1805 and is supposed to represent a battle that took place in 1797 (Plate 24). Though many horses appear on this robe, the prevalent weapons shown are bows, spears, and shields. An interesting early robe, donated to the Historical Museum in Bern in 1838 as a Crow robe, may also be of Mandan origin.

Occasionally a scene normally painted was imitated in quillwork (Plate 25).

Rawhide Decoration

In the decoration of their parfleches the Plains Indians achieved a distinctive style. Though the simplest geometric forms—straight lines, triangles, rectangles, diamonds—predominate, they are arranged in a variety of combinations, some of which characterize subdivisions of the area. The overwhelming number of specimens housed in museums are painted, but according to Dakota informants the patterns were originally incised, *i.e.*, an artist would scrape away portions of the pigmented layer of the buffalo skin, leaving sections of lighter or darker shading. Whatever may be the relative antiquity of the two procedures, incising was certainly practiced at one time, for two Crow samples are to be seen in the Chicago Museum of Natural History along with a few Eastern Dakota and Blackfoot specimens.

The two main parfleche flaps are symmetrically decorated; in addition, the northwestern tribes—Sarsi, Blackfoot, Crow, Assiniboin, Dakota, and the

ART 149

marginal Nez Percé and Kutenai—decorate the side flaps, though with less care. Straight lines preponderate, but curves crop up among several northwestern peoples, most of all among the Blackfoot. The Crow stand out for the precision of their lines, the Wind River Shoshone and Southern Ute coming next.

The decorative area is mostly oblong, but the northwestern tribes again show distinctiveness in substituting a trapezoid for the rectangle, this being always the case among the Sarsi and Kutenai, frequently among the Blackfoot and Assiniboin, occasionally elsewhere. Some tribes enclose the decorative field in a frame, which others completely lack.

A very common trait is a central stripe that extends through the middle of the flap and either forms the basis of a large central figure (Fig. 38) or divides the field into two symmetrical panels. Although there has doubtless been a great deal of trading back and forth in recent times, some patterns remain absent or rare in certain tribes and common in others. The Crow, for example, are fond of vertically unbisected large diamonds in the cen-

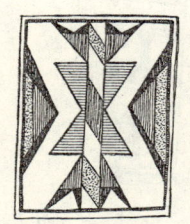

Fig. 38. Designs painted on parfleches: left, Crow; center, Cheyenne; right, Hidatsa.

ter, while favoring neither the clear-cut two-panel system nor the slender figures that often seem to divide the decorative field of the Arapaho or Cheyenne into five as against the three longitudinal units of the Crow. A framed central rectangle and a central hourglass figure are also common among the Crow. Details are at times continuously distributed, proving historical connection. Thus, the Crow and the Wind River Shoshone place solidly colored rectangles in the four corners of the field; less frequently this feature appears among the Nez Percé, Gros Ventre, and Dakota.

Altogether the northwestern tribes show marked similarities of treatment, and there is also a strong resemblance between the Crow and Shoshone styles. On the other hand, despite the affinity of

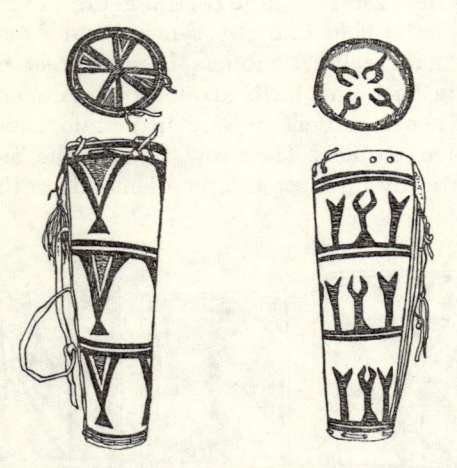

Fig. 39. Two painted rawhide cases used for ritual objects by the Arapaho. The design on the cover of the case is also shown.

Crow and Hidatsa in other respects, their parfleches reveal no specially close relationship.

Rawhide containers other than parfleches, such as the envelopelike square cases with a flap (Fig. 23), resemble the parfleches in ornamentation. This applies in part even to the cylindrical medicine bags; but since the shape of these objects modifies the visible decorative field, deviations may be expected to occur both on the main body and the cover. This certainly holds for Arapaho specimens, on which inverted tents and distinctive fishtail-like and stemmed crescent designs figure prominently (Fig. 39).

Embroidery

Since a draftsman enjoys far greater freedom than an embroiderer, we should expect a much wider range of decorative designs on rawhide containers and on nonpictographically ornamented robes than in quillwork and bead embroidery. Actually the reverse holds, the embroidered patterns being very diverse and sometimes markedly complex; a craftswoman might even succeed in quilling bird forms, horses, and mounted braves in full regalia (Plate 25). Elaboration, however, was a comparatively late development.

A chronological study by Frederic H. Douglas, based on early reports and drawings as well as on authentically early museum specimens, affords the following as the probable sequence of events. In the quillwork that unquestionably preceded beadwork, angular geometric designs predominated; floral patterns in the Plains were either intrusions from the Woodlands or, later still, due to French influence. This angular style, based on triangles, rectangles, and their combinations, is to be correlated with the prevalent "two-thread" technique (see page 71), but since "one-thread" sewing was not wholly lacking, some curvilinear effects were achieved, notably in the production of rosettes.

Bead embroidery hardly developed on the Plains prior to 1835–1840, when White traders began to introduce large china and glass beads on a considerable scale. The early beads, most commonly white and sky blue, are about ⅛ inch in diameter, nearly double the size of the beads brought in from about 1850 and thereafter. Again, the dominant technique employed, "lazy-stitch" sewing, affected the style, largely excluding curvilinear patterns. The figures worked out in this period seem to have been shared throughout most of the area; they include equilateral and isosceles triangles, generally resting on or hanging from a transverse stripe; chains of right-angled triangles; bars and oblongs; and series of concentric oblongs. The impression conveyed is one of massiveness. Characteristic of this earlier period is the general smallness of the beaded areas, even 6-inch bands being infrequent. In a study of the influence exerted by quilled decoration on its successor, this earlier beadwork style would obviously be of crucial importance.

The modern style set in with the availability of much smaller beads, whose precise character indicates the age of the decorated pieces, and came to fruition from 1880 to 1900. Tribal differences, both technological and stylistical, asserted themselves in this later period. The Dakota, Cheyenne, and Arapaho adhered to the lazy stitch; the Blackfoot, Sarsi, Plains Cree, and Flathead made exclusive use of the overlay; the Crow, Assiniboin, Gros Ventre, and

Plains Shoshoneans employed both techniques. In the south, where beadwork was used only for trimming, the lazy stitch was in vogue among the Pawnee, whereas the Omaha preferred the overlay.

In the ornamentation of long, narrow strips, say, on men's leggings, the style is rather uniform throughout the area. The forms that appear comprise almost exclusively solid triangles or hourglasses, characteristically stepped, circles, crosses, and rectangles. Though eclipsed by later elaborations, these elements, which are proved by photographs to have been the commonest everywhere in the area during the 1870s (Douglas), persisted into the most recent times.

Apart from the widespread features just listed, subareal differences evolved. We may distinguish a northwestern style typical of the Blackfoot, Sarsi, Plains Cree, and Flathead. Hundreds of little oblongs or squares are united to form large patterns, usually of a single color with borders of varicolored squares. The figures include stepped triangles, squares, diamonds, crosses, oblique wide bands with stepped long sides. The style is markedly simple and restricted as compared with that of other subareas and bears "the closest affinity of any of the Plains to that seen in porcupine quillwork" (Douglas). Highly characteristic of Blackfoot moccasins is the U-shaped figure on the instep, often associated with subsidiary designs. This decoration was the most fashionable on Crow moccasins in the second decade of the present century (Fig. 40); on the other hand, it is completely lacking in the large collections from the Arapaho and Gros Ventre to be found at The American Museum of Natural History.

The embroidery of the Crow and Shoshone suggests definite affinity with parfleche decoration; nor is the relationship confined to these two tribes. There may be something in the Dakota theory that painting preceded even quillwork and that before manipulating quills the Indian women painted moccasins with conventional patterns. Taking the area as a unit, we find in both embroidered and painted compositions the same arrangement of hourglasses, diamonds, and triangles. Thus, the Hidatsa parfleche (Fig. 38) shows essentially the same central figure as some Dakota pipe pouches. Generally speaking, the Crow-Shoshone style seems to be more massive than that of most other tribes; large triangles and their combinations, hourglasses and

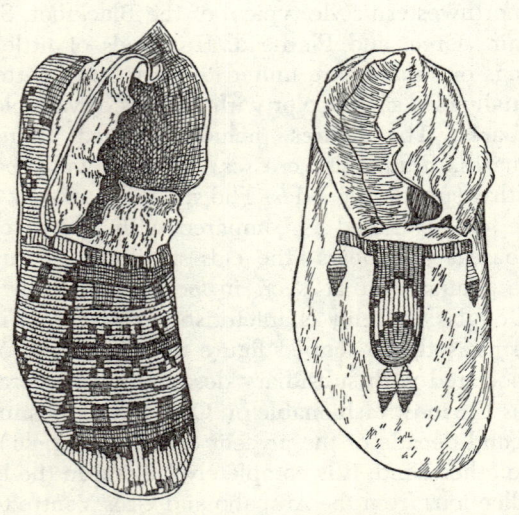

Fig. 40. The difference in moccasin designs is shown here in examples from the Arapaho (left) and the Crow (right).

lozenges, are characteristic; a vertical chain of them often has one triangle balanced on a transverse stripe resting on the apex of another.

As might be expected from their geographical position, the Crow share design features not only with the Blackfoot, but also with the Dakota, Arapaho, and Cheyenne. By and large, the efflorescence of bead embroidery can be best illustrated by Dakota and Arapaho specimens. To take only moccasin decoration, the poverty of the Blackfoot with their ever-recurring U motif contrasts with the profusion of designs among the two tribes mentioned (Fig. 40, Plate 26). The Dakota have names for the most popular of their design elements (Fig. 41), though not for the major compositions they build up from them. Typical of these latter are the patterns on pipe and tobacco bags, which have been called the culmination of Dakota decorative design (Plate 27). Dakota and Arapaho decorations generally impress one as comparatively light rather than massive. Both favor a small central diamond with symmetrical appendages, say, of "forked trees" (Fig. 41). The Dakota usually have these additions on all four corners of the diamond, while the Arapaho as a rule content themselves with a single pair; the former are also more inclined to insert crosses and stars by way of varying the background.

Scholars have shown that some of the simpler embroidered designs extend beyond our area; thus, the isosceles triangle enclosing the rectangle, often conceived on the Plains as a tipi with its door, crops up likewise in Pueblo territory. That there is a historical connection involved seems likely, but we

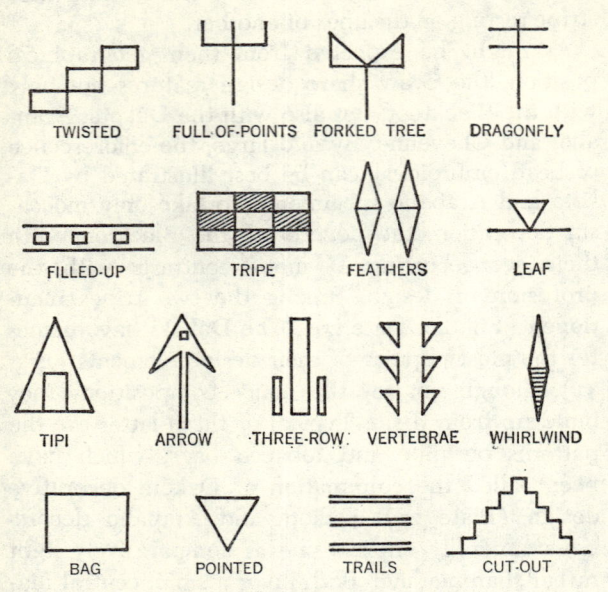

Fig. 41. Conventional design elements and their interpretation from the Dakota.

cannot be sure in what direction this motif and others spread.

Designs and Symbolism

Plains Indian art sheds light on an important problem. Among the design units of the Dakota there is one called "dragonfly" (Fig. 41), and the doubly crossed vertical line in question could easily suggest the shape of the insect. Since many primitive tribes interpret purely geometric forms as animals, plants, natural phenomena, or other parts of the real world, theorists once generally assumed that art began with an attempt to depict real objects. In later times, they suggested, the representations had become less and less like the originals until at last only the name remained as evidence of the original artist's intention. Everyone admits that this process, known as conventionalization, is possible and has at times actually taken place; the problem is whether *all* geometrical figures originated in this way. The question can be discussed from more than one point of view, and we shall confine ourselves to considerations pertinent to our area.

Turning first to our Dakota design names, we find that by no means all of them refer to any concrete object. There are such purely descriptive designations as "twisted," "full-of-points," "filled-up," "cut-out." The suspicion arises that they evolved for convenience of reference and that the whole of the nomenclature of which they form part is nothing but the craftswomen's technical vocabulary. That some shapes suggested either an animal like the dragonfly or an artifact like an arrow seems natural enough. In the case of the "whirlwind" sign, one simply cannot conceive of a native's first trying to give a lifelike picture of the phenomenon indicated, and it is equally inconceivable how such a picture would ultimately assume the semblance of a narrow diamond. The obvious inference is that native craftswomen were familiar with certain simple forms and, for convenience' sake, came to label them. In other words, the association between form and name is secondary.

There are even more cogent considerations. The attempt to link meaning with designs is by no means universal in our area. It seems to have been lacking among the Blackfoot and was very slightly developed among the Crow, though these latter do sometimes call a right-angled triangle a "spearhead," a couple of such figures with facing hypotenuses "two facing tipis," and a plain cross "a star." The only persistent association seems to be that of a diamond with an infant's navel cord. Incidentally, the Arapaho regularly symbolize the navel by the same figure, which however may bear a variety of other meanings. A strong urge to interpret typical geometrical forms is confined to relatively few tribes, such as the Arapaho and the Dakota; and even among them informants frequently declared that their decoration had no significance but served a purely aesthetic purpose.

It might be argued that the Indians had merely lost the memory of the original meanings, but here a vital point enters. Where meanings are offered for a particular design, they vary within the tribe. Among the Dakota, Wissler discovered that often the woman making a decorative pattern and the man wearing the garment bearing the design connected different meanings with the design. Obviously an interpretation was secondarily read into it, certainly by one sex. This is sufficient to prove that our Indians do tend to invest a given geometrical figure with meaning. In the present case we can even point out the underlying drives. Dakota males were obsessed with the objective of military glory, hence used any occasion to inject relevant ideas. So it came about that, while a woman beaded designs on moccasins merely for decoration, her husband wearing them would see in the designs a picture of warfare: a diamond became a man's body, triangles stood for the tipis around which a battle raged, straight lines represented arrows, pronged figures symbolized wounds. When women interpreted geometric figures, they naturally expressed interests of a different order. For instance, the Dakota believed that the turtle presided over female physiological functions; hence this reptile played a conspicuous role in feminine thought. Sometimes a woman might actually start with the idea of making a fairly lifelike representation of a turtle in shaping an amulet, and such efforts may be regarded as parallel to the men's paintings of their war records. But more commonly she would use the most diverse figures—the U on a dress, diamonds with pronged appendices on leggings, an arrangement of triangles on a rawhide case—to symbolize the turtle or its breast (Plate 28).

Another interesting symbol conceived by Dakota women is a series of parallel lines on cradles, saddle blankets, and moccasins to represent the childbearing stage in a woman's life. The identical arrangement on a moccasin is interpreted by the Arapaho as the poles of a sweatlodge. This decoration on footgear is so distinctive that it cannot have originated independently in two tribes of the same area; hence, we infer once more that the design existed before the interpretations, was diffused as a decoration, and used for different symbols by the Arapaho and the Dakota. Other designs shared by these tribes confirm the conclusion. A simple four-branched cross usually represents the morning star for an Arapaho but is rarely connected with an astral body by the Dakota, who more generally see in it the four quarters of the globe or corpses or the rescue of an imperiled fellow tribesman.

What is more, Arapaho explanations were highly variable within the tribe, depending on the individual informant and on the context. A triangle with a curved hypotenuse may be a horse's ear, a buffalo horn, a lake, or a fish. A solidly embroidered disk serving as a tent ornament stood for the sun or the whirlwind; near the top of a cradle it denoted the infant's head. The diamond was associated with no less than ten different meanings—the navel, a person, an eye, a lake, a star, life or abundance, a turtle, a buffalo wallow, a hill, a tent interior. Surely it is inconceivable that so many distinct attempts at realism should all converge by deterioration toward a diamond—apart from the fact that it is not easy to imagine how an artist could ever realistically represent "life or abundance." Further, the meanings cited also occurred with quite different figures: a square, a trapezoid, a triangle, a pentagon, a circle no less than the diamond symbolized a lake; the life symbol could be a small rectangle, a green square enclosing a white and red square, a diamond. Evidently both a set of forms and a set of symbolic concepts were conventional in the tribe and came to be variously combined.

The course of development may, then, be summarized as follows. The Plains Indian artist was familiar with a number of geometrical designs, some of which were named for obvious resemblances to natural phenomena or artifacts, others being associated for reasons no longer clear. But in any case the association was as a rule secondary, not due primarily to an urge toward realism, which found expression in pictography.

Plains Indian symbolism offers some points of interest apart from the problem of conventionalization. The Arapaho only exceptionally professed to represent plants, rather infrequently interpreted designs as human beings, and rarely as the larger mammals. Dogs and horses, deer and elk did not appear at all in this context, whereas small members of the animal kingdom were fairly common. Yet altogether animals loomed far less conspicuously than topographic features—mountains, rocks, the earth, etc. Of celestial bodies, only stars turn up very frequently, especially the morning star.

Information is too meager to permit tribal characterization from this point of view; yet a few facts of historical interest stand out. The marked paucity of interpretations among the northwestern tribes goes hand in hand with other resemblances, *e.g.*, in their parfleche decoration, so that they constitute a subarea. The Crow, however, show some kinship with the Dakota and the Arapaho. Like the former, though on a lesser scale, they had what looks like a technical nomenclature for design elements. On the other hand, the occasional identification of the cross with a star and the regular association of a lozenge with the navel point toward the Arapaho.

It remains to speak of the use of color. A white background is frequent in the beadwork of all tribes, being used almost exclusively by the Arapaho, while the Cheyenne showed an additional preference for yellow, the Shoshone for a light grayish blue. The Blackfoot were far less given to white than other tribes, employing rather light red, yellow, and blue backgrounds. As previously stated, the Omaha assert that blue was unknown to them in pre-Caucasian times. The same belief held among Crow informants.

Colors often had symbolic meanings, in art as well as in warfare (page 116) and in religion. With the Dakota, red suggested the sunset or thunder; yellow, the dawn, clouds, or earth; blue, the sky, clouds, night, or day; black, the night; green, the summer. Black betokened victory for the Crow, Arapaho, and probably other tribes. The Arapaho employed red to signify blood, man, paint, earth, sunset, or rocks; yellow, for sunlight or the earth; green, for vegetation; blue, for the sky, haze, smoke, far-away mountains, rocks, and night. White formed the normal background, but occasionally denoted snow, sand, earth, or water. The Crow used red paint to represent longevity and the ownership of property; it figured prominently in the Tobacco organization. White clay stood for ablutions intended to induce a vision and a knowledge of the future.

Music

Compared with African Negroes, the American Indians had only a few types of musical instruments, and those of the Plains are no exception.

Probably universal in the area was the flageolet (often referred to as a flute) used mainly by a lover when courting his sweetheart. By a code previously agreed upon, a young Assiniboin from a distance of a hundred yards could convey messages to his girl while she was inside her tipi without her family's catching on. He was able to express such ideas as, "I am here waiting for you," "I am watched," "Remain," "I'll come again," "Meet me tomorrow." An old Dakota specimen was 25 inches long and ⅝ inch in diameter. It consisted of a straight stick carved at one end into a crane's head with open beak; it has been described by Frances Densmore in Bulletin 61 of the Bureau of American Ethnology as "an open pipe with the usual whistle or flageolet mouthpiece." The Hidatsa speak of a "singing whistle," a flageolet of box elder wood with the pith removed; it had seven holes. Several forms of whistle made of the wing bones of birds or of wood were noted by Maximilian as distinctive of the several Mandan military societies.

Rattles were made of gourds mounted on a handle and enclosing pebbles or of rawhide shaped in the form of a pear, globe, or open ring (Fig. 42). The rawhide was stretched over a frame of woodwork while wet and dried, pebbles being inserted at holes in the top or handle. Rattles were shaken by doctors when treating their patients and also served as emblems of organizations or of officials in them. Often they were decorated with feathers. The "deer-hoof" or dewclaw rattle consisted of a stick to which deer or antelope hoofs were attached; among the Hidatsa it was one of the badges of Dog society membership (Plate 17).

What may be called a rasp was distributed over

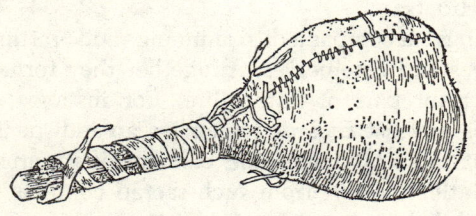

Fig. 42. A Blackfoot skin rattle (about 9 inches long); the handle is wood covered with leather and bound with thongs.

a large portion of the area and beyond. The Assiniboin type consisted of a 3-foot piece of wood that had notches cut along its edge. "The performer drew a stick backward and forward, along the notches, keeping time" (Henry). The instrument was the emblem of a Hidatsa organization (Fig. 43), being "played" at its dances, where the "female" stick was smoked with incense and propped up on two forked sticks; it represented a horned snake. The rasp was regarded as "male." The Ute employed the simple rasp to make music for their Bear dance, and the Paviotso used it for charming antelope.

Two main kinds of drums appear. The type more closely approaching ours was hollowed out from a section of a tree, with strips of hide serving as heads. A Wind River Shoshone sample, with decorated drumheads, is shown in Figure 43; the willow drumstick had its end wrapped with buckskin. This type could be suspended from forked sticks. Unequivocally aboriginal is the tambourine-like "hand drum" with a single skin head, the other side having a grip of cordage. This form figured in many situations, such as the military clubs, the Crow Tobacco organization, the Goose Women society of the Hidatsa.

Songs accompanied drumming and rattling at dances and ceremonies. Altogether they formed an important part of native life. For instance, some tribes at least regarded them as an indispensable, if not the most important, element of supernatural revelations. Apart from such sacred contexts, there were lullabies, secular songs distinctive of organizations, snatches composed in derision of a rival club or a personal enemy or a joking relative (page 127).

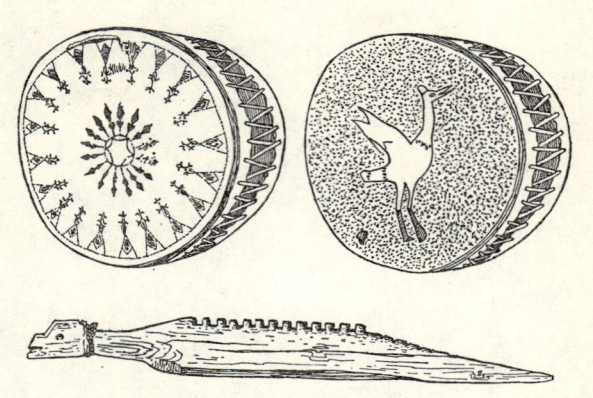

Fig. 43. Above, a Shoshone double-headed drum (about 22 inches in diameter and 14 inches deep). The bird representation appears on the reverse side of the drum. Below, a wooden rasp (a little over 4 feet long and 5 inches wide), the musical instrument of the Notched Stick Society, Hidatsa.

Investigations of this vocal music have been pursued for many years by Frances Densmore, but the highly technical results do not lend themselves to a brief popular summary. It seems noteworthy, however, that she finds the Dakota, Mandan, Hidatsa as presenting more similarities among themselves and with the Ojibwa than with the Ute.

6 SUPERNATURALISM

Beliefs

THE SUPERNATURAL

Magic, the use of supernatural techniques for gaining one's ends, is often contrasted with "religion," the appeal to supernatural beings. In the practice and theory of primitive peoples it is hardly possible to maintain a rigid distinction between the two concepts: for example, a magical cure may be taught by a benevolent spirit, and a magical rite may be held quite as holy by the performers as a ceremony dedicated to the worship of a god. Accordingly, it is useful to have a single term for the whole system of beliefs and practices involving power beyond that of mortal beings, and this combination of beliefs and actions may be called "supernaturalism."

Of course, the native cannot conceive of nature as the modern scientist does, and accordingly he cannot oppose to such a concept another that transcends what are called natural laws. But he can and does react vehemently to perceptions that are wholly out of the normal range of his experience. American Indians have a variety of words to describe what strikes them as mysterious, weird, or miraculous, thrilling or awe-inspiring. The Crow word is *maxpé*, corresponding to Hidatsa *xupá*, Dakota *wakan*, Algonkian *manitō*.

To the abstract notion so designated, a particular experience is or is not assimilated. The word and its derivatives may be applied to persons or things and may even be used as adjectives or adverbs. The Dakota said of a child who speaks surprisingly well for his age, *ie wakandagi*. A Crow who magically lured deer into a corral was described as a *maxpé* man; in the myths the same epithet is applied to heroes and witches; and a word from the same root, *xapāria,* designated tangible objects viewed with special veneration, such as feathers seen in a vision. It is quite possible for an Indian to assume different attitudes at different times toward the same object that is called "wonderful" by any of the preceding terms. Sometimes an inanimate object, because of its oddity, was treated as a "supernatural" person. A Crow who found a peculiarly shaped rock (Plate 29) suggestive of an animal would treasure it, grease it, wrap it up with beads and other offerings, and believe it capable of reproduction. Periodically the owner would pray to the rock to grant him long life and wealth.

The first thing that strikes an observer of most primitive peoples is the way in which supernaturalism pervades every sphere of social life. In the communal antelope hunt a Comanche magician tried to block the escape of the game by crossing certain sticks decorated with antelope hoofs. When the herd had been surrounded, he could supposedly kill a particular antelope by simply pointing one of his hoofs at it. Other tribes employed corresponding devices to lure and destroy buffalo. In a time of scarcity, the Mandan believed, the dance of the White Buffalo Cow women enticed the herds near the village. Elsewhere a hoop game was played in order to call buffalo. Much of the magic rested on the principle that mimicry of a desired event could produce it. Such "imitative magic" may appear unobtrusively in many different ways as part of a complex ceremonial. At one stage of the Tobacco Dance the Crow Indians raised their drumsticks aloft to symbolize and to promote the growth of the plant; and the semisedentary tribes of the area, skillful farmers as they were, did not rely solely on their knowledge of farming, but also on the efficacy of their agricultural rites.

As supernaturalism intruded into economic life, so it also asserted itself in warfare. A Crow brave did not venture on a raid without the prompting of a supernatural protector in a dream or vision. A Dakota shield was supposed to owe its efficacy more to the vision that had suggested the design on its cover than to the toughness of the hide. In a ceremony for bringing about the death of a tribal enemy, the Crow would blacken ceremonial articles since it was their custom to put black paint on one's face in token of a killing. Sometimes a warrior attempted to divine whether the party on which he was setting out would meet with success: if in peering into a mixture of badger and buffalo blood he fancied seeing an enemy's scalp, he felt encouraged to proceed; if he saw himself scalped, he abandoned the project.

The Arapaho even derived innovations in decorative design from inspiration by spirits. A generalizing Plains Indian is reputed to have said that while White men had new ideas, the Indians had dreams or visions; and one Blackfoot conceived the invention of the phonograph not as the achievement of a creative genius, but as the gift of a spirit that had revealed to the "inventor" just how the apparatus was to be constructed.

In short, for the Plains Indian supernaturalism was not the equivalent of churchgoing of a Sunday, but something that profoundly affected his daily life and offered an explanation of extraordinary occurrences.

VISIONS

Most North American Indians attached great importance to visions, and in the Plains these took precedence in the religious life. However, the spirits did not always appear to their prospective protégé, but might merely become audible to him, issuing instructions and promising definite benefits. In Siberia and parts of western North America supernatural visitants were not sought; in fact, often the spirit compelled a native to accept his guardianship much against the future protégé's wishes. In contrast, Woodland and Plains Indians deliberately went out to a lonely spot in order to obtain a revelation. Some Crow individuals received favors unsought when in a predicament. Occasionally it even happened that a spirit came under ordinary circumstances from a pure desire to befriend the mortal. However, the normal procedure was to go into solitude, fast and thirst for four days, and supplicate the spirits to take pity on the sufferer. A Crow usually cut off a finger joint of his left hand or in some other way mortified his flesh by way of arousing supernatural pity.

Certain tribal differences are noteworthy with respect to the vision quest. In the Woodlands, Ojibwa and Winnebago parents regularly instructed boys, possibly not over seven years of age, to fast in order to obtain the blessing of a spirit, and on the Plains the Hidatsa elders likewise prompted their children to seek a revelation at an early age. But no such admonition was customary among the Crow. There a lad grew up, constantly hearing that all success in life was derived from visions; hence, being eager for horses and for social recognition, an adolescent would go out to fast, praying for rich booty, for a chance to strike a coup, or for some other benefit. A mature man or woman would seek a vision whenever a special cause arose—if his children were sick, if he had lost his property, if he longed to revenge the killing of a close relative, and so on. Again, the Arapaho seem to have sought a vision only as adults.

We naturally wonder what really happened on such quests. There is no doubt that the vast majority of informants firmly believed in the reality of the experiences they described. In order to explain this phenomenon psychologically, several factors have to be considered. First of all, the god seeker was usually under a strong emotional impulse—either yearning to shine before his fellows or desiring relief from want or disease or the grief over an unavenged kinsman. By seclusion in a lonely spot, by his fast, by self-mutilation, he naturally intensified his emotional state. What is more, the myths told by his people and the accounts of the supernatural experiences of contemporary tribesmen had left an imprint on his mind and helped to shape the sense impressions that came to him. His longings at the time blended with the visionary pattern of his tribe and with the sounds or sights actually experienced under highly abnormal conditions so as to inspire an interpretation of things seen and heard. Individual peculiarities likewise entered: an Indian of a predominantly auditory type might imagine a whole series of distinguishable sounds—the call of a bird, the rustling of leaves, the neighing of a horse, the speech of an alien tribe, and what not. If his was a decidedly visual type, he would see specific details, as when a would-be raider caught sight of a mount he was to steal—say, a bay horse with docked tail, heavy mane, and a zigzag line painted down its legs. A man who subsequently arranged his sensations for his own enlightenment or to give a clear statement to an audience was in the position of ourselves when trying to give a coherent account of a dream. Without trying to deceive or to invent, he would unconsciously bridge over obscure points, filling in the gaps, adapting his memories of the experience to one of the tribal vision patterns familiar to him from listening to earlier accounts.

A good example of such a pattern is the following. Several Crow informants independently tell how on their lonely vigil they saw a spirit or several spirits riding along, how the rocks and trees in the neighborhood turned into enemies who attacked the horsemen, but were unable to inflict any harm. The symbolical meaning of these apparitions is that the spirits are making the visionary invulnerable. This is, of course, a generally prized blessing, but several persons could not independently conceive the identical image of spiritual riders shot at by transformed bits of the landscape, especially when the very same motif appears also in traditional stories apart from the narration of the teller's personal experiences. Evidently the image, however it may have originated, became part of tribal folklore and was readily worked into the report of their revelations by persons who particularly craved invulnerability.

Again, it was certainly a part of the tribal pattern that most Crow Indians obtained their spiritual blessing on the fourth night of their seclusion, four being the mystic number within the area.

The supernatural beings who befriend man vary enormously in character. Animals were very frequent visitants of Plains Indians. Buffalo, elk, bears, eagles (sometimes conceived as birds producing thunder by flapping their wings), and sparrow hawks constantly figure in the narratives, but so also do quite lowly beasts such as dogs or rabbits. A Pawnee legend even describes the invocation of mosquitoes, and according to Cree tradition a mosquito gave one tribesman the gift of chieftaincy. Curious contradictions do not seem to have been recognized as such by the Indians. In a Crow story a rabbit pursued by a hawk promises to give supernatural power to an Indian if he will shield him from the bird of prey. Correspondingly, a Pawnee boy gets supernatural aid from mice who are unable to extricate themselves from a relatively simple difficulty. That is, though animals are possessed of supernatural powers, they may be dependent on mortals for specific services, for which they reward them. Celestial patrons are also frequent, stars figuring prominently among the Pawnee. Fanciful creatures of more or less human shape likewise appear in visions, *e.g.*, a dwarf with a very powerful musculature. Sometimes the patron comes in human guise but in disappearing assumes his true shape or otherwise gives a clue to his identity.

The Crow interpreted the relationship between patron and protégé as that of a father and his child, and accounts of visions often explicitly quote the spirit as pronouncing the formula of adoption: "I will have you for my child." In any case the spirit normally taught the Crow a sacred song, instructed him just how he must dress in battle or if a man was to become a doctor what medicines or curing devices he must use, and frequently imposed certain taboos as to diet or behavior. Any infraction of the rules was liable to precipitate a loss of the guardian's protection or even a dire calamity. Often the visionary not only wore some token of his vision or painted it on, say, his shield cover, but also on the strength of successive visions assembled the ingredients to build up a "medicine bundle," a wrapper containing a set of sacred objects indicated by the spirit. A Pawnee bundle contained as a minimum one pipe, tobacco, paints, certain birds, and corn—all assembled in a container of buffalo hide that was hung from the wall of the lodge. The opening of a bundle and the treatment of its contents were accompanied by definite rites. As already stated, it is often difficult to tell whether the native consistently considered such objects sacred in their own right, in other words, made them fetishes wholly independent of any personal spirit, or whether they become sacred only as gifts of the spirit; very likely the attitude of a person varied at different times.

If because of visions, one individual worshiped above all a supernatural buffalo, another an eagle, and a third the morning star, the question arises how these several beings ranked in relation to one another. With the Comanche and the Crow this problem arose only when there was a clash of interests between tribesmen, each man falling back on the protection of his own guardian and the issue showing whose patron was the stronger. In the absence of a coherent system of the universe, the religious consciousness assigned priority to individual visitants. Thus, an Indian once told the author that a feather he cherished as a memento of his vision of a bird was the greatest thing in the world. At the opposite extreme stood the Pawnee (see page 182), who had brought their beliefs into a logical system, venerating a Supreme Being named Tirawa, a sky-dwelling creator who rules the universe, his commands being executed by lesser deities. Utterances by Dakota medicinemen suggest a similar fondness for metaphysical speculation and integration. A question that remains unanswered is whether the average Pawnee or Dakota individual in his daily life was actually guided by priestly generalizations or whether in practice, without overtly rejecting them, he followed the Crow pattern.

Though all persons coveted a revelation, not all were able to obtain one. Those who did not succeed naturally did not wish to be thereby doomed to failure throughout life. The Crow and some other tribes resolved the dilemma by permitting a successful visionary to sell part of his power to less fortunate tribesmen, adopting them as his supernatural patron had adopted *him*, making for each of his disciples a replica of his sacred paraphernalia, teaching him the sacred songs, and warning against breach of any taboo associated with his medicine.

SHAMANS

At the opposite pole from those unable to gain a personal vision were the Indians who, as demonstrated by their conspicuous success, had obtained exceptional power from the spirits. Such persons were said to be *maxpé* or *wakan* and in English may be called "medicinemen" or, to borrow a convenient Siberian term, "shamans."

According to the Wahpeton Dakota, their medicinemen lived a prenatal existence among the Thunders and enjoyed a knowledge, prior to birth, of all that would happen to them as mortals. Their social role began with maturity, when they received a sign from the Thunders to start performing shamanistic duties; any shaman disobeying the divine orders would suffer punishment or even be killed by the Thunders. The services rendered to tribesmen included curing the sick, discovering the whereabouts of the enemy, and helping to recover lost or stolen property. By way of proving his powers a shaman summoned people to large meetings, at which he performed tricks in order to establish himself as a wonder-worker.

The most elaborate organization for such miraculous performances appeared among the Pawnee. Their medicinemen in some measure partook of the nature of priests since they were trained, a great master of legerdemain being surrounded by a number of disciples. However, all medicinemen were supposed to obtain their powers from living creatures so that the subjective experience of the vision remained a vital element. In the late summer or early fall all the accepted masters at sleight-of-hand gathered in one of two earthlodges reserved in the village for that purpose and with the aid of pupils erected their several booths. A turtle effigy was modeled at the cleared fireplace, a new fireplace put on its back, and a ceremonially felled tree was planted by the Skidi Pawnee in the forked tail of an image representing a mythical water monster encircling the fireplace. The clay statue of a woman, life size, was set up on the south side, a large male figure of rawhide was placed upon a pole above the lodge, and many small human figures, also of rawhide, were attached about the assembly place. The fire symbolized the sun; the clay female, the moon; the large male effigy, the morning star; and the many little images, the stars.

After a dedication ceremony there was an impressive procession through the village, each shaman wearing a costume in mimicry of his animal protector. Then the participants reentered the lodge for a secret ritual, after which the door was opened for the spectacular show. Among other tricks there was the magical maturing of cornstalks before the onlookers' gaze; and the Bear shamans pretended to tear out a man's liver, to eat it, and then to make him rise unharmed.

Sleight-of-hand was a common technique for impressing the laity. The Iruska shamans of the Pawnee handled burning corn husks with their bare hands, took meat out of a kettle of boiling soup, and stood on red-hot rocks. These tricks were closely paralleled by the Dakota, who among other things shared a fire-walking feat with Arapaho, Gros Ventre, and Cheyenne performers. Another marvelous stunt, noted by Maximilian among the Mandan and Hidatsa, was to harbor some animal or plant inside one's body and have it emerge to the amazement of the spectators. The Prince actually saw a Hidatsa woman "dance a corncob out of herself," and another Indian professed to feel a buffalo calf kicking around inside his body. A Crow informant declared that when a certain song was sung a horse inside her would try to come out, protruding his tail from her mouth.

Sometimes Crow shamans offered a public competitive exhibition of their powers, one man or a group trying to overcome those pitted against them.

More important from the laity's point of view was the shaman's doctoring. The treatment of illness did not necessarily require supernatural power, for there were liniments, herbs, therapeutic potions, and other home remedies. However, in serious cases recourse was generally had to a practitioner who derived his techniques, even when rational, from a visionary experience. Because of the usually specific nature of the instruction given by the spirit, a doctor was likely to cure only particular ailments. Thus, he might treat only women in childbirth or men bitten by a snake.

Perhaps the commonest primitive theory of disease ascribes the cause to a foreign object in the patient's body; hence the physician tries to extract it, usually by suction, exhibiting to the patient and his kin the splinter, thorn, or what not that supposedly caused the disturbance. These notions occur also in the Plains. For example, in recent times a Crow named Bull-all-the-time cured several patients by sucking at the afflicted parts with a pipestem and pulling out, respectively, a bone, a black beetle, a morsel of meat, but he deprecated any competence in dealing with wounds or snake bites. The treatment by suction obviously implies sleight-of-hand.

Sickness would smite a shaman or his patient if rules laid down by his spiritual patron were disobeyed, whether willingly or not. Thus, it might be fatal for a sick man if a dog crossed his doctor's path. Anyone who ate food forbidden to him in a dream or vision was bound to suffer.

Though witchcraft was less pronounced than among the Pueblos, the Plains Indians did sometimes resort to effigy magic. In the 1890s, some Comanche suspected an interpreter of treason, made an image of him, and pelted it with mud; in consequence, they assert, he had a hemorrhage and died. The same people used to kill a sorcerer after he had repeatedly worked harm against his fellows. This act was in line with Basin custom, but at least the central Plains tribes probably did not proceed in this way, rather counteracting the malevolent shaman's magic by the aid of another shaman.

Other medical techniques included massage, smoking, bleeding, cupping, and applying burning sage. Arapaho doctors fumigated a sick infant with the smoke from heated roots or cedar twigs or made it inhale the fumes from herbs laid on hot coals. Though the sweatlodge (page 186) was prominent in ceremonialism, it was also used for medicinal purposes, at least by a number of tribes, such as the Arapaho and the Comanche.

PRIESTS

Whereas a shaman by definition acquires his status through a personal communication by supernatural beings, the priest need not have this face-to-face relationship with the spirit world but must have competence in conducting ritual. In other words, he has been trained for his activities. As stated, the medicinemen of the Pawnee were shamans by virtue of their animal mentors, but they were likewise priests in so far as they had to undergo special instruction. One might even speak of their ordination, for before being allowed to take a permanent place in the lodge each had to demonstrate his skill to the leaders, being ejected if he failed. However, the Pawnee had a number of other men who combined official standing with a knowledge of sacred songs in their sequence and of the meaning of ritual procedures. Accordingly, the tribe can properly be said to have had a priesthood. More particularly, the priests were associated with the sacred-bundle scheme that underlay Pawnee political organization. Each of the thirteen Skidi villages owned a bundle, which had to be opened at the first thunder in the spring, when the keeper made offerings and went through the traditional rites. Four of the bundles were preeminent, and a fifth, associated with the evening star, took absolute precedence; the priests of these bundles rather than the titular chiefs held supreme authority. Normally, the four priests in turn assumed responsibility for the welfare of the people for the period of a year and specifically for the success of the buffalo hunt. If this miscarried, the Evening Star priest was asked to supersede his officiating colleague. The priesthood was strictly hereditary, passing from its holder to the next of kin in the maternal line.

HEREAFTER

Some American aborigines, such as the Winnebago, were greatly concerned over the hereafter and the ability to travel thither in safety. This interest and anxiety seem to have been foreign to most Plains Indians. While sharing the universal aboriginal belief in a survival of the soul, the future was not a matter of great concern, there was no notion of rewards and punishments after death, no ancestor worship, no elaborate picture of posthumous exist-

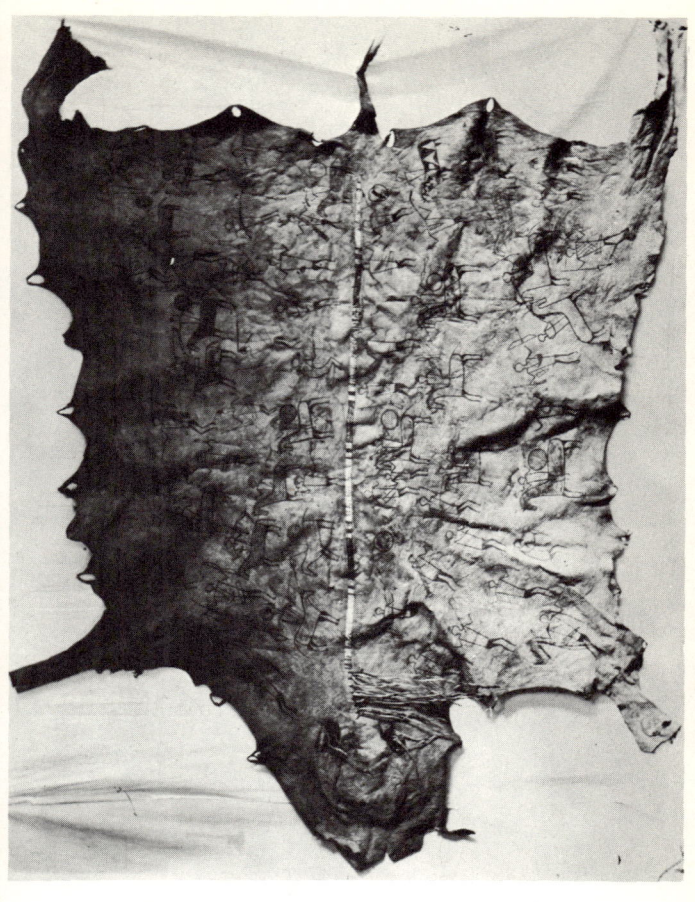

24. A painted buffalo-skin robe collected by Lewis and Clark from the Mandan in 1805. The scene is supposed to represent a battle that took place in 1797. Courtesy Peabody Museum, Harvard University.

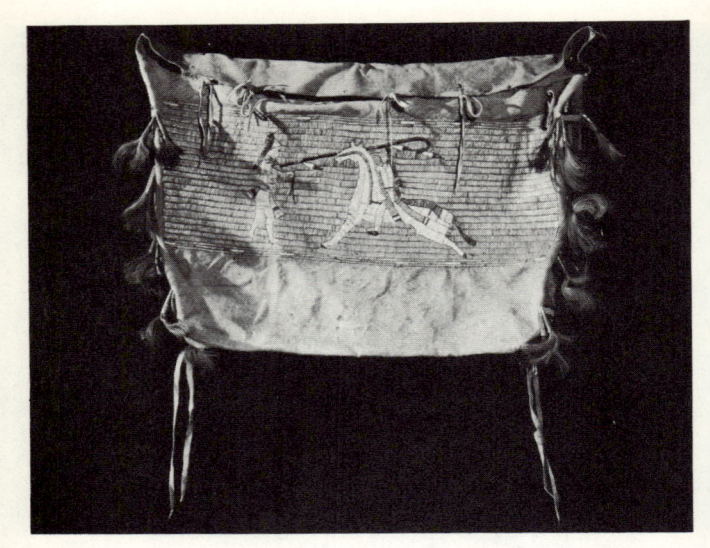

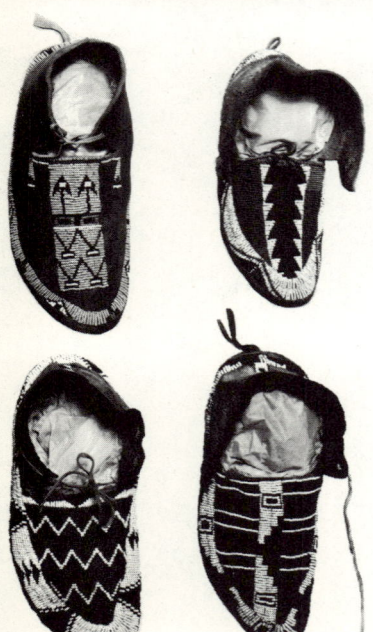

25. A quill-decorated saddlebag from the Dakota.

26. Dakota moccasins, illustrating the variety of design elements.

27. Beaded and quilled pipe and tobacco bag from the Dakota.

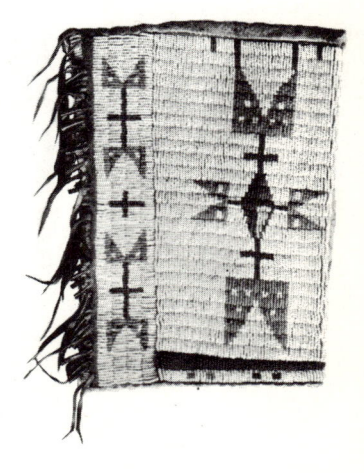

28. A Dakota woman's bead-ornamented legging.

29. Crow sacred rock and offerings.

30. Face paint, headdress, and necklace of a Blackfoot medicine man.

31. *Altar in the Adoption Lodge, Crow Tobacco Ceremony.*

32. *Entrance into the Adoption Lodge, Crow Tobacco Ceremony.*

33. The leader of the procession in the Crow Tobacco Ceremony leaving the Preparatory Lodge with her pipe.

34. The leader (center, with pipe) heading the procession to the Adoption Lodge, one of the stops on the way to the garden for planting, Crow Tobacco Ceremony.

35. A model, showing one phase of the Arapaho Sun Dance

36. The sacred doll of the Crow Sun Dance

ence. The usual conception was that the dead lived very much as they had while alive, hunting buffalo, playing games, and inhabiting the same sort of tipis as during their previous existence. Such beliefs as these rested largely on the reports of persons who had visited the spirit land, but returned to their fellows, *i.e.*, of people who were believed to have died but who recovered from their state of unconsciousness and sooner or later divulged their adventures while supposedly dead.

As might be expected, the Pawnee elaborated ideas on the subject, incorporating them into their general world view. Some souls traveled to the sky to turn into stars; cowards and men who died from disease joined the spirits in the south after traversing the Milky Way; chiefs and priests journeyed on a special road to a distinct destination; and shamans also had a spirit village of their own. According to one Pawnee view, the souls of people who died of illness, because seen by the Star of Disease, are taken to the South Star's home, whereas the Morning Star disposes of the fate of all others.

Concerning the soul concept itself, the Crow distinguished the ghost that haunts the grave and the soul that travels to the hereafter. They attributed souls to animals. According to the Mandan, a person had four souls, two of which, respectively, symbolized by white sage and the meadowlark, merged to form the spirit of the hereafter. The third was connected with its owner's lodge and loitered about it so long as traces of it remained, while the fourth sometimes left the village but periodically returned to frighten people.

WORLD VIEW

Whether the Plains Indians as a whole recognized a supreme deity is a knotty problem. A positive answer seems established for the Pawnee. Their Tirawa existed in the beginning, wedded to Atira (Born from Corn or Vault of the Sky). He ordered the other gods where to stand and issued further commands to them through the Evening Star, the Mother of all Things. In accordance with his will the Morning Star mated with the Evening Star and the Sun with the Moon; the girl issuing from the former union as well as the boy begotten by the Sun were put on the earth, and the two married. Other deities also created human beings. The earth-dwellers acquired the rudiments of Indian culture and received from the gods the gift of ceremonial bundles, the associated rituals being revealed by the Evening Star. The Pawnee thus developed a rather complex mythology, strongly emphasizing the importance of celestial characters, all of them subordinate to Tirawa.

Certainly most of the other tribes had nothing like so coherent a scheme. The Crow, for example, by and large regarded the Sun as the outstanding supernatural being—he was invoked in prayer and on the vision quest, though he very rarely appeared to a would-be visionary; the sweatlodge was preeminently in his honor, and albino buffaloes were invariably offered to him. However, these Indians were not wholly consistent in regarding him as most powerful. In a crisis they relied primarily on their individual patrons, and they sometimes failed to distinguish him from the mythological figure called Old Man Coyote (page 139) whom they generally associated with the creation of the world, of man, and of human culture, but who is also in many episodes of his cycle an utterly unscrupulous rascal.

Ceremonialism

It is difficult to separate faith and observance, for the native who believes in supernatural beings will try to placate them by some act; and if he thinks that a certain procedure would bring rain or any other desired end, he will apply it. Accordingly, the foregoing account of *beliefs* could not be divorced from some statements about associated *practices*. In the following pages, however, attention is focused on relevant activities, the sum total of which is called "ceremonialism" or "ritualism," while its elements are conveniently labeled "rites."

Except for the western marginal peoples, such as the Comanche, who herein reveal their ultimate affinity with the Basin and Plateau Areas, the Plains Indians were markedly given to ritualism. Indeed, in this respect the Pawnee approach the Pueblos, who attained the highest development on the continent. The observances may be simple and brief, as when an Iowa, before smoking formally, offered tobacco to the sky spirit, puffing a mouthful of smoke toward him. At the other end of the scale were such four-day festivals as the Sun Dance and the Okipa of the Mandan, both of which required weeks of preparation. Such major ceremonies involved the entire tribe, at least as spectators and also in considerable measure as minor performers, even when portions of the ritual were enacted in secret. Other rituals, such as certain bundle ceremonies, were the private business of a limited group or even of a single individual; the performances might be of the utmost importance to those concerned, but obviously could not fulfill the requirements of a theatrical spectacle.

Rich as the Plains were in ceremonials, certain types prominent among other primitive tribes were absent or restricted. Thus, elaborate puberty rituals for girls, of outstanding importance in California, were either lacking (Crow, Arapaho, Blackfoot) or held only for a favored daughter (Dakota). Locally, observances at a girl's coming of age led to a four days' seclusion (Cree, Assiniboin), during which she was forbidden to scratch her head, except with a special stick, ate very sparingly, and practiced feminine activities, but such customs were dwarfed by coexisting rituals of a different order. In contrast to the Australians and the Tierra del Fuegians, there was no obligatory initiation of boys into a men's society that terrorized women. As a matter of fact, though menstrual taboos imposed some restrictions on the female sex, wives often aided their husbands in sacred rites, and in specific instances the highest ceremonial offices were open to women. Positively, ceremonialism was strongly affected by the central position of visions, which led to infinite diversification in details since individuals could add to or modify a traditional procedure on the basis of personal revelations, could found new subdivisions or offshoots of a religious fraternity, adopt novices, and so forth. A common supernatural patron might lead to a special organization (Dakota, Omaha): Omaha Indians blessed by supernatural grizzlies or buffalo, respectively, formed societies and danced in imitation of the animals. This fact, incidentally, shows that there was *some* impersonation in Plains ritualism, though considerably less than among many other Indians.

ELEMENTS OF CEREMONIALISM

Many rites were performed either separately or as parts of a larger whole. They include offerings and prayers, the solemn unfolding of the packs containing sacred objects, painting of the celebrant's face or body (Plate 30), sweating, the singing of sacred songs. A few of these merit some further account.

Prayers and offerings were commonly made and frequently the suppliant vowed that he would render gifts provided his wishes were fulfilled. Indeed, the Arapaho evolved a votive pattern for all major ceremonies, even those of military societies, a man pledging a performance if he escaped sickness or danger. The contractual relation assumed between the spirit and the worshiper is illustrated in the invocation of the Sun by a Kansa war captain:

"I wish to kill a Pawnee! I desire to bring horses when I return. I long to pull down an enemy! I promise you a calico shirt and a robe. I will give you a blanket also, O Wakanda, if you allow me to return in safety after killing a Pawnee!"

Shields, being sacred, were normally kept covered. Before exhibiting his own, a Crow chief would take some live coals, burn wild carrot root for incense, hold his shield above the fire, raise it a little, lower it, raise it a little higher, continuing in this way until the fourth time, when he lifted it aloft and began removing the two buckskin covers. This instance illustrates the effect of a sacred number on ritual procedure, significant acts being repeated accordingly. Often there were three feints; when walking out of a tipi toward the ceremonial lodge, the leader of the procession simulated an exit three times, each time withdrawing the foot put forward, and finally at the fourth time made the real start.

Tremendous importance was attached to songs taught in a vision; a Blackfoot doctor's power was supposed to lie primarily in his chants, which he was not allowed to sell as he might other sacred property. Plains Indians repeated songs in accordance with their mystic number. The most prominent number was doubtless four, but seven might coexist in the same tribe; the Blackfoot sang ritualistic songs by sevens, though four figured when they picked up ceremonial objects after three feints.

In part of the area the vapor bath was prized for its therapeutic value, and in recent times Crow and Blackfoot Indians have indulged in it as a sport. Yet its outstanding importance was ceremonial; some tribes considered sweating a necessary purification before taking part in any major ceremony. For sweating, the Indians erected a low dome-shaped structure of willow saplings, dug a fireplace in the center, put into it rocks that had been heated red-hot, and covered the little lodge with skins, making it quite dark inside. Water was poured on the rocks, making the participants sweat profusely. In order to permit them to cool off, an outsider removed the covering for a short time, then the operation was repeated. After the final (probably fourth) sweating, the bathers, dripping with perspiration, dashed into the nearest creek or in the wintertime wallowed in the snow. The sweatlodge of the Crow was as a rule conceived as an offering to the Sun, but religious associations varied tribally, as did the details connected with the institution. The Blackfoot excluded women, whereas the Crow admitted them, though mostly as initiates into the Tobacco order. The number of willows for the frame varied according to the occasion: fourteen was usual among Crow and Blackfoot, but the Crow might use as many as a hundred, which number Blackfoot regarded as essential in the Sun Dance. As a rule, four persons joined in sweating themselves.

The sweatlodge is widely distributed in North America, being found from the Atlantic to the Pacific, though in California without vapor. The modern Finnish *sauna* and its Scandinavian equivalent in the sixteenth century involved procedures strikingly similar to the North American ones, thus raising the question whether the phenomenon could have been diffused from a single center.

A special space set aside in a ceremonial structure for arranging sacred objects or smoking them with incense is conveniently called an altar. The Blackfoot smudged their bundles in a plot behind the fire where the grass and surface soil had been removed. Their favorite incense was that from sweetgrass, but the plant varied with the bundle, as did the size and shape of the altar. The sacred plot was shaped into crescentic and other figures by means of colored earth. For one type of bundle it was proper to clear a 2-foot square of grass and cover it with white earth, then the crescent moon was worked out in black, bordered by yellow; two circles of the same colors symbolized the sun and the morning star, and two narrow oblongs in red represented sun dogs.

Altars of a different type were set up in the Sun Dance lodges of several Plains tribes, buffalo skulls being formally arranged in an excavated or cleared area. Near the center of the adoption lodge of the Tobacco order the Crow similarly cleared an oblong space at whose head the members afterward put down their medicine bags. Each of the longer sides was bounded by a row of willow arches resembling croquet wickets, and outside each row there was a parallel log of equal length. Within the altar were laid four rows of juniper sprigs (Plate 31). The altar represented the tobacco garden— the juniper, the tobacco itself in its green state— the logs were reckoned sacred, hence must not be burnt for firewood, but animal droppings placed on the altar might serve to light a pipe and to burn incense.

Compared with other primitive groups, the Plains Indians present some striking negative features in their ceremonial details. Masks were not wholly absent, for the Bull Dancers of the Mandan (Plate 19) wore buffalo heads and the Fool society of the Assiniboin, who acted like clowns in obedience to a spirit's revelation, wore grotesque masks. It remains true, however, that such disguise was markedly rare, in contrast to the Northwest Coast, Pueblo, and Iroquois Indians who had a profusion of masks. To some extent the absence of masks is explained by the slight development of carving in our area. In correlation with this deficiency, attempts at impersonation of deities were also rare, though by no means entirely absent. A conspicuous exception, besides that mentioned previously, occurred in the Okipa, where actors did assume the role of outstanding mythological characters.

MAJOR CEREMONIALS

Ceremonials of outstanding importance were not always the most spectacular. This applies to most of the rituals connected with bundles. The Arapaho recognized a "flat" pipe as the great tribal fetish. It was kept in a painted tipi (Plate 9), wrapped in a large pack of many pieces of cloth, and suspended so as never to touch the ground. An Arapaho might invoke the pipe to grant him long life and happiness, and he might present it with offerings. The keeper was the only one familiar with the orthodox version of the tribal myth and took four consecutive nights to tell the story. He directed the Sun Dance as well as other great ceremonies and was regarded with the utmost awe. But the observances connected with the holy of holies itself were unimpressive: the pipe had to be held and handled in the traditional way. Any dramatic features were coincidental, inasmuch as the pipe figured in the Sun Dance, and they were shared by tribes without this particular fetish.

Similar considerations apply to many forms of sacred pipe bundles in the area, some seventeen varieties of one type being found among the Blackfoot alone. The owners all enjoyed great esteem, but did not form an organization. The original pipe was revealed by the Thunder, a supplementary variety stemming from a bear who had thereby repaid a Blackfoot for the favors his daughter had granted the animal. The numerous appurtenances enclosed in the bundle include the fetus of a deer; squirrel, muskrat, mink, and bird skins; necklaces; and many other objects. It was obligatory for the owner to open the bundle at the first thunder in the spring, also when someone in distress had vowed to the Sun to dance with the pipestem or when the bundle was transferred to a purchaser. Outsiders were supposed to derive benefits from a bundle, but above all they redounded to the glory of the owner and afforded him protection. He was, however, obliged to submit to many fanciful and in part burdensome rules: he was not allowed to point with any digit but his thumb nor to pick up any object he found; he had to hold his pipe in a particular way; he must never sit on his bedding; and so forth. His wife had to make smudge every morning and shift the position of the bundle in fixed sunwise sequence; and under no condition was it to touch the ground. The importance of these sacred pipes in Blackfoot society is manifest. Yet again the correlated ritual is devoid of the spectacular element. When about to open his pack, the owner invited an experienced ritualist as aide and a few others to help with the singing. The ceremony itself consisted merely in opening the pack, in singing songs by sets of seven, and in simple dancing—all this before a restricted audience.

Intermediate in dramatic elaboration between such performances and the Sun Dance are the mystic rites that correspond to the Grand Medicine Dance of the western Woodland tribes. Typical of the Woodlands is supposed to be the Midewiwin, the secret Medicine society of the Ojibwa, where the candidate for admission was magically shot with a shell, fell forward apparently lifeless, and was restored by the older members. Actually this feature is equally characteristic of Southern Siouans, such as the Iowa and Oto; indeed, the Omaha had two organizations, the Shell and the Pebble society, of which the supposed shooting and resuscitation was a cardinal characteristic. Apart from "killing" the novice, the members shot at one another to demonstrate their magical power. In short, this aspect of these societies was simply a startling shamanistic exhibition of power.

CROW TOBACCO SOCIETY

The Tobacco order of the Crow—which, as a result of new visions, split up into a number of chapters—planted a sacred tobacco, *Nicotiana multivalvis,* that was different from the species they smoked, *N. quadrivalvis* (page 28). Benefits accrued from the planting both to the members and to the tribe at large, and the prestige connected with affiliation induced people to pay heavy initiation fees to the sponsor who gave him the seeds and instructed him as well as usually also the tyro's wife, assuming a parental relationship toward them. During the winter the novice was usually taught four Tobacco songs and attended dances by his "father's" chapter. In the beginning of spring the highest officials of the several chapters met to discuss their dreams about the proper place for planting and settled on a site. These officials had received bags containing the members' seeds and prepared them for planting by mixing them with water, the droppings of game animals, roots, and other ingredients. For this labor the mixers were paid.

On the day after the preparation of the seeds the members, sometimes accompanied by the whole camp, set out for the garden after having been painted by the mixers. Outsiders were controlled by the military society serving as police at the time. The women carried large bags with seeds on their

Fig. 44. Tobacco bags used in the Crow Tobacco Ceremony.

backs (Fig. 44). Everyone assembled in a lodge, and the musicians intoned a song. One woman was far ahead of the line, and her chapter took precedence, for she carried a specially sacred otterskin. After four songs had been sung in the lodge, a woman walked round it and led the procession outside, being followed first by the other women, then by the men of her chapter, who took up a position to the right of the women. Then came the other chapters in turn until all of them formed a horizontal line. They proceeded toward the garden site, halting four times, and singing four songs at each stop. At the last station, possibly 100 yards from the goal, those carrying their tobacco bags turned them over to fast runners, who raced to the garden, where they laid down the bags; the winner of the race was sure to enjoy good luck that year and to have a good crop of tobacco. Various observances were followed at the stops, where the otterskin bearer offered the mixers a pipe to smoke, and they announced their dreams about the tobacco.

After the race the members came up to the site, cleared it, and prepared it by setting fire to the grass. The mixer of each chapter counted out a number of rows according to the size of the membership till the whole garden was divided up, a stick marking each group's plot. For each chapter a famous brave ran across the short side of the oblong that formed the garden and back again, reporting in a low voice, that he had been on a war party, struck a coup, and on his return found the tobacco prospering. The mixer, after proclaiming the message aloud and after three feints, punched a hole in the ground, thus ushering in the planting of the seeds.

When a chapter had completed this task, husband and wife cooperating, the men sang, both sexes danced in position and then feasted. After the planting, members would lie down at the edge of the garden, hoping to get a vision and a song about the tobacco.

A crudely fenced garden inspected in 1910 was about 60 by 6 yards, divided into six plots for the several chapters, each bounded by a row or rows of little willow wickets. Each couple within the chapter marked its section off by little stones and by setting up a distinctively shaped digging stick at either end. Two miniature sweatlodges were constructed at opposite sides of the garden to foster the growth of the sacred weed, and incense was burnt in them. A short distance from the site there was a large sweatlodge.

Formerly the adoption of novices took place immediately after the planting, but in later times it was postponed until the week of the Fourth of July festivities. Members of any chapter might attend the initiation, but only the initiating chapter received presents. The right to put up the adoption lodge with its altar was a greatly prized prerogative. There was a procession to it from a smaller preparatory tipi, in which the novice and the older members were decorated with face paint; the designs had all been revealed in visions, hence were the visionary's copyrighted property that could be transferred only by payments. Gray-bull had paid his own mother a horse, an ermine-skin shirt, quilts, and money for the right to use her pattern and sold it to Plenty-coups for four horses. When all members had been painted, dances were held in the preparatory tipi, the men drumming, a few shaking rattles, and the women gently swaying their bodies in position as they held unwrapped sacred articles. The wife of the man who owned the adoption lodge, holding a pipe, took up a position at the exit, while the men drummed and sang. After three feints she passed out of the tipi, followed by the women and then the men in a single file (Plates 33, 34). They halted four times, and at each stop four songs were sung. Then they entered the lodge, the musicians seating themselves on the west side of the altar, the women to the south and north. Immediately after the entrance a warrior went through roughly the same procedure as at the planting.

A man privileged to do so lit a pipe with trade

tobacco—never with the sacred species—and it was solemnly smoked by the men. Thereafter the drummers beat drums and sang, and members, mostly women, would dance in accompaniment. Each held a weasel skin or willow sprig or eagle feather fan or the like in her hands. The dance simply consisted in moving the body in place while alternately advancing and drawing back, or raising and lowering, the clenched hands with a convulsive movement. Sets of dancers took turns. It was essential that each novice should dance jointly, *i.e.*, in a horizontal line, with the four men who had taught him songs during the winter. These procedures occupied most of the day except at noon during an intermission for a feast and a distribution of gifts from the novice's kin to the adopters. In the late afternoon the terminal song was intoned, and at its close the members all lifted willow sprigs or drumsticks to symbolize and promote the growth of the tobacco.

Either immediately after this ceremony or the following morning, the novice or the married couple who had been initiated joined their instructors in a sweatlodge with tobacco bags on top of it. The following morning the newly adopted was allowed to pick out any "medicine" objects, including sacred tobacco bags, paying for each article in turn and for any coveted ceremonial privileges.

Between the planting and the harvest, members of the order had to observe various rules, *e.g.*, they must not play shinny after the sprouting of the plant, lest it break down. During this period the members often danced, in the simple way described, in order to hasten the growth of the tobacco. There were four formal inspections of the garden, either by the mixers or by inspectors reporting to them. When the wild cherries were ripe, the members—theoretically of all chapters on the same day—harvested the crop, returned to camp, and danced as they had during the adoption. If some plants were not yet mature, subsequent visits were made to the garden. After the final crop the members danced with the newly plucked tobacco in the adoption lodge. Finally the stems and leaves were plucked out, cut up fine, and thrown into a creek.

The Crow Tobacco society affords a good insight into Plains Indian ceremonialism. The ceremonies are highly composite. There is no central idea to which the various activities are logically subordinated. All the Crow identified the sacred tobacco with a star, but it is impossible to detect in the procedures a consistent astral cult. The origin tales do bring in one or more stars as founders of the order, but the chapters traced their beginning to all kinds of sources—weasels, a lizard, a crane, buffalo, or an eagle as the Sun's messenger. The performances themselves combine characteristic ritual ideas of the area—the altar, sweatlodges, incense smoking, facial paint, fourfold repetition. The notion that visionary blessings are transferable finds expression in the creation of innumerable special privileges, all finding payers of extravagant prices. Since the culture stresses military prowess, warriors get an opportunity to recount their deeds before a sizable audience, though their coups have nothing to do with either the stars or the avowed purpose of the ceremonies—the tribal welfare.

THE SUN DANCE

The Sun Dance ranks as the most conspicuous religious festival of about twenty Plains tribes. It was not performed by the Pawnee, Wichita, Omaha, and several other Southern Siouans, but elements of it appeared among the Pawnee and Omaha. Because of the self-torturing associated with most of its forms, the Department of the Interior prohibited its performance in 1904, the ban being removed in 1935, so that sundry tribes have held the Dance since then, though modern conditions have introduced alterations. The festival was most highly elaborated among the Arapaho, Cheyenne, and Dakota, most meager and recent among the western marginal tribes. The Comanche, after being mere spectators of the performance by their Kiowa neighbors, worked out a simplified copy of it in 1874; the Ute adopted the dance about 1890 and subsequently made it their principal ceremony.

What holds true of the Crow Tobacco ceremonial holds equally for the Sun Dance: it does not revolve about the worship of a particular deity, the popular English name for it being a misnomer, but is a composite of largely unintegrated elements prominent in the area at large. The remarkable thing about it is the wide distribution of many objective features, while the interpretations and ostensible motives for holding it vary widely. Quite general was its tribal character: the Dance was performed after the reassemblage following the winter dispersal, *i.e.*, either in the late spring or early summer. Though in many tribes the performance was annual, it hinged on some distressed tribesman's vowing to have it held if he were relieved of his worries. Among the Crow the only motive was an inconsolable mourner seeking revenge upon the tribe that had killed a close relative of his, so that years might elapse between successive ceremonies. A priest acquainted with the ritual conducted the Dance, first instructing the pledger in a preparatory tipi, while a large number of tribesmen not concerned with esoteric aspects brought in the requisites for the great ceremonial structure. Most groups stressed the solemnities associated with the central or the first pole to be set up for the lodge: they scouted for a suitable tree, had a specially qualified person—say, a chaste woman—chop it, and treated the fallen tree as an enemy on whom coup was to be counted. Before raising this pole, the builders put a bundle of brush, a buffalo hide, and offerings into the fork of the log. Commonly this bundle was explained as an eagle's or thunderbird's nest. The exceptional structure of the Crow was merely a huge tipi in shape; typical was a circular enclosure from whose crossbeams rafters extended to the fork of the central pole (Plate 35). Within the enclosure a cleared area with buffalo skulls figured as the altar. Before the main celebrants entered, warriors came in to dramatize military exploits (Crow, Kiowa, Arapaho, Cheyenne, Oglala, Hidatsa).

Generally the pledger and his associates, such as the members of his club among the Cheyenne, fasted and thirsted for several days, steadily gazing at the top of the central pole as they danced and prayed for power. The Crow pledger had to stare at a sacred doll (Plate 36) provided by his priestly mentor until it granted him a vision of a scalped enemy. Not absolutely general was the torture feature: certain participants had their breast or back punctured so that skewers could be inserted, ropes were attached at one end to the center pole, at the other to the skewers, and the dancers strained against the ropes until they had torn themselves loose. The dance was extremely simple, the performers merely rising on their toes while blowing whistles. As for the torture feature, it was completely lacking among the Kiowa, Ute, and Shoshone; only among the Dakota and Ponca did the main celebrant practice such self-mortification, while elsewhere it was voluntary, though usual, for other dancers.

So many of the objective traits were alike throughout most of the area that they must have diffused from a single source. Yet the alleged aims of the ceremony vary widely. We must infer that the ceremonial *behavior* in the festival was older and that the assumed objectives were subsequent additions. It is also clear that the Dance was only in part a religious ceremony and in large measure served for the aesthetic pleasure and entertainment of the spectators.

MODERN MOVEMENTS

Two modern religious movements require notice—the Ghost Dance and the Peyote Cult.

The Ghost Dance derives its name from the belief that the Indians were to be reunited with their dead. Its earlier form (1870) was developed by a Paviotso Indian in Nevada who went into trances and preached that the deceased were about to return to earth and that the ancient life was to be restored along with the game animals then growing scarce. In about 1888 the prophet's younger kinsman Wovoka renewed the message. On the basis of a personal revelation granted to him, he taught his fellow tribesmen a dance that was to bring about the reunion with the dead. He combined this doctrine with ethical teachings, prohibiting fighting and enjoining peace with the Whites. Sometimes he blended Christian with pagan ideas, at one time even pretending to be Christ returning to renew the aging earth. This need for renovating the earth is an old and widespread American Indian conception.

Whereas Wovoka's predecessor had aroused no interest in the Plains Area, the younger messiah appeared at a time far more favorable to the reception of his cult. For one thing, means of communication had greatly improved, so that interested Indians living at a distance could easily visit the prophet. Secondly, by 1888 the disappearance of buffalo had wrought great hardships, which were aggravated by misunderstandings with the agents of the United States government. The Teton Dakota, Arapaho, Cheyenne, and Kiowa more especially seized upon what they supposed to be the new faith, though actually they completely changed its import. The peaceable Paviotso had never dreamt of rebellion against the government, whereas among the warlike Plains tribes this became a cardinal point of doctrine. Goaded into fury by their grievances, the disciples of Wovoka in the Plains substituted for his policy of amity a holy war in which the Whites were to be exterminated. As far as possible the dress and the ways of the hostile race were to be tabooed, while vestiges of the old life, such as the traditional games, were eagerly fostered. In revivalist mass meetings men and women worked themselves into hypnotic trances and, on coming to, announced what visions they had seen—deceased kinsfolk, vast herds of buffalo, and so forth. The Dakota more particularly devised a kind of shirt, symbolically decorated, that was supposed to make the wearer bulletproof.

Under the impetus of this cult, hostile demonstrations broke out among the Teton under the leadership of Sitting Bull, who was killed by Indian police on December 15, 1890. A fortnight later there was a battle at Wounded Knee, where 31 soldiers and 128 Dakota were killed. The armed insurrection virtually ceased with this engagement, but the excitement persisted for some time among several of the tribes.

The most suggestive facts about the movement are the radical change by the Plains Indians of the imported Basin cult and the minor variations created within the Plains by the leaders of the several tribes affected. Particular developments are likewise of interest, such as the religious flavor imparted by the votaries to old games. The Pawnee, for instance, carried shinny balls or hoops in their dances and tried to induce visions with their aid; they also came to treat the hand game as a ceremony, its proper procedure being revealed in visions.

Weston La Barre in his study of the Peyote Cult describes peyote (*Lophophora williamsii* Lemaire) as "a small, spineless carrot-shaped cactus growing in the Rio Grande Valley and southward." Its round top, the only part visible above the ground, is cut off and dried to form the "button." The plant is not to be confused with the north Mexican mescal (*Agave americana*). Containing nine narcotic alkaloids, peyote produces visual hallucinations and other physiological derangements, including dilated pupils. The first effect is exhilaration, followed by depression, nausea, and wakefulness, and ultimately the partaker has brilliant color visions lasting for several hours.

The cult centering about this narcotic is recent in the Plains, not reaching the Kiowa before *ca.* 1870 and hardly becoming conspicuous there until about fifteen years later; but Mexican natives used the plant as early as the sixteenth century, and the Cora practiced a peyote ritual in 1754. Since the species is not indigenous north of Texas, most of the Plains peyotists are obliged to make expeditions to its home or to purchase it. As in the case of the Ghost Dance, the Plains Indians greatly modified the religious notions developed in the original center of diffusion. In Mexico the main objective of the seasonal ritual was curing, success in war and in corn growing or the deer hunt; there was considerable dancing, but no society of peyote eaters, no exclusiveness, even women taking part in the performances. In the Plains, doctoring, though as a rule important, was not essential; warfare was stressed in the earlier period; dancing was generally lacking; the ceremony can be performed at any time; and the peyote worshipers form an organization, which at first excluded women. The Mexicans assemble outdoors, the Plains Indians in a tipi; the Plains tribes stress smoking, which plays no great role in Mexico, but do not combine their Peyote Cult with ritual races and ball games, which loom large in Mexico. Notwithstanding such noteworthy differences, there are likewise many parallels in the two areas. To mention only a few, in both regions peyote is collected on a ceremonial trip, the sessions are held at night, followed by a ritual breakfast, in which parched corn, sweetened water, and boneless meat are prominent.

The earliest form of Plains peyotism, as practiced by the Kiowa, exhibits a number of features characteristic of ancient Plains supernaturalism. Meetings are held in accordance with a vow, on the pattern of a Sun Dance; the desire for a vision through the peyote takes precedence of the doctoring motive; there is a preparatory sweatbath; and four appears as the sacred number. As to organization, the sponsor of the meeting is responsible for the expense involved and supplies the peyote; he selects the leader of the ceremony, who is assisted by a drummer and a fire tender. The leader's regalia include a staff, a gourd rattle, an eagle-bone whistle, a drum partly filled with water, and cedar incense. Essential for a performance is the peyote altar, usually built of clayey earth in a crescent shape.

Given the Plains pattern of visionary experiences as the basis for modifications in ritual, the Kiowa prototype came to be considerably altered in accordance with leaders' individual revelations. In some tribes even Christian elements entered, including Bible reading; the three Osage officials are said to represent the Trinity; a bird image of ashes made by the Oto is interpreted as the Spirit descending at Jesus' baptism. As a matter of fact, peyotism is shot through with symbolism, both pagan and Christian. The leader's staff is the "staff of life" for a Wichita, the Saviour's staff for an Iowa.

Because of the supposedly evil effects of peyote—a mooted issue—many attempts have been launched to prohibit its use. As a countermeasure an intertribal Native American Church was founded. It is worth noting that the cult spread to various Woodland and Basin groups as well as to originally Southeastern tribes settled in Oklahoma.

7 PREHISTORY AND HISTORY

The earliest finds of archaeological material in the Plains date back possibly over 10,000 years—so far back that its makers cannot be regarded as the ancestors of the Indians under consideration in this book, though they were doubtless of the same race. It is, however, interesting to note that the area was inhabited thousands of years ago by hunters who manufactured tools of the ancient types known as "Folsom" points, *i.e.*, thin stone points skillfully worked by pressure, large longitudinal flakes being removed from one or both faces.

Of direct relevance to our subject have been the archaeological researches of the past twenty years by William D. Strong, Waldo Wedel, William Mulloy, and others. Working back from sites known to have been occupied by particular tribes in historic times, they have been able to unfold the story of culture in earlier periods, though so far only in limited portions of the total area. Nevertheless some definite results stand out. Before the coming of the horse, Nebraska and the Dakotas appear to have been for some time inhabited by semisedentary peoples. That is, contrary to the picture of later times the Pawnee and the Mandan rather than pure hunters set the tone in this region. Pawnee sites of *ca*. A.D. 1800 indicate large villages of earthlodges with plenty of horse remains and articles of Caucasian origin as well as distinctive aboriginal pottery. Sites of the same district on the Platte and Loup rivers, Nebraska, probably dating back to A.D. 1600, reveal no signs of contact with Whites, and the large earthlodge villages of this period harbored far superior pottery and a greater abundance of stonework. The conclusion is that during the two centuries aboriginal Pawnee culture declined.

To a still earlier period belong many small villages with mostly, though not exclusively, square earthlodges. Pottery is abundant, and ornaments of shells indigenous to the Gulf coast prove connection with the Southeast. Roughly contemporary are settlements of small, scattered, unfortified earthlodges, half underground, rectangular or square dwellings being definitely in the majority. Clay rather than stone pipes of elaborate and realistic shape are characteristic; abundant vegetable remains, such as charred maize, and many bone hoes demonstrate considerable farming. Just south of the Platte-Missouri confluence a unique site has plenty of remains of squashes and gourds but no trace of maize, and deer bones outnumber those of buffalo. Typical of the same settlement are small houses with reed-thatched roofs and a dearth of stone implements, compensated for by much fine work in bone and antler, including awls and beads.

At Signal Butte, in westernmost Nebraska, Strong found clearly separable layers, the top one containing earthenware like that on the Upper Republican, while the two older strata have no pottery at all. In stone projectile points, the highest and the lowest horizon differ sharply. The upper stratum has tiny chipped points resembling those of the Upper Republican and of the earliest historic Pawnee. In the lowest stratum leaf-shaped points recall those found in Nebraska and elsewhere in association with extinct species of mammals.

The sequence in the subarea best explored to date, then, is as follows: At first there was, as elsewhere, a purely hunting stage. Later, agriculture, mainly based on maize, was developed to a considerable degree, though hunting remained important. The economy was thus intermediate between that of the virtually altogether agricultural Pueblos and of the purely hunting equestrians of the historic Plains.

A star example of the changes undergone by some tribes is furnished by the Cheyenne. In the eighteenth century they occupied a settlement on the Sheyenne River in east-central North Dakota; this was destroyed by the Ojibwa in *ca.* 1770. Excavation demonstrated a village of possibly seventy circular earthlodges very much like the type found on the Upper Missouri in historic times. Cache pits contained vegetal remains, broken pottery, buffalo bones, and various indications of White contact. By way of contrast, a Cheyenne camp site of the early nineteenth century showed no trace of agriculture or of earthlodges but contained numerous trade objects. It would seem that within the space of fifty years the formerly semisedentary Cheyenne had completely given up farming and permanent dwellings in favor of buffalo hunting and tipis.

If several centuries ago Nebraska and the Dakotas were inhabited by natives of a relatively complex way of life, Montana seems to have had outposts of that culture. About five miles southeast of

Glendive, in the easternmost part of the state, William Mulloy discovered a site with one small earth-lodge and twenty cache pits. Abundant remains in the neighborhood suggest that perhaps most of the occupants of the settlement lived in temporary dwellings. Several circumstances render this site especially noteworthy. The district lies within the territory of the historic Crow, whose language is so close to Hidatsa that they cannot have separated more than a few centuries ago. A westward migration is supported by both Crow and Hidatsa tradition, and this movement was accompanied by a loss of farming, so that Crow history broadly parallels that of the Cheyenne. Given these basic facts, a transitional stage is a reasonable assumption, and the site near Glendive meets the conditions. Buffalo shoulder blades indicate the sort of hoeing practiced until recently by Hidatsa women and the pottery—not made by the historic Crow—seems most closely related to that of the Mandan-Hidatsa (Plate 15), both in its uncoiled technique and its simple decoration. The stone tools point in the same direction, duplicating types previously known from the Mandan. Many small scrapers chipped only on the back and worked into a flat convex edge at one end closely resemble an authentically Mandan blade in the United States National Museum.

Though the correspondence is not complete and should not be expected to be so, it is thus likely that the occupants of the Glendive site were Crow Indians still retaining a good deal of their Hidatsa cultural heritage "before they had sloughed off entirely their old semisedentary mode of village life and pottery-making and when they had not yet acquired the horse" (Wedel).

Another significant series of archaeological discoveries proves that pottery without agriculture was once very widely distributed in Montana, even in the extreme North and Northwest. The relations of this ware are as yet obscure; some details point toward the western Great Lakes or the upper Mississippi Valley. We cannot contend that the ceramic art ever *flourished* in Montana or is very ancient there. In Pictograph Cave, near Billings, the single stratified site so far examined, pottery exists only in the upper layer and with Caucasian remains, indicating manufacture by the direct ancestors of historic inhabitants of the region. Nevertheless, the finds enlarge the range of the ceramic art in North America and support traditions of northern Plains tribes hitherto treated with reserve (page 61).

The archaeological exploration of Texas has also brought to light interesting connections. In the Panhandle, many-roomed stone and adobe buildings prove Pueblo influence, while the pottery points overwhelmingly to the utilitarian cord-marked ware of the central Plains. The few Pueblo-like sherds that have been found help, however, to fix the approximate date of the culture as between A.D. 1300 and 1450. In the contemporary eastern Pueblo of Pecos, New Mexico, various implements connected with the hunt and skin dressing prove that the borrowing extended in both directions. The people of the Panhandle practiced at that period partly an agricultural, partly a hunting economy. Possibly, because of serious droughts, they migrated, so that Coronado found the Canadian River Valley to be the home of nomadic buffalo hunters.

In the Texas section of the Llano Estacado the remains are quite different, the pottery discovered indicating a marginal Pueblo culture. The same influences appear to the south.

In north-central Texas, on the Upper Brazos and Upper Red Rivers, a few sherds of trade Puebloan pottery accompany a mixed economy of semisedentary Plains type and Pueblo hand mills. It has been suggested that the bearers of this culture were Wichita, but prior to 1700 evidence is lacking that this tribe lived south of Oklahoma; it can be traced archaeologically only as far south as central Kansas. Thus north-central Texas in, say, A.D. 1450 was inhabited by an as yet unidentified semisedentary people. Still farther east the sites fall within the Caddoan section of the Southeastern Area. The Caddoans visited there by the Spaniards in 1542 had cotton blankets and turquoise, both of which they must have obtained from the Pueblos. A connection between the Southeast and the Southwest, say, in 1400, is further suggested by ceramic resemblances due to mutual borrowing and greater than can be ascribed to mere trade. However, there is very little similarity between Southeastern sites in the wooded sections of eastern Oklahoma, western Arkansas, northwestern Louisiana, and northeastern Texas on the one hand and central or southern sites of clear-cut Plains type. At present the Pawnee cannot be archaeologically connected with fellow Caddoans to the south and southeast, though linguistic affiliation points in that direction.

As the Cheyenne and Crow cases illustrate, a combination of archaeological with historical and linguistic findings greatly aids us in the reconstruction of the past. For some tribes the written records suffice to give us a fairly clear picture of cultural developments.

The Plains Cree are one of the best-known instances. When first mentioned by the chroniclers of the *Jesuit Relations* in 1640, the Cree had nothing to do with our area, being an eastern Woodland people living toward Hudson Bay. In 1666–1667 they were roving hunters, canoers, and gatherers of wild rice who shared with other forest dwellers the region between Hudson Bay and Lake Superior. Hostile to the Dakota, they were friendly to the Assiniboin. With the coming of the Hudson's Bay Company, the Cree turned trappers to supply the traders with furs. The demand for beaver made them penetrate farther west, displacing the older inhabitants with the aid of the Europeans' guns. By about 1730 a detachment of Cree was reported south of the Saskatchewan, and they had certainly reached Lake Winnipeg. Though not yet adapted to the new habitat, they had already largely changed their old economy for, as a result of their specialization as trappers, they were now depending on the traders for weapons, clothing, utensils, and even food. They still paddled about in canoes, thus enjoying great mobility. The advantage due to firearms, however, decreased as other tribes likewise got guns.

The change, which affected only part of the Cree, was rapid, but came by stages. In 1772 the western advance guard was impounding buffalo, but still clung to the canoe. In fact, a few survivals of the old culture, such as snowshoes, remained for good. But to all intents and purposes the Plains Cree, after somewhat tardily taking up equestrian life, became thoroughly assimilated Plains people, sharply separated in outlook and customs, though not in speech, from the Eastern Cree.

Other Woodland tribes, who lived farther south, sharing the widespread maize culture of the East, completely abandoned farming in favor of the buffalo chase. The Cheyenne have already been cited in this connection. When first mentioned in 1673 they lived in westernmost Wisconsin and the section of Minnesota between the Mississippi, Minnesota, and Upper Red River. Pressed by the Dakota, who were themselves pushed out by the Ojibwa, they migrated westward. In 1804 Lewis and Clark found them in the Black Hills country of present South Dakota. The Cheyenne, too, turned into pure buffalo hunters, but also played the part of middlemen in procuring English goods from the Hidatsa and passing them on to the Arapaho and other tribes. It is probable that the basic mutation did not affect all the Cheyenne at once, but at first only their westernmost outposts while the laggards were still to some extent raising corn.

The story of the Dakota runs parallel with that of the Cheyenne. When first seen by Whites in the seventeenth century, they were a forest people occupying the territory from the Upper Mississippi to the headwaters of the Minnesota. They embraced many politically distinct subdivisions, but a sense of unity persisted, and their three dialects did not differ materially. "They fought other people, but ordinarily not each other" (Mekeel). The Teton, migrating as far as the Black Hills, Wyoming, and southeastern Montana, became the embodiment of Plains nomadism, while the Santee and other eastern sub-groups retained the old semi-agricultural economy. The differentiation cannot be wholly due to European contact, for as early as 1700 Le Sueur notes the Teton's lack of canoes and wild rice. At all events, the Dakota as a unit must have been an originally Woodland people, a large branch of which became buffalo hunters to the exclusion of farming.

The Assiniboin speak a language closely akin to the N dialects of Dakota. In 1640 they were already distinct from the parent tribe and inhabited the vicinity of the Lake of the Woods and Lake Nipigon in southern Ontario. They became intimately connected with the Cree, sharing in the transformation undergone by that tribe. In Lewis and Clark's day they were also in close contact with the villagers of the Upper Missouri. As might be expected, their culture is largely a blend of Dakota and Cree traits.

The Southern Siouans may be summarily dealt with. None of them occupied *high* Plains country, and some of their traditions indicate the lower Ohio River as an earlier home. What is more, the language of the Iowa-Oto is closely related to Winnebago, the speech of an unquestionably Woodland people. Skinner finds a series of stages between the Winnebago at one extreme and the Ponca at the other, the Iowa, Oto, Omaha, and Ponca marking the steps toward a full-fledged Plains culture. None of them turned into pure hunters, but even the historic Iowa surrounded buffalo, dressed skins with elk-horn scrapers, crossed rivers in bull-boats, traveled with travois, and had rival military clubs. The Omaha also had some military societies, though overshadowed by other organizations. They lacked the Sun Dance, but did practice the ceremonial chopping down of a tree that is so conspicuous and widespread a feature of that festival. Among the Ponca there were several military organizations; in part they obtained them from the Teton and passed them on to the Omaha. The Ponca also celebrated a full-fledged Sun Dance. All in all, the Southern Siouan culture was a mixture of Plains and Woodland features.

While all the tribes just considered came from the eastern Woodlands, the Caddoans of the Plains —Pawnee-Arikara and Wichita—can be connected specifically with the Southeast. This holds true especially if, in accordance with many scholars, the Iroquois of New York are regarded as originally native to that area. In this connection it is worth emphasizing that eminent linguists consider Iroquoian and Caddoan closely related stocks and that the unquestionably Iroquoian Cherokee were met by De Soto (1540) in the southern Alleghenies. To the great resemblance between Pawnee and Iroquois pottery may be added the exceptionally large number of small triangular, unnotched arrowheads found in Iroquoian and Caddoan sites. The Southeast as a whole is marked by the deposition of human remains in bone-houses; and though such ossuaries are not known from the historic Pawnee, early sites indicative of the Pawnee do reveal such structures. Again, prehistoric square earthlodges on the Republican River strongly recall a type discovered in Arkansas. Unknown in the period of Caucasian contact, they may well represent the antecedent of the historic circular earthlodge. Grass houses, typical of the modern Wichita and observed by Coronado in 1541 along the Arkansas River, are a variant of this type. A striking parallel between the Skidi Pawnee and the Natchez of the Lower Mississippi is the torture of a captive stretched out in a frame. The cutting open of the victim's breast is reminiscent of an Aztec ceremony (southern Mexico), but the immediate historical connection seems to be with the Natchez. Considering that the Caddo proper and other members of their family are indigenous to the Southeast, it is justifiable to trace the Plains Caddoans to the vicinity of the Gulf of Mexico, say to southern Texas, even though clear-cut archaeological proof is lacking. We may picture the Pawnee as originally skillful Southeastern farmers, who also did considerable hunting. As they pushed farther west and north, they probably—like the historic Caddo—took more and more to the buffalo chase. This explains the abundance of buffalo bones on archaeological sites within their territory. However, in getting more and more horses the Pawnee tended to emphasize this aspect of their economy, and though they kept on farming, the art of pottery declined. Considering that in the later periods they often raided the Southwest, they remained remarkably free from Pueblo influences. Thus, the stone hand mill, so characteristic of the Pueblo Area, was conspicuously rare, wooden mortars of the Eastern type prevailing.

The Arikara must be considered a fairly recent offshoot of the Pawnee since their speech differs only dialectically. They moved north, became neighbors of the Mandan and Hidatsa, and are probably responsible for some elaborations in the culture of the Upper Missouri.

In all the foregoing cases the Plains were invaded from the east. There were likewise incursions from the opposite direction. From the subarctic Athabaskan region came the Sarsi, linguistically an offshoot of the Beaver Indians first discovered toward the end of the eighteenth century around the upper Saskatchewan and Athabaska Rivers. Numerically weak, they attached themselves to the Blackfoot and assimilated the ways of their more powerful neighbors, even achieving sketchy replicas of the military associations and the Sun Dance.

Of much greater importance in Plains history were the Uto-Aztecans. The three groups significant in this context—the Wind River Shoshone, Comanche, and Ute—all belong to the Shoshonean branch of the family. Some other Shoshoneans also partook of Plains culture, but only sporadically and to a minor degree. Since by far the majority of Shoshonean tribes lived in the Basin Area and southern California, our three groups doubtless ultimately came into the Plains as relative newcomers from the west; *i.e.*, they formerly inhabited an area of marked simplicity. Accordingly, on the whole they passively took on Plains features, absorbing essentially material rather than social and religious traits. One vital exception, however, must be made. The Shoshone provided horses for the Crow and the Blackfoot (page 42). In the southern Plains, the Comanche, being near the Spanish settlements, played a corresponding role; the Ponca regarded them as their masters in horsemanship and in packing horses. Apart from such services, it is possible that the distinctive parfleche style of the Crow was influenced by the Shoshone.

How soon the Shoshoneans turned into Plains Indians remains uncertain. The "Teyas" of the Spanish chroniclers have been regarded as Comanche, but this is merely a possible interpretation. The earliest unquestionable reference to this people goes back to 1701 and places them near the headwaters of the Arkansas (Colorado); in 1705 they were found in New Mexico. Since Comanche and Shoshone differ only dialectically, their separation cannot date back many centuries. That they or the parent tribe had adopted buffalo hunting as their main subsistence basis by *ca.* A.D. 1700 may be accepted as certain.

The Blackfoot and the Arapaho-Gros Ventre languages, though Algonkian, differ so sharply from other Algonkian tongues as to indicate for their speakers a long period of separation from eastern and central members of the stock. It is therefore plausible to assume that they are "ancient occupants of the northern true plains, or rather of the foothills of the Rockies and the plains tributary thereto" (Kroeber). In the south, the Kiowa cannot be traced outside the Plains Area on the basis of historic documents. Linguistically, some scholars link them with the Tanoan family of the Rio Grande region, in other words, with the easternmost Pueblos. The Athabaskan Kiowa-Apache, too, are apparently old inhabitants of our area, centering in southwestern Oklahoma. As a small group they attached themselves to the Kiowa for the celebration of the Sun Dance as though a band of the larger tribe, but otherwise preserved their identity; the two peoples communicated with each other mainly by gestures. The case of the Plains Apache (page 9) is problematic. The "Querechos" or "Vaqueros" described by sixteenth-century Spanish chroniclers as nomadic hunters have been generally identified as "Apache"; but the Jicarilla Apache who seem to have come closest to the Plains pattern turn out to have practiced considerable farming before the American occupation, and the oldest survivors in 1934 insisted on the ancillary and comparatively recent use of the tipi. In consequence, doubt is cast on the traditional equation "Querechos = Apache." Finally, the archaeological evidence cited indicates prehistoric Pawnee residence in the Plains, as does the Spanish reference to grass houses of presumably Wichita and almost certainly Caddoan construction.

Thus, though many other groups may well have been in the area in aboriginal days, the strongest claim for early Plains residence may be made for the eastern Shoshoneans, the Blackfoot, Arapaho-Gros Ventre, Kiowa, Kiowa-Apache, Pawnee, and some other Caddoans.

8 ACCULTURATION

Acculturation has been defined as the changes produced in the cultures of peoples in continuous contact with each other. When the two groups differ in complexity, the simpler culture is likely to be more receptive than the other. Such was the relative status of Indians and Caucasians, the latter more frequently playing the donor's role. Thus occurred the assimilation of the White man's clothing, utensils, tools, firearms, and horses. Yet the process was not wholly one-sided, for maize was the Indian's gift to European civilization, and the specific variety planted on the Upper Missouri proved a boon to White settlers in the area.

Automatically the recipients of laborsaving devices dropped their ancient handiwork and processes of manufacture except where emotional attachment led them to retain what was old, as in ceremonials. In this sense there were cultural losses as well as gains. By no means all possible material traits were accepted, even where the advantages were obvious. The Plains tribes accepted cattle as the closest approach to the moribund buffalo herds, but did not take at all kindly to milking, churning, or cheese making. Further, some elements of the Caucasian culture were, for some reason, introduced much later than necessary; the Crow, for instance, did not get wagons until 1874.

It is necessary to distinguish acculturation that happened through the sheer contact of Indians with Whites and the acculturation due to deliberate planning on the part of the United States government. Far-reaching results were caused by the mere coming of traders and later by the construction of railroads. The rapid interchange of ideas by different tribes at the time of the Ghost Dance would not have been possible in the era of more primitive transportation.

The general policy of the government was to civilize the natives in the sense of making them literate, English-speaking, Christian farmers like their White neighbors. This aim created formidable problems. In the first place, many tribes, having either always or at least for decades been nomadic hunters, did not wish to take up fixed residences. But even the semisedentary Plains Indians were not ready to emulate the example of Caucasian agriculturists. For one thing, their farming tools were hoes and dibbles, involving techniques quite different from ploughing with domestic livestock. No less serious was the sociological transformation involved, for in the old days women planted, whereas under the new order the men were expected to do the work. At first, then, any men who took up ploughing were likely to lose face and to be jeered at. Apart from everything else, much of the land allotted to the natives was unsuitable for husbandry or required irrigation. The task of the agency officials appointed to teach the Indians farming was therefore an arduous one. Some Indians managed to lease their land to Whites, some simply killed off and ate whatever cattle were issued to them. Again, in matrilineal tribes, confusion arose when officials insisted on having land inherited from father to son.

One outstanding change in adaptation to an industrial civilization was in the direction of individualism. The Plains Indians were indeed intensely individualistic in matters of prestige, but economically they were often the reverse, sharing food freely with anyone and other chattels at least with kinsfolk. A potentially successful farmer would thus be held back in his economic progress by a host of needy spongers if he clung to tribal ethics. On this point individuals widely varied, some for a long time being willing to forego material prosperity rather than to flout ancient custom.

With regard to education, the government provided schooling on and off the reservations. For a long time the boarding schools like that at Carlisle, Pennsylvania, were far more effective since the children, removed from parental and tribal influences, had to learn English and to make adjustments to American life. In other respects the results were less advantageous: alienated from his people, the returning young man or woman was at least for some time a stranger in his own country. These "educated Indians" could, however, play an important part as interpreters and as spokesmen of their people in dealings with United States officials.

An important personality problem, for the males, was finding a suitable substitute for the ancient goals. With the buffalo gone and warfare a thing of the past, they found it very hard to discover any objectives that made life worth living. Some strongly expressed the sentiment that they preferred the old existence with all its hazards, but with the chance for glory, to the pedestrian career of a farmer or mechanic.

Education was to a considerable extent offered by missionaries of various denominations. The effectiveness of their religious instruction is difficult to judge. It depended on the length of time the Indians were exposed to such efforts and on the individual character of both the natives and the missionaries. With the older people, aboriginal paganism lingered for a very long time. Moreover, aboriginal religion was definitely neither propagandist nor dogmatic, so that an Indian could very well combine Christian doctrines with ancient belief in the reality of spirits who appeared in visions. In those recent cults which favored proselytizing, such as the Peyote Cult, Christian teachings easily blended with native ideas.

Conditions have been so different for the several groups on the Plains that no generalizing sketch of their acculturation can do justice to all the facts. The issue has depended on such factors as when the particular tribe was put on a reservation, whether they remained in their historic territory, whether or not they had had markedly hostile clashes with government agencies, whether missions or schools had been established. Within the last half century, assimilation to White ways has certainly progressed. To take the Omaha, in 1910, of those under forty years of age 90 per cent had some knowledge of English, many of them spoke it well. All lived in houses, using tents only in the summer. Except for about twenty men in a population of 1,270, all males dressed in citizens' clothes, while the older women had taken to a compromise between native and White dress and some of the younger ones wore White clothing. Ninety-five per cent of the people used carriages and buggies. Ninety per cent of the children spent a reasonable portion of the year in school. Two Omaha were lawyers, two merchants, three or four engaged in real estate or stock business, several in government service, a large number were making good homes for themselves as farmers.

Although the Omaha, then, largely attained the goal originally set by the Bureau of Indian Affairs, there were currents and crosscurrents in the recent history of the Plains Indians. From 1933 until 1945 Commissioner John Collier headed the Bureau and applied the policy of fostering native custom so far as it did not conflict with the necessities of modern civilization. Thus became possible the revival of the Sun Dance in modified form.

Apart from developments directed from above, there have been "pagan" survivals, such as exist even in remote rural communities of western Europe and of America. In 1931 an old Crow would not eat a cake till he was assured that it had not been made with eggs, which had been tabooed to him in a vision. A middle-aged man at that time carefully kept his medicine bundle where it could not be polluted by the presence of menstruating women. The Arapaho were rigidly maintaining the mother-in-law taboo only twenty years ago and probably still are. Rather generally there has been the omnipresent struggle between progressives and conservatives, the former favoring rapid adaptation to modern conditions, the latter trying to salvage what they could of ancient usage.

9 CONCLUSION

A few general facts emerge from a consideration of the data. The tribes dealt with are properly regarded as representing a distinctive mode of life during the period of Caucasian contacts. Dependence on the buffalo, residence in skin-covered tipis, use of the horse for the hunt and for transport, the peculiar style of decorative and of pictographic art, the sign language, the ideology of warfare, the Sun Dance and less conspicuous features of supernaturalism are outstanding features widely prevalent in our area and not similarly combined elsewhere.

However, culture areas are merely convenient ways of classifying peoples, and we must recognize that a different alignment is possible and equally legitimate. The semisedentary tribes clearly form a subgroup within our area; and they could properly be united with the western Woodland tribes of Wisconsin and Illinois to form a Wisconsin-Southern Plains Area. This consideration applies with special force to the Southern Siouans. The Omaha, Oto, and Iowa share with the Winnebago, Menomini, Sauk, and Fox many traits not typical of the high Plains. To take one feature, the game of lacrosse is highly characteristic of the eastern half of the United States and suggestively lacking in our area—except among the Iowa, Oto, Eastern Dakota, and their offshoot, the Assiniboin. To take another feature from a different sphere of culture, the Southern Siouans have the same form of patrilineal clan organization as the Central Algonkians and the Winnebago, and with it went the same mode of classifying relatives (page 103). In vital aspects of social life, the Omaha resemble the Algonkian Menomini of the Woodlands more than they do their fellow Siouans. It is a matter of choice whether we stress the set of traits connected with the buffalo hunt and, in later times, with the horse or stress the complex which the Southern Siouans brought from the Woodlands in migrating westward.

From a broader point of view, we must first of all recognize Plains traits that go back to a hoary antiquity and were pan-American, *e.g.*, the technique of stone chipping, the dog as a domesticated animal, the firedrill. Then there are elements not so widely found, yet general north of the Rio Grande; the vision quest, lacking only in the Pueblo Area, would be an example. Another set of traits would include those penetrating from the west and southwest. Under this head fall the sinew-backed bow, hard-soled moccasins, and probably some decorative designs. This influence, however, is overshadowed by the features shared with the Eastern tribes of the continent and, like the Cree snowshoes, demonstrably carried west in the contact period. Altogether the Plains culture thus appears as a specialization of the Woodland cultures, modified by subsequent borrowings from elsewhere and by regional adaptations to a new environment.

The horse stimulated mobility and with it brought far-reaching contacts among hitherto remote tribes so that over an immense territory cultural leveling occurred. This was most noticeable as regards external features, but was by no means confined to them. The Comanche, peripheral to the typical representatives of the Plains, retained vestiges of their affinity with the Basin Area. Yet it is remarkable how many specific items they came to share, though some of them very late, with the most typical peoples of the Plains. Their mystic number was four, not five, as of some Basin Shoshoneans. Their practice of the vision quest and their attitude toward guardian spirits strongly recall Crow phenomena. Though in slightly developed form, military societies existed and so did a whole series of sentiments and practices associated with warfare on the Plains. There was the glorification of valor, the axiom that a man ought to die young as a warrior, the recital of coups, the scouts' swearing on a pile of buffalo droppings, the theoretical appropriation of all loot by the leader of a raid, the occasional assumption of a "contrary" role (page 113) by men courting death.

Leveling of another kind occurred when some tribes lost earlier features and at the same time adopted the horse and a fuller adaptation to the buffalo chase. Thus, those Cree who entered the Plains lost the canoe and became equestrian nomads; the previously corn-growing Cheyenne lost agriculture and fixed habitations as they specialized in buffalo hunting; the Pawnee did not go so far, but grew less intensive cultivators and more ardent hunters.

Important as Caucasian contacts were in precipitating westward migrations and in introducing the horse, the *creative* power of the innovations should not be exaggerated. The consequences seem merely "a logical development of the type of life described by Coronado" (Eggan). It is a curious fact that what figures as the fully developed Plains culture did *not* evolve among the tribes that first acquired horses; neither the Apache nor the Shoshone-Comanche nor the Nez Percé were Plains tribes in the fullest sense. The simple explanation is that many essential aspects of Plains culture were preexistent in the "Eastern Maize Area," not dependent on horse breeding, and came to be imported into the Plains by migration either of peoples or of ideas from the Woodlands. This appears clearly from the earlier sources.

In the first place, the buffalo was far from unknown in the East and probably a much more important game animal in prehistoric times than it became later. Robes of buffalo skin were worn in the Southeast, shields were of buffalo hide, the horns furnished ornaments on headdresses as well as material for spoons and dishes. As among the Hidatsa, hoes were made of buffalo shoulder blades. The hair was woven into cords, belts, and garters, which recalls the bags of buffalo wool seen among the Oto, Kansa, and Osage (Skinner). Though the animals grew scarce in the Southeast in colonial days, they occurred in large numbers in what is now Kentucky, northeastern Arkansas, Tennessee, especially in the western section of the Gulf region. The Creek even had a Buffalo clan in ancient times.

Farther north there were likewise local differences in the distribution of the species. The Menomini wove buffalo wool and wore a cap of buffalo skin in one of their dances, but in Catlin's day (1832) they had to go far to hunt the animal. The Winnebago went to the prairie after buffalo, and one of their clans was named for the species; the Ojibwa drove herds into enclosures. For the Miami, buffalo were the principal game and furnished the material for robes; these Indians set fire to the dead grass and surrounded the herd, driving it toward the hunters' ambush. Attention has been called to the effectiveness of such methods in early contact times.

What is more, though the relative importance of fishing, hunting, and cultivating varied from one Eastern tribe to another, the economic pattern of the Illinois and Miami was precisely that of the semisedentary Plains peoples. The Illinois of *ca.* A.D. 1700 would leave their villages in communal quest of large game in the winter, returning toward May to plant maize, beans, and pumpkins; as among the Mandan, Hidatsa, and Omaha, women farmed and men hunted.

Nothing was more characteristic of the Plains than the functioning of a police force during the collective hunt or in travel. It so happens that our earliest report of the institution (1680) is for the Santee Dakota, properly a Woodland group. Louis Hennepin, who wrote *A New Discovery of a Vast Country in America* (London, 1698), had met a company of men from that tribe and been offered of their meat when suddenly came retribution:

> Fifteen or sixteen Savages came into the middle of the Place where they were, with their great Clubs in their Hands. The first thing they did was to over-set the Cabin of those that had invited us. Then they took away all their Victuals and what Bears-Oil they could find in their Bladders, or elsewhere, with which they

rubbed themselves all over from Head to Foot. . . .

We knew not what these Savages were at first; but it appear'd they were some of those that we had left above the Fall of St. Anthony. One of them, who call'd himself my Uncle, told me, that those who had given us Victuals, had done basely to go and forestal the others in the Chase; and that according to the Laws and Customs of their Country, 'twas lawful for them to plunder them, since they had been the cause that the Bulls were all run away, before the Nation could get together, which was a great Injury to the Publick; For when they are all met, they make a great Slaughter amongst the Bulls; for they surround them so on every side, that 'tis impossible for them to escape.

All the characteristic elements of this phenomenon, the so-called soldier killing, appeared in other western Woodlands groups either during journeys or when engaged in a major economic enterprise. At the rice harvest the Menomini and the Winnebago police forbade anyone to trespass on the fields before the day fixed. The war chiefs of the Sauk and Fox restrained tribesmen from singly returning to the village from a hunt and destroyed a transgressor's canoe and property. In about A.D. 1700 an Illinois

would not dare separate from the mass to go and hunt when they are on land, for immediately a band of young men who are guards would run after him to make him return, break his arms and tear off all that he had on him. These savages have established this kind of law

CONCLUSION

among themselves because those who go in advance would cause the animals to flee while killing only a very few of them, which would oblige them to go much farther to find some.

In other words, this typical "Plains" institution was observed east of the Plains by the earliest travelers and as quite independent of any direct or indirect stimulus due to White contact.

Turning to supernaturalism, the Delaware and other Indians of the Atlantic Coast—not to mention tribes farther west—sent boys to fast for a vision at or before puberty, as did the Hidatsa and the Omaha. The sweatbath of the Huron and the subsequent plunge into a river figure in Lafitau's work on Indian customs (1724). The Huron shamans practiced the Pawnee trick of putting their arms into boiling water and handling live coals as early as 1620, and similar miracles are reported from New York Indians fifty years later.

The roach found in certain ceremonial organizations of the Plains was the characteristic daily men's hairdress among the Pawnee, Osage, and Iowa. It was equally typical of the Sauk and Fox and in 1665 attracted the attention of David Pieterz de Vries on Manhattan Island: "Their hair is shorn at the top like a cock's comb."

Finally, Plains militarism, which sharply contrasts with Pueblo, Basin, and Plateau attitudes, corresponds closely to the spirit of the tribes east of the Mississippi before and after the coming of the horse. The suggestion sometimes offered that the craving for horses or other economic values was required to evoke warlike undertaking is preposterous in the light of the evidence. The Powhatan of Virginia, early colonial observers expressly state, seldom warred "for lands or goods, but for women and children, and principally for revenge." In later times, the theft of horses naturally became a main objective in the Southeast, but prior to their introduction retaliation and social advancement were the motives for war expeditions, the main difference from the Plains being the inordinate importance attached to scalps. Just as in the Plains, a leader lost standing if he lost any followers, religious sanctions loomed large, and the raiders carried with them the equivalent of a war medicine bundle.

The same attitude prevailed farther north. In 1632 an observer declared that the Huron went to war "without other pledge or hope of recompense than of honor and praise, which they value more than all the gold in the world." Something very much like the coup existed among several Eastern tribes: a Huron or Illinois took an enemy prisoner by merely touching him. An Illinois captain had to pacify the family of a follower killed on a raid. The Miami leader reaped all the glory of success, but also the disgrace of failure. The system of sending out scouts and having them make a formal report offers another parallel. Naturally, the resemblances multiply as one approaches the Plains. Thus, the war-bundle concept, rudimentary among the Delaware of 1774, flourished full-blown among the Menomini, Sauk, Fox, and Winnebago. Recital of one's deeds in public was characteristic of Menomini and Winnebago. The latter valued touching a foeman higher than killing him, they taught their young the universal Plains maxim that it was well not to die of old age but as a young fighting warrior, and, like Cheyenne or Crow, they swore oaths to affirm the correctness of their claim to a war honor.

In short, vital ingredients of the Plains culture existed before European influences, though not necessarily all *in* the Plains. Further, in the Plains themselves Coronado in 1541 already distinguished the two main subcultures of the area—the villagers' and the nomads'. The people of Quivira planted corn and built houses of "straw," and there were "other thickly settled provinces around it [one settlement] containing large numbers of men." By way of contrast, the Querechos and Teyas "do not have any crockery . . . do not make gourds, nor sow corn, nor eat bread. . . ." They depended for sustenance on the flesh of buffalo, for fuel on buffalo dung. "A Teya was seen to shoot a bull right through both shoulders with an arrow, which would be a good shot for a musket." These people lived "in tents made of the tanned skins of the cows," and the tents were transported by pack dogs. Pemmican, travois, the sign language are specifically attested by the Spanish chroniclers. However much the Woodland Indians and Caucasians brought into the Plains later, the ecological pattern of the culture area had been created before the discovery.

Imperfect as the picture of the natives by their earliest White visitors is, we do not get the impression that the nomads of the Plains were laboring under the wretched standards of living of the aborigines of the Basin. Coronado's men came upon a settlement of 200 tipis, which suggests a band of, say, 1,000 people. Later, but still before the horse had reached them, possibly in 1740, the Piegan could muster against the Shoshone 350 warriors, representing a probable population of 1,500. Finally, at least the southern nomads were in a position to enrich their life by trading with the Pueblos, exchanging robes for corn and what not; this intercourse could easily involve additional cultural loans.

It remains true that the Plains Indians at any period we can clearly grasp are not so sharply set off from the Woodland peoples as these are from the Basin or the Southwestern tribes. Nevertheless, the effective ecological exploitation of the buffalo created something distinctive, and the cultural complex resting on this basis obviously antedated the horse, the fur trade, or any other White influence. On this fact rests the justification for speaking of an aboriginal culture area.

HINTS FOR FURTHER READING

There are a number of not over-technical books giving more or less complete descriptions of particular Plains tribes. The following may be recommended:

BOWERS, ALFRED W., *Mandan Social and Ceremonial Organization*, University of Chicago Press, Chicago, 1950.

CURTIS, EDWARD S., *The North American Indian*, Vol. 4 [Crow], The University Press, Cambridge, Mass., 1909.

FLETCHER, ALICE C., and FRANCIS LA FLESCHE, "The Omaha Tribe," 27th Annual Report, Bureau of American Ethnology, Washington, D.C., 1911.

GRINNELL, GEORGE BIRD, *The Cheyenne Indians*, Yale University Press, New Haven, 1923.

LOWIE, ROBERT H., *The Crow Indians*, Farrar & Rinehart, Inc., New York, 1935.

MC CLINTOCK, WALTER, *The Old North Trail* [Blackfoot], Macmillan & Co., London, 1910.

WALLACE, ERNEST, and E. ADAMSON HOEBEL, *The Comanches; Lords of the Southern Plains*, University of Oklahoma Press, Norman, Oklahoma, 1952.

There is no general book on the archaeology of the area, but the following essays give a fair picture of modern methods and results:

CHAPMAN, CARL H., Culture Sequence in the Lower Missouri Valley, in *Archeology of Eastern United States*, pp. 139–151, James B. Griffin, ed., The University of Chicago Press, Chicago, 1952.

EGGAN, FRED R., The Ethnological Cultures and Their Archeological Backgrounds, in *Archeology of Eastern United States*, pp. 35–45, James B. Griffin, ed., The University of Chicago Press, Chicago, 1952.

MULLOY, WILLIAM, The Northern Plains, in *Archeology of Eastern United States*, pp. 124–138, James B. Griffin, ed., The University of Chicago Press, Chicago, 1952.

STRONG, WILLIAM DUNCAN, From History to Prehistory in the Northern Great Plains, in *Essays in Historical Anthropology of North America*, Smithsonian Miscellaneous Publications, Vol. 100, pp. 291–352, Washington, D.C., 1940.

WEDEL, WALDO R., Culture Sequences in the Central Great Plains, in *Essays in Historical Anthropology of North America*, Smithsonian Miscellaneous Publications, Vol. 100, pp. 291–352, Washington, D.C., 1940.

Among the numerous more popular books on the area a few may be cited as interesting and instructive:

GRINNELL, GEORGE BIRD, *Blackfoot Lodge Tales*, Bison Books, University of Nebraska Press, Lincoln, Nebraska, 1962.

LINDERMANN, FRANK B., *American: The Life Story of a Great Indian* [Crow], The John Day Company, New York, 1930.

LINDERMANN, FRANK B., *Red Mother* [Crow], The John Day Company, New York, 1932.

MARIOTT, ALICE, *The Ten Grandmothers; a Contribution to the Ethnology of the Kiowa Indians*, University of Oklahoma Press, Norman, Oklahoma, 1945.

SCHULTZ, J. W., *My Life as an Indian* [Blackfoot], Doubleday, Page & Co., New York, 1907.

SCHULTZ, J. W., and JESSIE L. DONALDSON, *The Sun God's Children* [Blackfoot], Houghton Mifflin Company, Boston, 1930.

The best of the early observers often give a marvelously clear picture of Plains Indian life before it was thoroughly modified by White influence. Some remarks on several of the authors listed below are indicated.

Catlin (1796–1872) was an American painter who visited many tribes in the United States and is especially good on the Mandan, whom he observed in 1832. Prince Maximilian of Wied Neuwied (1782–1867), a trained German naturalist, had already distinguished himself by his travels in Brazil when in 1832 he set out for a two years' journey to the Indians of the Upper Missouri. He studied the Mandan shortly after Catlin and gave an excellent description of their culture a few years before they were reduced by the smallpox, besides offering briefer observations on various other tribes. Carl Bodmer, a Swiss artist who accompanied the Prince, made numerous drawings of high documentary value. Henry and Thompson were intelligent British fur traders in the Blackfoot country about the turn of the nineteenth cen-

HINTS FOR FURTHER READING

tury. Denig became a bookkeeper for the American Fur Company at Fort Union near the mouth of the Yellowstone in about 1843 and played a prominent part in that region. Married to an Assiniboin chief's daughter, he enjoyed exceptional opportunities for observing his wife's tribe and also neighboring Plains peoples. The work cited was probably written about 1854. Lewis and Clark's famous expedition (1804–1806) was stimulated by President Thomas Jefferson. Starting from St. Louis, they ascended the Missouri and the Jefferson Rivers, crossed the Rockies, descended the Columbia, and reached the Pacific. They recorded many priceless observations on the Indians met. In addition to their Original Journals there are several works summarizing their scientific results.

BRADBURY, JOHN, *Travels in the Interior of America, in the Years 1809, 1810 and 1811*, Smith & Galway, Liverpool, 1817.

CATLIN, GEORGE, *Illustrations of the Manners, Customs and Conditions of the North American Indians*, Henry G. Bohn, London, 1848.

DENIG, EDWIN THOMPSON, "Indian Tribes of the Upper Missouri," 46th Annual Report, Bureau of American Ethnology, Washington, D.C., 1930, pp. 375–628.

HENRY, ALEXANDER, and DAVID THOMPSON, *New Light on the Early History of the Great Northwest*, edited by Elliott Coues, Francis P. Harper, New York, 1897.

KURZ, RUDOLPH FRIEDRICH, Journal; an Account of His Experiences among Fur Traders and American Indians on the Mississippi and the Upper Missouri Rivers during the Years 1846 to 1852, Bureau of American Ethnology, Bulletin 115, Washington, D.C., 1937.

LEWIS, M., and W. CLARK, *Original Journals of the Lewis and Clark Expedition* (Thwaites edition), Dodd Mead & Co., New York, 1904.

MAXIMILIAN, PRINCE OF WIED, *Travels in the Interior of North America*, translated by H. Evans Lloyd, London, 1843.

WINSHIP, GEORGE PARKER, ed., *The Journey of Coronado, 1540–1542, from the City of Mexico to the Grand Canyon of the Colorado and the Buffalo Plains of Texas, Kansas, and Nebraska, as told by himself and his followers*, A. S. Barnes & Co., New York, 1904.

Technical monographs on Plains cultures or particular phases of them will be found in Bulletin XVIII and in the Anthropological Papers of The American Museum of Natural

History; the Annual Reports and Bulletins of the Bureau of American Ethnology; and the Anthropological Series of the Field Museum of Natural History, Chicago.

Most monographs on the Plains Indians give bibliographies in which additional references may be found. In addition, a very useful compendium, the *Ethnographic Bibliography of North America*, by G. P. Murdock (third edition), Human Relations Area File, New Haven, Connecticut (1960), lists a great many books, short papers, etc. on the areal cultures.

INDEX

Acculturation, 219–23. *See also* White men
Adobe, 6, 209
Adolescents. *See* Boys; Girls; Puberty
Adornment, personal, 55–56, 119. *See also* Clothing; Face paint; specific ornaments
Adultery, 82, 141
Africa, 14, 81, 90, 121
Age-societies, 106–11
Agriculture, 21–25, 82, 169, 220–21, 227, 229. *See also* specific crops
early, 206 ff, 213, 215
Air-*vs.*-water myths, 141
Algonkian family, 9, 105, 134, 141, 226. *See also* specific tribes
languages, 5, 167, 217
Allegheny Mountains, 214
Altars, 187–88, 194, 196, 198, 203
Ancient Society, 96
Animals, 39–46, 173, 177, 181, 184. *See also* Hunting; specific animals
in art, 147, 148, 156 ff, 161
and clan names, 100–2
in folklore, 138 ff
as patrons. *See* Societies; Visions
Antelope, 15, 18, 164, 168
Antlers. *See* Horn

Apache tribes, 5, 9, 43, 217–18, 228
population, 12, 13, 14
Aprons, deerskin, 49
Arapaho tribe, 5, 13, 27, 39, 46, 117, 217, 218
arts and crafts, 60, 61, 62, 63, 66, 68, 69, 71, 152, 162
design in, 150, 151, 153, 154, 155, 158, 159–61, 169
families and social organization, 81, 85, 86, 94, 95, 105, 223
bands, 93–94
children, 46, 84, 89–90
societies, 106, 109, 112, 113, 185, 189, 197, 198
games, 136
hunting, 15, 48
medical techniques, 179
and menstruation, 90, 184
pipes, 58, 189
religion, 113, 169, 171, 200
ceremonies, 49, 177, 185, 189, 197, 198
societies, 106, 109, 112, 113, 185, 189, 197, 198
tipis, 32, 33, 34
Archaeology, 205–10 ff. *See also* specific relics, sites

Archery, 136. *See also* Bows and arrows
Arikara tribe, 5, 8, 12, 33, 42, 48, 214, 215
  agriculture, 21, 22, 28
  crafts, 60
  families, 85
  games, 135
  societies, 110
Arizona, 6
Arkansas (state), 210, 228
Arkansas tribe, 9–10
Arrowheads, 20, 58, 206–7, 214
Arrows, 58, 72, 75, 76, 128. *See also* Arrowheads; Fishing; Hunting
Art, 8, 82, 143–65, 225. *See also* Crafts; Embroidery; Painting
Ash-wood bows, 72
Assiniboin tribe, 5, 21, 33, 42, 52, 211, 213, 225
  arts and crafts, 148–49, 152–53, 162, 164
  folklore, 141
  games, 134, 136, 137
  and hunting, 15, 17, 18
  population, 13
  and puberty, 184
  social organization, 97, 110, 188
  warfare, 117–18, 119
  weapons, 76
  weaning of children, 89
Athabaska River, 216
Athabaskan family, 5, 9, 216, 217. *See also* specific tribes
Athletics, 134–36
Atira, 182
Aunts, 84, 103
Australia, 90, 99, 106, 184
Awls, 58, 69, 70, 206
Aztecs, 5, 215

Babies. *See* Infants

Backrests, 34, 38, 89
Bags, 59, 60, 64–66, 67. *See also* Decoration; specific types of bags
Baking, 26
Ball games, 134–36, 202
Bands, 92–94, 97
Bannock tribe, 9
Barter. *See* Trade
Basin peoples, 6, 7, 8, 216, 227, 231, 233, 234. *See also* specific tribes
  folklore of, 138
  and Peyote Cult, 204
  property destruction and, 91
  and sinew-backed bows, 72
  sorcerers, 179
Baskets, 7, 23, 60
Beadwork, 71, 82, 151–62, 206
Bear Dance, 164
Bear shamans, 177
Bears, 173, 184, 189
Beaver furs, 211
Beaver tribe, 11, 216
Beds, 34, 38
Belden, James S., 74
Beliefs, 167–83. *See also* Ceremonies; Religion
Belts, buffalo-hair, 228
Berrypicking, 82, 131
Billings, Montana, 209
Birds, 151, 163. *See also* specific birds
  naming for. *See* Clans; Societies
Birth. *See* Childbirth; Infants
Black Hills, 2, 212
Black Mouths, 111
Blackfoot tribes, 5, 10, 11, 35, 48, 169, 216, 217, 218. *See also* Blood tribe; Piegan tribe
  arts, crafts, 59, 60, 61, 65,

Blackfoot tribes (*cont'd*)
  120, 121, 148–49, 152
  color in, 161
  design in, 153, 155, 158
  music, 163
  ceremonialism, 129, 186–87, 189–90
  clothing, 50, 52
  cradles, 46
  and dogs, 40, 42
  family and social organization, 81, 86, 97, 100
    children, 46, 83
    societies, 106, 109
    status, 124, 127, 128
  and food, 18, 19, 26, 56
  games of, 132
  hairdress, 53
  and horses, 43, 121
  pipes of, 30, 58
  population, 12
  and puberty, 90, 184
  societies, 106, 109
  tipis, 32, 33, 34
  and tobacco, 27–28, 29–31
  tools, implements, 27, 56 ff
  warfare, 117, 119, 120, 121
  weapons, 58, 72–74, 75, 76
Blankets, 15, 128, 210
Bleeding, medicinal, 179
Blood tribe, 5, 10, 12
Boats. See Bull-boats; Canoes
Bodmer, Carl, 112
Body paint, 55–56, 112, 185
Boiling of food, 26
Boiling-water test, 113, 231
Bone-houses, 214
Bone implements, 57, 58, 71, 206. See also Awls
Bones, disposal of human, 91. See also Bone-houses

Bowls, wooden, 62, 133
Bows and arrows, 72–76, 118, 226. See also Arrowheads; Hunting; Warfare
Boxes, rawhide, 66
Boys, 83–84, 90, 116–17, 170–71, 184, 231. See also Brothers
  comradeship of, 87–88, 90
  in folklore, 140
  games of, 131, 136
  joining of societies. See Societies
  and social rank, 123, 124
Braids, 53, 54, 89
Bravery, 112, 116–17 ff, 227. See also Recitation of deeds
Bread, 130
Breechcloths, 49
British, the, 42, 130
British Columbia, 8, 141
Broiling, 26
Brothers, 80, 81, 84, 85, 96
  and kinship terms, 103, 104
Brushes, 52, 53, 144
Buffalo, 6, 9, 15–18, 21–22, 43, 46, 207–17 *passim*, 225 ff, 228–29, 233, 234
  disappearance of, 68, 200, 219, 221
  droppings, 25, 115, 227, 233
  hair, woven, 59, 60, 228
  heads, wearing of, 112, 188
  hides, uses for. See Robes; Shields; Leather; Rawhide
  horn, uses for. See Horn
  magical calling of, 136, 168
  offered to Sun, 182

Buffalo (*cont'd*)
  policing of hunts, 16, 111, 125–26, 229–31
  robes, 21, 51, 82, 129, 228, 229
    hunting with, 15, 18
    painting on, 143–48
  skulls, 112, 187–88, 198
  supernatural, 173, 184
  tongues, 46, 52
  transporting of meat, 40
  weapons for, 15, 57, 76. *See also* Weapons
Bull-all-the-time, 178
Bull-boats, 36, 41, 49, 213
Bull society, 112, 188
Bundles. *See* Medicine bundles
Bureau of American Ethnology, 13, 131, 163
Bureau of Indian Affairs, 223
Burial, 60, 88–89, 91
  in bone-houses, 214
Burning objects, handling of, 177, 231
Button game, 131–32, 201

Caches (storage pits), 24, 38, 207, 208
Caddoan family, 5, 9, 38, 43, 210, 214, 215, 218. *See also* specific tribes
Calendric hides, 146
California, 18, 28, 184, 187, 216
Camas roots, 26
Camp circles, 7, 15, 93, 94, 132
Campbell, W. S., 33
Canadian River Valley, 209
Canoes, 48, 211, 213, 227
Caps, 52, 228
Captives, 106, 116, 123, 215
Carlisle, Pa., 221
Carrying straps, 48
Carvings, wood, 62, 63, 143, 144, 188

Cass County, Nebraska, 60
Catfish, 19
Catlin, George, 67, 72, 228
Catlinite, 58
Cattle, 219, 220
Cedar-wood bows, 72
Ceramics. *See* Pottery
Ceremonies and ceremonialism, 8, 45, 83, 128–29, 137, 169, 183–204, 215, 231. *See also* Dances; Feasts; Medicine bundles; Societies
  clans, moieties, and, 99, 101
  dog-eating, 39–40
  hunting, fishing rituals, 16, 19, 136, 168
  lodges for. *See under* Lodges
  music for, 164. *See also* Songs
  priests and, 179–80
  puberty rites, 88, 90, 184
  shamans and, 176–77. *See also* Medicinemen
  tobacco, 29–30, 191–97
Champlain, Samuel de, 18
Chants. *See* Songs
Chastity, 79
Chaui Pawnee band, 94
Cherokee tribe, 214
Cherries, wild, 56, 196
Cherry pounders, 56, 63
Cherry-wood bows, 72
Cheyenne tribe, 5, 12, 51, 177, 207, 227
  arts, crafts, 60, 69, 149, 150, 152, 155, 161
  family and social organization, 80–81, 92, 94, 96, 110, 111
  government, 125, 126
  games, 134, 135, 136
  rituals, 110, 197, 198, 200
  societies, 110, 111

INDEX

Cheyenne tribe (*cont'd*)
  tipis, 32, 33, 93
  trade, 21, 27, 130, 212
  warfare, 117, 127
  weapons, 72, 74, 75
Chiefs, 118, 123 ff., 181
Childbirth, 14, 86–87, 159. *See also* Infants
Children, 83–84, 86–88, 89–90, 129, 168, 223. *See also* Boys; Girls; Infants; Matriliny; Patriliny
  games of, 131
  killing of, 119
  and kinship units, 95, 96, 97, 99, 102
  orphans, 123, 124, 140
Chippewa group. *See* Ojibwa group
Christianity, 200, 203, 220, 222
Clans, 95–103, 123, 127, 226
Clark, William. *See* Lewis and Clark
Cliffs, driving game down, 15, 16, 18
Cloth, 49, 130, 147
  buffalo-hair, 59, 60, 228
Clothing, 49–52, 59, 67, 82, 130, 219, 222–23. *See also* Cloth; Headgear; Robes
  ceremonial, 47, 50, 112
  embroidered. *See* Embroidery
  warriors', 112, 119
Clowns, 142, 188
Clubs, stone, 56–57, 72, 76, 118
Coffee, 130
Collier, John, 223
Color, use of, 161–62
Colorado, 217
Comanche tribe, 5, 27, 33, 46, 216–17, 227, 228
  bands, 92

  crafts, 60, 69, 145
  games, 136
  and horses, 45, 91
  population, 13
  supernaturalism, 168, 174, 183, 197, 227
  sweatlodges, 179
  and trade, 130
  weapons, 72, 74, 76
Comb cases, 69
Compound bows, 75
Comradeship, 88, 90
Containers, 62–67, 151. *See also* Bags; Parfleches
"Contrary" role, 113, 142, 227
Cooking. *See* Food
Cora tribe, 202
Cords, buffalo-hair, 228
Corn (maize), 21–25, 129, 206, 207, 219, 229, 233
Coronado, Francisco de, 21, 38–39, 42, 57, 58, 129, 148, 211, 233
Corpses. *See* Burial
Coup, 117–18, 119, 122–23, 198, 232
Courtship, 79, 162
Cousins, 104–5
Cradleboards, 46–48, 87
Crafts, 7, 59–72. *See also* Art; Beadwork; Pottery
Cree tribe, 5, 11, 40, 48, 87, 173, 211, 213
  arts, crafts, 61, 152, 153
  bands, 93, 94, 110–11
  burial, 91
  clothing, 51, 52
  dwellings, 31, 92, 93
  folklore, 141, 173
  games, 135
  hunting, fishing, 18, 19, 130, 211
  life cycle, 86–89
  population, 13

Cree tribe (cont'd)
  and puberty, 88, 184
  tattoos, 56
  and tobacco, 27, 29
  warfare, 117, 118, 121
  and weapons, 72, 76, 130, 211
Creek Confederacy, 117, 122, 228
Crow tribe, 5, 25, 26, 27–28, 44, 46, 208, 219, 223
  arts, crafts, 62, 77, 148–51, 152–55, 158, 216
  color in, 70, 161, 162
  clothes, 49–51, 52
  and corpses, 90
  and dogs, 41, 42
  economic values, 128
  family and social organization, 8, 84 ff, 96, 124 ff
    bands, 93, 94, 95
    children, 46, 82
    kinship terms, 104
    kinship units, 98, 100, 101
    societies, 110, 111, 143, 144, 191–96. See also Tobacco society
  folklore, 137, 139
  games, 131–36 passim
  hairstyle, 53, 54
  population, 13
  religion and ritual, 167–88 passim, 191–96, 198. See also Tobacco society
  societies, 110, 111, 143, 144, 191–96. See also Tobacco society
  tipis, 32–33, 34
  and trade, 129
  warfare, 114, 117, 118
  weapons, 57, 74, 75, 76, 77
Culin, Stewart, 132, 134
Cultural Areas of Native North America, 13
Cup-and-ball game, 136, 137
Cupping therapy, 179

Dakota tribes, 5, 11, 46, 52, 110, 119, 212–13. See also Santee Dakotas; Teton Dakotas
  arts, crafts, 69, 70, 71, 146, 148–49, 152, 154
    design in, 77, 144, 150, 155–60, 162
  music, 165
  and dog-eating, 39–40
  dwellings, 32, 33
  Eastern. See Santee Dakotas
  games, 131, 134, 136
  hairstyle, 54
  language, 10, 167, 168
  Oglala. See Oglala Dakotas
  population, 13
  religion, 175, 176, 177, 184, 197, 199, 201
  social organization, 97–98, 100, 104
  weapons, 75, 77, 114, 169
  Western. See Teton Dakotas
Dances, 107, 108, 110, 112, 137, 190. See also Sun Dance; Tobacco society
  music for, 164
  women's, 113–14, 116, 137, 168, 202
Danger, flouting of, 112, 118–19. See also Bravery
Death, 14, 88–89, 90–91, 127, 139. See also Burial; Ghosts; Killing
  defiance of, 119, 122, 227
  life after, 180–81

INDEX

Decoration, 143–62. *See also* Beadwork; Embroidery; Shells; Personal decoration
Deer, 58–59, 67, 69
  bones, 206
  -hoof rattle, 163
Delaware tribes, 231, 232
Denig, Edwin T., 27, 70
Densmore, Frances, 163
Department of the Interior, 197
Descent, rule of. *See* Matriliny; Patriliny
Design, 8, 144–62, 169, 194
De Soto, Hernando, 214
Dewclaw rattle, 163, 165
Dialects. *See* Language; specific tribes
Diamond design, 157, 158, 160
Dibbles, 220
Dice, 131–33
Diegueño tribe, 28
Discipline, 83–84, 127. *See also* Police
Disease. *See* Sickness
Dishes, 60–62, 228. *See also* Pottery
Doctors. *See* Medicinemen
Dog sleds, 48
Dog society, 106, 108–11, 163
Dog travois, 40–42, 43, 44
Dogs, 7, 39–42, 43, 44, 173, 226, 233
Doll, sacred, 198
Dorsey, J. O., 124
Double standard, 79
Douglas, Frederic H., 71, 72, 151, 153
Dragon, in myth, 141
Dragonfly design, 156
Dreams, 114, 169, 191, 193. *See also* Visions
Dress. *See* Clothing
Droughts, 1–2, 209

Drums, 164, 165, 203
Dwellings, 31–39. *See also* Earthlodges; Grass lodges; Tipis
Dyes, 69, 70

Eagle feathers, 119
Eagles, in folklore, 173
Earrings, 55
Earthenware. *See* Pottery
Earthlodges, 8, 31, 32, 34–38, 62, 82, 91
  ceremonial, 38, 176. *See also under* Lodges
  prehistoric, 205–6 ff, 214
Economic values, 127–30
Economy. *See also* Agriculture; Horses; Trade
  acculturation and, 219–23
  prehistoric, 207–10
Education, 83–84, 221, 222, 223
Effigy magic, 179
Eggan, Fred R., 228
Elk, 15, 68, 173
  horn, 74, 213
  teeth, 50–51
Elopements, 80
Embroidery, 7, 69–72, 82, 151–62, 206
English, the. *See* British, the
English language, 220, 221, 222
Ermine skins, 51, 119
Eskimos, 91
Evening Star, 180, 182
Ewers, John C., 147
Exogamy, 97, 99
Eyebrows, removal of, 55

Face paint, 55, 128, 185, 194, 196
Families, 79–91, 95–103, 226
  and bands, 91–94
  of languages, 4
  kinship terms, 103–5
  and rank, 123–24

Farming, 21–25, 82, 169, 220–21, 227, 229. See also specific crops
  early, 206 ff, 213, 215
Fasting, 170, 171, 198, 231
Fathers. See Families; Men and inheritance. See Inheritance; Patriliny
Fathers-in-law, 85–86
Feasts, 88, 89, 108, 124, 195
Feathers, 7, 112, 122, 163
Festivals. See Ceremonies
Finger mutilation, 91, 170
Fire, 138–39. See also Fuel
  hunting by, 15–16, 18, 229
  walking on, 177. See also Burning objects, handling of
Firearms. See Guns
Firedrills, 25, 26, 130, 226
Fish, fishing, 9, 19–20, 60, 229
Flageolets, 79, 162–63
Flathead tribes, 9, 43, 152, 153
Fleshers, 58, 59, 63
Fletcher, Alice C., 48
Flint knives, 58, 130
Floor mats, 60
Flutes (flageolets), 79, 162–63
Folklore, 137–42, 172. See also Myths
Folsom points, 205
Food, 15–27, 82, 130, 138–39. See also Farming; Hunting; specific foods
Fool society, 188
Foot races, 136
Fortifications, 31, 116
Fox society, 108–9, 111, 112
Fox tribe, 54, 66, 105, 225, 230, 231, 232
French, the, 42, 130, 151
Fuel, 20, 25, 40, 82, 233

Fumigating, medicinal, 179
Fur trade. See Trade

Gambling, 131–34
Gambling trays, 60, 132
Game. See Hunting; specific animals
Games, 99, 102, 131–37, 168, 201, 225
Garters, buffalo-hair, 228
Gelding of horses, 44
Geometric designs, 8, 144, 148, 156–62
  embroidered, 8, 151–52 ff
Ghost Dance, 199–201, 220
Ghosts, 181, 199–201
Gifts, 80, 86, 124, 130, 185, 195
Girls, 84, 96, 131, 140. See also Marriage; Sisters
  puberty rituals, 88, 90, 184
Glendive, Montana, 208
Glue, 74, 144
Goose society, 113, 164
Gorgets, shell, 55
Gossip, 127
Gourds, 163, 206, 233
Government, 123–27. See also United States government
Grand Medicine Dance, 191
Grandparents, 87
Grass, 1–2
  firing of, 15–16, 18, 229
  weaving with, 60
Grass Dance, 40
Grass lodges, 9, 38–39, 214, 218, 233
Grinnell, G. B., 134
Gros Ventre tribe, 5, 18, 33, 52, 75, 117, 217, 218. See also Hidatsa tribe
  crafts, 59, 150, 152, 153
  population, 13
  social organization, 97, 100, 105, 106

INDEX

Guessing games, 133–34
Guns (firearms), 42, 75–76, 117, 118, 130, 211, 219

Hair, 52–54, 89, 101, 118
  weaving with, 59, 60, 228
Hairy-coat, 38
Half-shaved Head society, 112
Hallucinations, 202. *See also* Visions
Hammers. *See* Mauls
Hand drum, 164
Hand (button) game, 131–32, 201
Hand mills, 25, 210, 215
Harvests, 23–25. *See also* Corn
Hasinai Confederacy, 43. *See also* Caddoan family
Hawks, in folklore, 173
Hays, Kansas, 1
Headgear, 52, 113, 228
Heads, cutting off of, 118
Hennepin, Louis, 229
Henry, Alexander, 164
Hereafter, the, 180–81
Heredity. *See* Kinship units
Heyōka association, 113
Hickory-wood bows, 72
Hidatsa tribe, 5, 8, 56, 72, 79, 167, 208
  agriculture, 23–24, 28–29
  and animals, 42, 44, 45, 48
  arts, crafts, 60, 62, 66, 144, 149, 154
  music, 163, 164, 165
  and death, 91
  dwellings, 31, 33, 34–38
  family and social organization, 81, 86, 94–95, 96, 101, 104, 106 ff
  joking relatives, 127
  games, 136
  population, 13
  religion, 129, 170–71, 177, 198
  societies, 106, 107, 108, 109
  and trade, 212
Hides. *See* Skins
Hilger, Sister M. I., 90
History, 205–18
  in paintings, 147
Hoes, 58, 206, 208, 220, 228
Hoop-and-pole games, 135–36, 168, 201
Horn, uses of, 52, 58, 206, 228
  bows, 72, 74, 75
Horses, 7, 42–46, 84, 206, 215, 225, 226
  after owner's death, 89, 91
  hunting with, 15, 16, 18, 225
  in paintings, 147, 148
  races, 136
  and trading, 21, 43, 128, 129–30, 216, 219
  and war, 114, 115, 118, 119–21, 124, 231
  and weapons, 72, 76
Hot Dance, 144
Houses, 222. *See also* Lodges
  bone-, 214
  Osage, 39
  Pueblo, 6, 209
Hudson Bay, 211
Hudson's Bay Company, 211
Hunting, 6, 15–19, 31, 82, 228–31. *See also* Buffalo
  with dogs, 40
  in folklore, 139
  magic for, 113–14, 168
  police and, 16, 111, 125–26, 229–31
  prehistoric, 207–15 *passim*
  trade and, 68, 130, 211
  weapons for. *See* Weapons
Huron group, 231, 232

Husbands. *See* Marriage; Men
Hyde, George E., 22, 25

Idaho, 8
Illinois (state), 122, 225
Illinois tribe, 122–23, 229, 230–31, 232
Implements. *See* Tools; Utensils
Impounding, 15, 16–19, 211
Incense, 187, 188, 193, 196, 203
Incest, 139, 141
Incising of rawhide, 148
Individualism, 221
Infants, 46–47, 86–87, 90, 179
  birth names, 87, 101, 102, 117
  birthrate, 14
  navel cords, 87, 158, 161
Inheritance, 91, 127, 221. *See also* Matriliny; Patriliny
In-laws, 85–86, 223. *See also* Marriage
Interment. *See* Burial
Introduction to Pawnee Archaeology, 36
Iowa tribe, 5, 13, 20, 76, 118, 213, 225
  ceremonialism, 183, 190, 203
  clans, 97, 98
  crafts, 60, 66
  games, 134
  hairdress, 231
Iron blades, 68
Ironwood bows, 72
Iroquoian family, 18, 188, 214. *See also* Huron group
Iruska shamans, 177

Jesuit Relations, 211
Jicarilla tribe, 9, 13, 217–18

Joking relatives, 127, 164

Kansa tribe, 5, 13, 23, 43, 185, 228
  kinship units, 97, 98, 100
Kansas, 25, 38, 210
Kentucky, 228
Kickapoo tribe, 66, 105
Killing. *See also* Hunting; Warfare
  of enemies, 118, 124, 169, 198, 230, 232
  murder, 96, 126–27
Kinietz, W. Vernon, 122
Kinship. *See also* Families
  terms, 103–5
  units, 95–103
Kiowa tribe, 5, 13, 20, 33, 92, 217, 218
  ceremonialism, 106, 197, 198, 199, 203
  cradleboards, 46, 47
  crafts, 20, 60, 69, 146
  and modern cults, 200, 202, 203
Kiowa Apache tribe, 5, 12, 14, 217, 218
Kit-fox society, 108–9, 112
Knife cases, 67
Knives, 57, 58, 130
Kroeber, A. L., 13, 217
Kutenai tribe, 8–9, 13, 46, 68, 149

La Barre, Weston, 201
Lacrosse, 102, 134, 225
Ladders, 62
Ladles, 62
Lafitau, J. F., 231
La Flesche, Francis, 48
Lake of the Woods, 213
Lances, 76, 112
Language, 4–6, 10–11, 167–68, 212 ff
  English, 220, 221, 222
  sign, 5–6, 52, 225, 233
Lapps, 18, 33, 91

INDEX

Law, 123, 125–27
Lazy stitch, 71, 152–53
Leather, 63, 67. *See also* Clothing; Skins
Leggings, 49, 50, 153
Le Sueur, C. A., 213
Levirate, 80
Lewis, Meriwether. *See* Lewis and Clark
Lewis and Clark, 21, 30, 148, 212, 213
Life cycle, 86–91
Linton, Ralph, 91
Liquor, 31, 130
Llano Estacado, 210
Lodges, 34–39, 111, 181
   ceremonial, 38, 176, 185–86, 187–88. *See also* Sweatlodges
   for Sun Dance, 198
   for tobacco rites, 192 ff
   earth. *See* Earthlodges
   grass, 9, 38–39, 214, 218, 233
   sweat-. *See* Sweatlodges
Louisiana, 210
Loup River, 43, 206
Lovers, 79, 162
Lumpwoods, 111, 143

Magic, 105, 136, 167–70, 176–79. *See also* Ceremonies
Maidu tribe, 18
Maize. *See* Corn
Mandan tribe, 5, 8, 19, 42, 48, 205, 208
   agriculture, 21 ff, 25, 28
   arts, crafts, 60, 61, 148, 163, 165
   clans, 96, 101
   dwellings, 31, 32, 33, 92
   marriage, 80
   population, 13, 14
   religion, 168, 177, 181, 183, 188
   societies, 106, 107, 109, 111, 112
   villages, 31, 94
Mandelbaum, D. G., 92
Marriage, 12, 79–86, 123. *See also* Families; Men; Women
   bands and, 94
   of captive women, 116
   courtship, 79, 162
   kinship units and, 96 ff
   by purchase, 45, 80
Masks, 188
Massage, 179
Matriliny, 12, 95, 96, 97, 104, 220
Mauls, 27, 56, 63
Maximilian, Prince, 109–10, 112, 163, 177
Meat. *See also* Hunting; specific animals
   cooking of, 26
   pemmican, 27
   sharing of, 128
   storage of. *See* Caches
Medicine bundles, 113, 128, 129, 138, 174, 180, 182
   bags for, 59, 64
   menstruation and, 88, 90
   in rituals, 180, 185, 187 ff
   war, 115, 117, 232
Medicinemen (shamans), 87, 174, 175–79, 186, 231
   after death, 181
   and rattles, 163
   and smoking, 29, 30
Mekeel, Scudder, 212
Men, 14, 29, 82. *See also* Chiefs; Medicinemen; Clothing; Hair; Warfare
   and art, 144, 158–59
   and civilization, 220–21, 222
   and marriage, 79 ff. *See also* Marriage

Men (cont'd)
  patriliny, 95, 96, 97, 104, 226
Menomini tribe, 20, 91, 225, 226, 228, 230, 232
  crafts, 66, 228
  and kinship units, 101–2, 105
Menstruation, 88, 90, 184, 223
Mescal, 201
Metates. *See* Hand mills
Mexico, 27, 201, 202, 215
Miami tribe, 16, 17, 122, 229, 232
Mice, 173
Midewiwin, 190
Military societies, 106–13, 137, 191, 213, 214, 216, 227. *See also* Warfare; specific societies
  and musical instruments, 163
  and prayers, offerings, 185
Minnesota, 43, 58, 212
Missionaries, 222
Missouri Indians. *See* Oto-Missouri tribes
Missouri River, 49, 207
Mi'tutak (village), 94
Moccasins, 51–52, 67, 134, 226
  decorating, 69, 153, 154, 158–59
Moieties, 98–100, 102
Monsters, mythical, 140, 141
Montana, 8, 25, 93, 207–9, 212
Moon, 177, 182
Mooney, James, 13
Morgan, Lewis H., 96
Morning Star, 161, 177, 181, 182
Mortars and pestles, 25, 62, 215
Mosquitoes, 173

Mothers. *See* Children; Families; Matriliny; Women
Mothers-in-law, 85, 86, 223
Mountain Crow band, 93, 94, 95
Mountain-sheep horn, 74
Mourning, 89, 91, 198
Mulloy, William, 205, 208
Murder, 96, 126–27
Music, 79, 162–65. *See also* Dances; Songs
Mutilation, self-, 55–56, 91, 170
Myths, 9, 11, 138–42, 168, 182–83, 188, 189

Names, 87, 90, 101, 102
  of clans. *See* Clans
  of designs, 157–61
Narcotics, 20, 199–204
Natchez tribe, 215
Native American Church, 204
Navahos, 28
Navel cord, 87, 158, 161
Nebraska, 20, 23, 25, 60, 205
Necklaces, 55, 112
Nephews, 84, 85, 104
Nevada, 28, 45, 91, 180
New Discovery of a Vast Country in America, 229–30
New Mexico, 7, 9, 42, 209, 217
New York, 214
Nez Percé tribe, 9, 13, 43, 46, 73, 74, 228
  crafts, 68, 149, 150
Nicknames, 87, 93, 100
Nieces, 84, 96
Nipigon, Lake, 213
North Dakota, 25, 205, 207
Notched Stick society, 165
Numbers, mystic, 186, 203, 227

Numbers (cont'd)
   in tobacco rites, 191–96 *passim*
Núpta (village), 94
Nursing of babies, 87, 89–90

Oaths, 115, 122, 127, 227. *See also* Vows
Obscenity, 86
Ocean, in myth, 140–41
Oglala Dakotas, 106, 112, 113, 124, 198
Ohio River, 213
Ojibwa group, 5, 20, 91, 165, 207, 212
   hunting, 229
   Medicine society, 190–91
   and visions, 170
Okipa, 183, 188
Oklahoma, 204, 210, 217
Old Man Coyote, 139–40, 182–83
Old Woman's Grandchild, 140
Omaha tribe, 5, 10, 15, 19, 48, 55, 225, 226
   and acculturation, 222–23
   arts, crafts, 59, 61, 62, 67, 69–70, 153
   color in, 70, 161
   clothes, 49, 51, 52
   dwellings, settlements, 31, 32, 33, 34–36, 116
   family and social organization, 84–85, 96, 97, 99, 100–1, 124–25
   kinship terms, 104
   marriage, 80
   games, 134, 135, 136
   government, 125, 126
   hairstyles, 52, 53, 54
   population, 13
   societies, ceremonies, 184, 190–91, 197, 213–14
   weapons, 58, 72, 76
Onas, 141
One-thread sewing, 152

Ontario, Canada, 213
Opler, Morris, 9
Oregon, 28
Ornamentation. *See* Beadwork; Shells; Embroidery; Personal decoration
Orphans, 123, 124, 140
Osage orange-wood bows, 72
Osage tribe, 5, 13, 23, 51, 56, 203, 228
   hairstyle, 54, 231
   house, 39
   kinship units, 97, 99, 101
Ossuaries, 214
Oto-Missouri tribes, 5, 13, 33, 134, 213, 225
   ceremonialism, 190, 203
   clans, 96–97
   crafts, 66, 228
Overlay stitch, 71–72, 152–53

Paint bags, 67, 68
Painting, 8, 82, 119, 128, 143–51, 154
   body, 55–56, 112, 185
   face, 55, 128, 185, 194, 196
Palisades, 31, 38, 116
Panhandle (Texas), 209
Parents. *See* Children; Families; Kinship
Parfleches, 64–66, 67–68, 143, 148–51, 154, 216
Patriliny, 95, 96, 97, 104, 226
Paviotso tribe, 164, 199, 200
Pawnee tribe, 5, 8, 205–6, 210, 214, 215, 218, 227
   agriculture, 21, 23, 24
   arts, crafts, 58, 60, 61–62, 153
   arrow smoothers, 57
   clothing, 51, 52

Pawnee tribe (*cont'd*)
  cradleboards, 47
  dwellings, 31, 36, 38
  family and social organization, 81, 85, 94, 97, 99
    children, 47
    societies, 106, 110, 113
  games, 132, 135
  hairstyle, 54, 231
  and horses, 43
  population, 12, 14
  religion, 173, 181 ff, 197
    sacred bundles, 113, 174
    shamans, 175–80 *passim*
  societies, 106, 110, 113
  and tobacco, 29
Pebble society, 190–91
Pecos, New Mexico, 209
Pemmican, 27, 56, 64, 233
Personal decoration, 55–56, 119. See also Ceremonies; Clothing; Face paint; specific ornaments
Peyote Cult, 199–204, 222
Phonograph, 169
Phratries, 98, 99–100
Picks (digging tools), 58
Pictograph Cave, 209
Pictography. See Painting
Piegan tribe, 10, 12, 109, 233
Pipe pouches, 154, 155
Pipes, 29–31, 58, 61, 206. See also Smoking
  sacred, 174, 189, 190
Plains Cree. See Cree tribe
Plains Indian Painting, 147
Plains people, 6 ff, 26, 72, 231. See also specific tribes

Platte River, 43, 206
Police, 8, 106, 111, 115, 191, 229–31. See also Military societies
  and hunting, 16, 111, 125–26, 229–31
Political units, 10–11. See also Clans; specific tribes
Polyandry, 81
Polygyny, 81
Ponca tribe, 5, 10, 13, 33, 54, 116, 213, 216
  crafts, 66
  kinship units, 97, 98, 100
  and Sun Dance, 199, 214
Pond, Samuel William, 22
Poor, the, 44–45
  giving to, 124, 128
Population, 11–14
Porcupine quills, 52
  embroidery with, 7, 69–72, 82, 148, 151–52 ff
Pottery (ceramics), 26, 60–62, 215
  remains of, 206 ff, 214
Pouches, 60, 67, 68, 154
Poverty. See Economy; Poor, the; Property; Rank
Powhatan Confederacy, 231–32
"Prairie," definition of, 1–2
Prayers, 87, 168, 182, 185, 198. See also Visions
Prehistory, 205–18. See also specific relics, sites
Pressure flaking, 58
Prestige, 123–26, 129, 221. See also Rank
  horses and, 44–45
  polygyny and, 81–82
  tattoos and, 55–56
  warfare and. See Warfare
Priests, 126, 179–80, 181, 198
Prisoners, 106, 116, 123, 215

Property, 91, 123–24. *See also* Inheritance; Trade; Wealth
shamans and stolen, 176
Puberty rituals, 88, 90, 184
Public opinion, 82, 127, 129. *See also* Prestige
Pueblo people, 6, 7, 178, 209, 210, 215, 226, 234. *See also* specific groups
agriculture, 21, 207
cradles of, 46
and design, 155
and ritualism, 183, 188
Punishment. *See* Discipline; Police

Quapaw tribe, 9–10
Querechos, 217–18, 233
Quill flatteners, 71
Quills, for brushes, 52
Quillwork, 7, 69–72, 82, 148, 151–52 ff
Quivira, 233

Races, 136, 192–93
Radin, Paul, 122
Rafts, 48–49
Raiding. *See* Warfare
Railroads, 220
Rainfall, 1–2. *See also* Droughts
Rank, 123–26. *See also* Prestige
of women, 82–83
Rasps, 163–64, 165
Rattles, 163, 203
Raudot, Antoine Denis, 122
Rawhide, 51, 63–67, 163
decoration of, 148–51
Receptacles, 62–67, 151. *See also* Bowls; Parfleches
Recitation of deeds, 6, 118, 119, 196, 198, 232
Recreation, 131–42

Red River, 43, 210
Relatives. *See also* Families; specific relatives
joking, 127, 164
Religion, 105, 126, 167–204, 222. *See also* Ceremonies; Myths; Visions
Republican River, 206–7, 214
Reservations, 221, 222
Respect relationships, 84
Rice, wild, 20, 211, 213, 230
Ridicule, 127. *See also* Teasing
Riding gear, 44
Rio Grande, 217
Ritualism, rites. *See* Ceremonies
River Crow band, 93, 94, 95
Roaching of hair, 54, 231
Roasting of food, 26
Robes, 21, 51, 82, 129, 228, 229
hunting with, 15, 18
painting on, 143–48
Rocks, belief in, 168
Romance, 79
Rope, 59
Rosettes, embroidered, 71
Ruhptare, 94

Sacred bundles. *See* Medicine bundles
Saddles, 44
Sage, 179, 181
Santa Fé, New Mexico, 42
Santee (Eastern) Dakotas, 10, 11, 16, 20, 212–13, 229
agriculture, 20, 22
and clans, 98
crafts, 66
games, 134, 135, 225
police, 229–30
population, 13
Wahpeton shamans, 176

Sarsi tribe, 5, 11, 27, 33, 52, 75, 216
  art, 148, 149, 152, 153
  families, 105
  population, 13, 14
  societies, 110, 216
Saskatchewan River, 211, 216
Sauk tribe, 54, 66, 105, 225, 230, 231, 232
Saulteaux tribe, 91
Sauna, Finnish, 187
Scalps and scalping, 86, 117, 118, 122, 232
  ceremonies and, 116, 169, 198
Scott, Hugh Lenox, 6
Scouts, 115, 227, 232
Scrapers, 57, 59, 208, 213
Self-mutilation, 55–56, 91, 170
Self-torture, 197, 198–99
Settlements, 31–32, 116, 233. See also Kinship units; Lodges; Villages
Sewing, 52, 58, 59, 71, 152–53. See also Embroidery; specific items
Shamans. See Medicinemen
Shasta tribe, 28
Shell society, 190–91
Shells, 55, 206
Sheyenne River, 207
Shields, 76–77, 82, 114, 147, 169, 228
  exhibiting of, 185
Shimkin, D. B., 46
Shinny, 134, 195, 201
Shirts, 49, 51, 119, 201
Shoshonean family, 8, 30, 33, 46, 52, 74, 216–18, 227. See also Comanche tribe; Wind River tribe
  arts, crafts, 60, 68, 150, 153–54, 161, 165
  bands, 91–92
  and horses, 43, 46
  and Sun Dance, 199
Siberia, 170
Siblings, 80, 84, 85, 103, 105. See also Brothers; Sisters
Sickness, 14, 90, 99, 178, 179, 181. See also Medicinemen
  and new names, 87, 90
  smallpox, 14, 94, 108
Sign language, 5–6, 52, 225, 233
Signal Butte, Nebraska, 206
Sinew-backed bows, 72–74, 226
Sinew thread, 52, 59, 69, 71
Siouan family, 5, 8, 47, 54, 213–14, 225–26. See also specific tribes
  social organization, 98, 99, 100–2, 104, 105, 226
  societies, 110, 190, 213–14
Sioux. See Dakota tribes
Sisters, 80, 81, 84, 85, 96
  and kinship terms, 103, 104
Sitting Bull, 201
Skidi Pawnee band, 94, 176, 180, 215
Skinner, Alanson, 213, 228
Skins, 7, 82, 143–48. See also Buffalo; Clothing; Rawhide; Trade; specific items
  dressing of, 58, 62–63, 68–69, 209, 213
Skulls, 112, 141, 187–88
Sleds, dog-, 48
Small-ankle, 38, 81
Smallpox, 14, 94, 108
Smoke vents, 33
Smoking, 27–31, 89, 107–8, 183, 193, 194–95. See also Pipes
  in Peyote Cult, 202

Smoking (*cont'd*)
  of skins, 67
  as therapy, 179
Snow snake (game), 136
Snowshoes, 11, 15, 48, 211, 226
Social mobility, 123
Social organization, 79–130, 226
Social standing. *See* Prestige
Societies, 105–14, 190–99. *See also* Ceremonies; Dances; Military societies
  and hairdress, 54
  and musical instruments, 163, 164, 165
Soil, 1–2
Soldier killing, 230–31
Songs, 164–65, 175, 180, 185, 186, 190
  buying of, 108, 174
  Tobacco society, 191 ff
  visions and, 164, 174, 186
  warlike, 111–12
Sons. *See* Boys; Children
Sororate, 80, 81
Souls, 180–81
South Dakota, 205, 212
Spaniards, 7, 42, 130, 210, 216, 217, 218, 233. *See also* Coronado, Francisco de; De Soto, Hernando
Sparrow hawks, 173
Spearing of fish, 19–20
Spears (lances), 76, 112
Spirits. *See* Ghosts; Visions
Spokane tribe, 9
Spoons, 62, 228
Sports, 134–36
Stars, 161, 173, 177, 180, 181, 182, 196
Status, 123–26. *See also* Prestige
  of women, 82–83
Steward, Julian H., 45

Stone boiling, 26
Stone houses, 6, 209
Stone implements, 56–58, 82, 206–7, 208, 226. *See also* specific tools
Storage pits. *See* Caches
Storytelling, 137–42. *See also* Recitation of deeds
Strike-a-lights, 25, 130
Strong, William D., 60, 205, 206
Stunts, 113, 177, 231
Subclans, 98, 100, 101
Sugar, 130
Sun, 127, 177, 182, 185, 186
Sun Dance, 8, 31, 183, 189, 197–99, 217, 225
  adoption of, 9, 197, 213–14, 216
  altar for, 188–89, 198
  camp circle for, 32
  revival of, 223
  sweatlodge for, 187
Supernaturalism, 167–204. *See also* Ceremonies; Myths; Religion; Visions
Supreme Being, 175, 182–83
Surround, use of, 15
Swanton, J. R., 13, 122
Swearing. *See* Oaths; Obscenity; Vows
Sweating, 185 ff, 203, 231
Sweatlodges, 179, 182, 187, 193–94, 195, 196
Swimming, 48, 49
Symbolism. *See also* Supernaturalism
  in design, 156–62

Tabeau (trader), 22
Taboos, 31, 84, 85–86, 174, 175, 223
  clan names and, 101
  menstrual, 88, 90, 184
  at puberty, 88, 90, 184
  of Whites, 200

Tahiti, 124
Takelmas, 28
Tanning of hides, 67
Tanoan family, 217
Tattooing, 55–56
Teasing, 86, 127
Temperature, 2
Tepees. *See* Tipis
Tennessee, 228
Tents. *See* Tipis
Teton (Western) Dakotas, 10, 11, 13, 33, 212, 213
  games, 136
  religion, 200, 201
Texas, 209, 210, 215
Textile crafts, 59–60. *See also* Cloth
Teyas, 216, 233
Thompson River tribe, 28
Thunderbird, 141
Thunders, the, 176, 189
Tierra del Fuego, 141, 184
Tipis (tents), 6–7, 31, 32–34, 82, 106, 218, 225, 233
  ceremonial, 189, 198
  at death, 89, 91
  modern use, 222
  pictures on, 33, 119, 120, 121, 145–47
Tirawa, 175, 182
Tobacco, 27–31. *See also* Smoking; Tobacco society
Tobacco society, 162, 164, 169, 187, 188, 191–96
Toilet bags, 67
Tools, 22, 56–59, 206–10 *passim*, 220. *See also* Trade; Utensils; specific crafts, tools
Tops, spinning, 131
Tornaeus (missionary), 18
Torture, 106, 197, 198–99, 215

Totems, 100–2
Trade, 21, 55, 67–68, 127–30, 207, 211, 212, 220
  of cloth, 49, 130, 147
  effect on arts, 69, 147, 152
  of horses, 42–43, 128, 129–30
  of tobacco, 27
Transportation, 7, 39–49, 213, 220, 225, 233
Trapping, fur, 211
Traps, fishing, 19–20, 60
Travois, 40–42, 43, 44, 213, 233
Trees, 20, 88, 91, 198, 214. *See also* Wood
"Tribe," defined, 10
Tricks. *See* Magic; Stunts
Trunks, rawhide, 66
Tunics, 49, 51
Turnips, 20, 26
Turquoise, 210
Turtle design, 159
Two-thread sewing, 71, 152

Uncles, 84, 85, 96, 103, 104
United States government, 220–21, 222, 223. *See also* specific bureaus
Ute tribe, 5, 8, 13, 28, 33, 47, 72
  arts, crafts, 59, 60, 149, 164, 165
  Sun Dance, 197, 199
Utensils, 25–27, 34, 56, 61–62, 130, 219. *See also* Pottery; Tools; specific utensils
Uto-Aztecan family, 5, 9, 11, 216. *See also* specific tribes

Vapor baths. *See* Sweating
Vaqueros (Querechos), 217–18, 233
Vérendrye, Pierre de la, 21

INDEX

Villages, 31–32, 94–95, 97. *See also* Earthlodges; Settlements
Virginia, 231–32
Visions, 128, 142, 170–76, 186, 226, 227
   and designs, 77, 169
   girls and, 88
   Ghost Dance and, 201
   Peyote Cult and, 202, 203
   and Sun, 182
   tobacco rites and, 193, 194, 196
   and warfare, 114, 174
Visors, rawhide, 52
Vows, 185, 203
Vries, David Pieterz de, 231

Wagons, 219
Wahpeton Dakotas, 176
Wallis, Wilson D., 32
War bonnets, 52
Warclubs, 56–57, 72, 76, 118
Warfare, 7–8, 114–23, 124–25, 137, 158–59, 169, 225, 227, 231–33. *See also* Killing; Military societies; Weapons
   against U.S. government, 200–1
   in art, 119, 120, 121, 147, 148
   and braided hair, 54
   captives, 106, 116, 123, 215
   comradeship and, 88
   and naming, 87
   oath on exploits, 127
   Peyote Cult and, 202
   recitation of deeds, 6, 118, 119, 196, 198, 232
Washakie, 10
Washo tribe, 18, 28
Water, 82
   boiling, stunt with, 113, 231
   throwing of, 83, 86
   -*vs*.-air myths, 141
Wealth, 44–45, 124. *See also* Economic values
Weaning, 89–90
Weapons, 72–77, 82, 118, 148. *See also* Bows and arrows; Guns; Hunting; Warfare
Weasel skins, 119
Weaving, 7, 59, 60
Wedel, Waldo R., 36, 205, 209
Weirs, 19–20, 60
Whirlwind sign, 157
Whistles, 163, 203
White Buffalo Cow society, 113–14, 168
White men, 52, 169, 200, 219–23, 231. *See also* British; French; Spaniards; specific men; Trade
Wichita tribe, 5, 13, 33, 55, 66, 203, 210
   grass houses, 38, 214, 218
Widows, 89, 106, 124
Wild plants, 20. *See also* Rice
Will, George F., 22, 25
Will, Oscar H., 25
Wind River tribe, 5, 46, 110, 149, 150, 164, 216
   population, 13
Winnebago tribe, 60, 170, 213, 225, 228, 230
   games, 134
   social organization, 101–2, 105, 226
   and warfare, 122, 232
Wisconsin, 102, 122, 212, 225
Wissler, Clark, 48–49, 64, 86, 97, 113, 127, 129, 158
Witchcraft, 179

Wives. *See* Marriage; Women
Wolf tails, 119
Women, 14, 29, 82, 116, 137, 184, 186. *See also* various crafts
- and agriculture, 22–23 ff, 82, 208, 220, 229
- and art, 144, 151 ff. *See also* Embroidery; Painting
- captive, 116
- and clothing, 49–51, 52, 222–23. *See also* specific items
- and firewood, 40, 82
- and games, 132, 134, 135
- hairstyle, 53
- and infants, 46–47, 86–87
- killing of, 118
- and marriage, 79 ff. *See also* Marriage
- matriliny, 12, 95 ff, 104, 220
- menstruation, 88, 90, 184, 223
- saddles for, 44
- societies of, 106, 113–14, 164, 168, 191 ff
- and tipis, 32, 82
- widows, 89, 106, 124

Wood, for fuel, 20, 40, 82
Woodland people, 7, 211–14, 225, 226, 228, 233, 234. *See also* specific tribes
- arts, crafts, 8, 60, 66, 151
- and corpses, 91
- folklore, 138
- games, 134
- hairstyle, 54
- kinship units, 98, 101–2, 105
- and police, 229–31
- religion, 170, 190, 204
- and warfare, 121

Woodwork, 7, 62, 143
- bows, 72–74, 75
- utensils of, 62, 82, 130, 215

Workbags, 68, 69
World view, 182–83
Wounded Knee, battle at, 201
Wovoka, 200
Wristguards, 76
Written records, 211
Wyoming, 46, 93, 212

Yahgans, 141
Yakima tribe, 9
Yellow-head, 81
Yellowstone River, 93
Yokuts family, 18

Zuñis, 28

AMERICAN MUSEUM SCIENCE BOOKS

American Museum Science Books are a series of paperback books in the life and earth sciences published for The American Museum of Natural History by the Natural History Press, a division of Doubleday & Company, Inc.

* Alland, Alexander, Jr. *Evolution and Human Behavior* B7
* Asimov, Isaac *A Short History of Biology* B6
* Bennett, Wendell and Junius Bird *Andean Culture History* B9
* Bohannan, Paul *Africa and Africans* B8
* Branley, Franklyn M. *Exploration of the Moon* (Rev. ed.) B1
* Bronowski, J. *The Identity of Man* B15
* Curtis, Helena *The Viruses* B14
* Deetz, James *Invitation to Archaeology* B16
  Drucker, Philip *Indians of the Northwest Coast* B3
  Hartley, W. G. *How to Use a Microscope* B10
* Lanyon, Wesley E. *Biology of Birds* B2
  Linton, David *Photographing Nature* B7
  Lowie, Robert *Indians of the Plains* B4
* Michelmore, Susan *Sexual Reproduction* B11
  Oliver, Douglas *Invitation to Anthropology* B5
* Silvan, James *Raising Laboratory Animals* B13
  Wallenquist, Åke *Dictionary of Astronomical Terms* B12

* Also available in a Natural History Press hardcover edition.

AM 1C